642.4092 STR
Strange, Frances, 1942-
Don Strange of Texas : his
life and recipes

WITHDRAWN

FEB 21 2017

D0744434

DURANGO PUBLIC LIBRARY
DURANGO, COLORADO 81301

DURANGO PUBLIC LIBRARY
DURANGO, COLORADO 81301

DON STRANGE of TEXAS

Celebrate Every Day!

Frances Strange

His Life and Recipes

by Frances Strange with Terry Thompson-Anderson

featuring the photography of Tracey Maurer

SHEARER PUBLISHING FREDERICKSBURG, TEXAS

Copyright © 2010 by Frances Strange
Food photography copyright © 2010 by Frances Strange

Shearer Publishing
406 Post Oak Road
Fredericksburg, Texas 78624
Toll-free: 800-458-3808
Fax: 830-997-9752
www.shearerpub.com

All rights reserved. No portion of this book may be reproduced—mechanically, electronically, or by any means, including photocopying—without prior written permission of the publisher.

Library of Congress Cataloging-in-Publication Data

Strange, Frances, 1942–
  Don Strange of Texas : his life and recipes / by Frances Strange; with Terry Thompson-Anderson; featuring the photography of Tracey Maurer.
      p. cm.
  Includes bibliographical references and index.
  ISBN 978-0-940672-81-9 (alk. paper)
1. Strange, Don, 1940–2009. 2. Don Strange of Texas.
3. Caterers and catering—Texas—History. I. Thompson-Anderson, Terry, 1946– II. Title.

  TX910.5.S76S77 2010
  642'.4092—dc22
  [B]
                              2010021195

ISBN 978-0-940672-81-9

10 9 8 7 6 5 4 3 2

Production by Asia Pacific representing Phoenix Offset

Printed in China

The quotation on page 11 is from *Delights and Prejudices* by James Beard, rev. ed. (New York: Atheneum, 1981).

"Party a la Mexico" by James Beard is published by permission of Reed College.

The images on pages 30 and 31 are from articles originally published on June 18, 1960, and November 16, 1964, respectively, by the *San Antonio Light*. Copyright Hearst Corporation. Reproduced with permission.

———————

Christmas Bacon, Cranberry Pecan Sauce, Double-Barrel Brownies, Grilled White Wings, Hot Mustard Sauce, Jalapeño Béarnaise Sauce, Kendall Creek Honey Bars, Texas Two-Bite Pecan Tarts, and the Texas Grill Pardner are trademarked by Don Strange of Texas, Inc.

To Don

Thank you for inviting me to come along on the journey of *your*

life that became *our* life. Between the mountain highs and the

valley lows, it was quite a wonderful journey

CONTENTS

First Row: Jason, Parker, Mandy, Olivia, Kelly, Matt, Alexandra, Molly, Shanan, Emily, Austin, Jake
Second Row: Frances, Don, Brian.

PREFACE

For a number of years I, along with so many of his friends and fans, had been telling my husband, Don Strange, that he should write a book about his life and his work, which are pretty much interchangeable. I finally realized that there were two reasons why this would never happen. First, he was far too busy. If he wasn't out actually working at an event, then he was planning several. Second, Don could never focus on himself and his accomplishments to the extent required to actually write a book about his life. So in the spring of 2009, we agreed that I would write the story of Don Strange from my perspective, with his stories intertwined.

It turned out to be a very providential decision. Don passed away on November 11, 2009. He will be missed beyond measure, not only by his family but by the legions of friends and clients who loved him for his homespun humor and personality. He was respected far and wide as a man who was humble, honest beyond reproach, unassuming, and the most gracious host anyone would ever know. This book is the story of the man behind the legend of his catering company, Don Strange of Texas, Inc. It's a story told through his stories and our family's memories.

ACKNOWLEDGMENTS

There are so many people who gave tremendous help in the writing of this book. When Don's death came unexpectedly about two-thirds of the way through the writing, I wasn't sure if I had it in me to continue. Between family, friends, and employees, I was able to finish writing the story that Don and I had begun together.

First, my amazing family. Not only were they dealing with their own grief with the loss of their father but they stood very strongly behind me and pushed me to continue when I didn't know if I could. "The boys," Brian, Matt, and Jason, have given me courage that I didn't know I had. Shanan, Kelly, Mandy, Emily, Alexandra, Austin, Molly, Jake, Parker, and Olivia—all have been inspirations to me and have made my life happy at times when I didn't know if I could be happy.

Friends who had encouraged both of us to write our story. Their enthusiasm never waned. Even though they had heard these stories all through our friendship, they never tired of listening to the progress of the book.

All the employees of Don Strange of Texas, who are like family. Many dropped what they were doing to do research for the book. They have been invaluable. Di-Anna Arias, director of sales and marketing, was always my go-to person. Without her help and encouragement many details would have been missed.

And finally, Terry Thompson-Anderson and Kathy Shearer, who guided me through these new waters. Starting a new career at my age still seems a little crazy.

I am so grateful to have my life and be able to share it.

Three Wheels and a Brick

"Like the theater, offering food and hospitality to people is a matter of showmanship, and no matter how simple the performance, unless you do it well, with love and originality, you have a flop on your hands." James Beard's words of wisdom could have been uttered by Don Strange, the amazing man I married, as they so aptly describe his theory on the presentation of good food with a huge dose of showmanship. Don would probably add, "The real gist of it all is that the people have a great time, so I make every party the greatest one the host has ever been to."

It seems that Don and Mr. Beard thought very much alike on the subjects of food and hospitality. The quote is even more significant when considered in the context of the story of Don Strange of Texas. In the spring of 1976, we had the distinct pleasure of entertaining James Beard in our home. The occasion was a series of "celebrity chef" cooking schools, fund-raising events hosted by the San Antonio Junior Symphony and planned by a committee on which I was a member. In conjunction with his appearance, Don and I agreed to host a cocktail reception honoring Mr. Beard.

During the evening Don and Mr. Beard discovered that they had many things to talk about. Don was immensely impressed with the man we all know by the moniker bestowed on him by his contemporary, Julia Child: "The Dean of American Cooking." And it seems the admiration must have been mutual. A few months after the reception Mr. Beard wrote one of his nationally syndicated newspaper columns about Don Strange!

Following is a copy of Mr. Beard's article, which appeared in newspaper food sections nationwide on May 19, 1976. I thought it would be a fitting introduction to this book about Don Strange.

Party a la Mexico by James Beard

Occasionally you go to a party done with such thought, planning and imagination that you wish everyone would entertain as well. One such party I recently attended in San Antonio was given by two delightful friends, Don and Frances Strange. While one of the factors that made it a success was that Don is in the catering business, there are very few caterers who have his flair. I just wish I had him near at hand whenever I give a party.

Being in San Antonio, the party had distinct Mexican overtones, but though the thinking was Mexican, the style was pure Strange. Rather than the cocktail food being passed, the party spread through the house and into the garden in a fascinating parade of good things to see and sample. A beautiful buffet table was set up in the dining room, and on and around the terrace there were a tortilla booth, an omelet table, a big charcoal brazier where shrimp were being grilled and a huge barrel, the top covered with fine cheese.

The first thing to catch my eye on the buffet table was an enormous platter of artichoke bottoms stuffed with crabmeat and covered with remoulade sauce, and avocado halves surrounded by a choice of dressings to fill the cavities—Russian dressing, Green Goddess dressing, oil and vinegar dressing, an Italian sauce and caviar and sour cream. A huge melon basket was filled with fruits and another big platter held slices of cold marinated roast tenderloin and very thin rye bread and tiny rolls, so you could make your sandwiches. As if this was not enough temptation, there was a picadillo with tortilla chips.

My favorite of the evening, however, was something very different—stuffed, fried jalapeño peppers. These were the pickled jalapeños you find in a great many shops, divested of all their hot little seeds, stuffed with grated Munster cheese, rolled in a cornmeal-flour mixture, dipped in an egg-and-milk batter, again rolled in the cornmeal and flour and fried in an inch or so of hot fat until beautifully browned. After being allowed to cool, they were stacked on a platter. I found them so delicious I'm sure I ate far more than my fair share. Jalapeños are always considered to be volcanically hot, but these, while hot, were not mouth-searing, and their piquant taste was perfectly balanced by the softness of the cheese and the crunchy cornmeal coating.

Out in the garden, two women were making

drinkers, eager to taste whatever it was that smelled so good. This would be a very easy thing to duplicate for a summer barbecue . . . .

There was so much tempting food that as you wandered around, drink in hand, you felt you were at a dinner rather than a cocktail party. Suddenly, just when we thought we had tasted everything, along came platters of tiny grilled French lamb chops, seasoned only with salt and pepper. Then, for the finale, we were given huge wine glasses filled with a sweet, foamy iced drink the Stranges call Café Mystique, that served as both dessert and coffee.

. . . . This was a delectable, invigorating drink that kind of tempered the palate, a perfect finish to that feast of varied and interesting tastes and textures.

If I have waxed enthusiastic over this most delightful party, which had a little of Japan, a lot of Mexico, and a tremendous amount of Don Strange in it, it's because it is as much of a joy to recollect as it was to attend.

What an honor it was to Don to have his hard work and creative efforts extolled by a man of such great stature. I believe it was a turning point in his life—like being told "Fabulous job, Don. Keep up the good work!" by America's leading food authority. Knowing that a person so steeped in knowledge and experience thought he was doing an admirable job seemed to give Don the confidence to expand and grow the company, using his endless innovative and entrepreneurial skills to create ever greater events.

In the company's beginning there wasn't much money for fancy and expensive new equipment. Don would buy used equipment, which often was not in the best shape. A number of portable steam tables were among his found bargains. Many had only three wheels, one wheel or another having broken off and been lost. Don would maneuver the tables into place at events and lodge a brick under the corner that was missing a wheel. It became one of his can-do mantras over the years, remembering the days of "three wheels and a brick." He always said that it served as a reminder of how he'd started and that the only way to

tortillas from scratch at the tortilla booth, patting the dough flat between their palms, baking the tortillas on a griddle, filling them with a wonderful mixture of meat, grated cheese and hot sauce and rolling them up for you to munch on. The omelets at the omelet table were flat, in the Spanish and Mexican fashion, with a most unusual filling of grated Jack cheese, avocado chunks and hot sauce.

Everything I tasted seemed to have a new twist, including the little appetizers on the charcoal brazier. Raw shelled shrimp of medium size (the kind called 24 to 32 count in markets because that's the amount you get in a pound) had been wrapped first in smoked bacon, then in small pieces of boned chicken breast that had been pounded paper-thin, secured with a toothpick and marinated in teriyaki mix for 24 hours before being grilled over charcoal. The tantalizing smell of charcoal broiling brought a crowd of eaters and sustain the company's growth and maintain its reputation was to make every new event as good as or better than the preceding one. It's a story that perfectly illustrates his knack for overcoming challenges.

To those who knew Don, it comes as no surprise that he loved to tell stories. And while there was always some basis of fact to his stories, his embellishments were often grandiose. Our son Brian says he was in high school before it occurred to him that his dad never really did play for either the Boston Celtics or the Green Bay Packers. For much of the boys' childhoods he would begin a story with "Back when I played for the Boston Celtics" or "Back when I played for the Green Bay Packers." The day after a party, he might have talked for thirty minutes about a conversation he had with someone at the party, and it was, as often as not, with the bus driver who drove the partygoers to the ranch, or one of the security guards, or maybe just a couple who came by to say they were having a great time. My brother, Ben Singleton, adds, "And if that couple happened to mention that they were from Sheboygan, Wisconsin, then Don would come up with some obscure fact about Sheboygan to share with them, and after thirty minutes, after their tenderloin sandwich had gotten cold, they would move along, with everyone happy. They had just had a surprisingly engaging conversation with the famous caterer, and Don had just met a couple of very nice people and learned yet another obscure fact about Sheboygan." Our family has often joked that there are probably a few telemarketers out there who never dreamed they'd be looking for excuses to get off the phone until Don answered their dinnertime call!

During most of our married life I was a stay-at-home wife and mom to our three sons, Brian, Matt, and Jason. Don managed to build the humble enterprise begun by his parents into one of the largest catering companies in the state; yet he wanted to play a very active, hands-on role in the raising of our children. As the business began to really grow, I found myself taking on more roles. In addition to making a home life for the boys that was as normal

as possible, I strived to make our home a place where Don could leave the stress of the job behind him. I was the disciplinarian to our three boys, making sure that they grew up to embody the values, work ethic, and positive attitude that both Don and I held dear. The boys went through life with their dad telling them how wonderful they were, and with me going behind him and telling them not believe everything he told them!

Because Don usually worked all night and often slept until long after they had left for school the next morning, I found unorthodox ways to create family time for Don and our three young boys. I would often bathe them at night and get them ready for bed, then drive them to wherever Don was catering a party that night. At a prearranged time, Don would come out to the car and spend some time with the boys, talking about their homework, hearing about their day at school, and telling a few stories about his experiences that evening. Then I'd drive home and put them to bed. They recall those evenings much more vividly than most of us who were tucked into bed at night by our parents.

Don Strange of Texas has catered events from the White House to the Hollywood hills, countless weddings, corporate functions, private parties, and myriad other events for numbers ranging from 6 to 35,000. The big events the company has done were some of Don's greatest challenges, but he amazed me anew each time he rose to a new level of accomplishment, meeting each of those challenges head on and turning them into amazing events.

Don had more energy and stamina and worked harder than anyone I've ever known. I'd say he was driven to work, a trait he most likely got from his mother, who was a very rigid taskmaster. Her credo was that if you weren't doing something involving work, then you were wasting precious time. I always called her "Mrs. Strange"—and was never invited to address her in any other manner!

One of Don's qualities that contributed to both the success and popularity of the company was his remarkable creativity. He figured out a way to make every event totally innovative and spectacular. When Don saw a unique concept or idea, he immediately found a way to give it his own spin and to incorporate it into his repertoire of catering razzle-dazzle.

Don was the first caterer to break free of the traditional styles of catering around which the industry had thrived for years—the buffet meal line or the formal seated dinner. He began to customize each event to fit the client's wishes, even their personalities, stopping only at the impossible to make an event sparkle. And there weren't many "impossibilities" in his bag of tricks. He was a can-do person. Those who have witnessed events that Don catered were often amazed that what he started with ended up looking and working like it did! It seemed that Don worked his most memorable magic when things went wrong, as they often do in the catering business. At Don's memorial service my brother, Ben, mentioned in his eulogy that "Don could turn a broken chafing dish into a centerpiece that was so creative that future clients would demand it be a part of their event!" And one of hallmarks of a Don Strange event was that it exuded his captivating Texas spirit.

I've heard him tell our staff a hundred times, "I want every party that we do to be the best party that host has ever attended." Our son Matt so simply and eloquently summed up his dad the morning after he passed away: "To Don, it was never about Don. It was always about you." While Don certainly attracted the spotlight, he never sought it. Catering was his craft, but his talent was in focusing on what would make you feel that you were the most important person on the planet. The thousands of accolades he received and the fame he garnered were not because of self-promotion, but because of that determination to make every event the most memorable experience you could dream of. Whether the event was the Congressional Barbecue on the White House lawn, a Hollywood birthday bash, or feeding 2,000 people displaced by Hurricane Katrina at Kelly Field, this was *your* event, and he wouldn't relax until it was perfect.

If you ever had the opportunity to watch Don at one of the events he catered, you noticed two things. First, he was always watching, scanning the event to see how things were flowing—and he never missed even the most minute detail. Second, it was always a given that he was going to change something, generally at the eleventh hour. If you worked at his events, you learned to try to stay out of his line of sight when he had that look; otherwise he'd give you an assignment, and it wouldn't be an easy one like "go pick up that fork off the floor." It'd be something more like "let's you and me move all those cars over to the north pasture" or "let's you and me put up eight banquet tables over there and set up a coffee service." But without those changes, it wasn't a Don Strange event. It was never possible to argue with genius. The staff became adept at scanning events through Don's eyes, anticipating the changes he would most likely want and then making them before the last minute.

Don introduced the concept of serving stations, creating elaborate settings for serving one portion of a dinner. At Don Strange parties guests graze from station to station, selecting hand-patted and grilled gorditas with various toppings at one kiosk; then they mosey to a bar station for beverages, to another location for grilled beef tenderloin, to yet another for avocado halves with a choice of fillings, plus much more, with desserts interspersed at stations around the event.

The inspiration for the station concept came from the colorful two-wheeled carts of Mexico's street vendors, which Don's father had discovered. Don eagerly sought someone in San Antonio to fabricate similar carts to his specifications. They were equipped for cooking and serving, with canopy tops that could be changed to match the

color theme of the client's event. Don would transport the bright, festive carts to events by trailer, along with a caravan of refrigerated food trucks, other trucks full of props, grills, and various equipment, and vans carrying the staff. While traveling to one event, he heard two truckers talking on their CB radios, one trucker exclaiming, "Look at that! Do you suppose it's some kind of carnival going down the highway?"

All of the foods served by Don Strange of Texas are made by hand. Freshness was always Don's priority, long before it became a national trend. He was proud to say, "We make our foods from scratch so our clients know what's in the food we serve. We buy locally grown produce whenever possible—wherever we go. We source all of our meats from Texas, and all of the fish we serve is wild-caught."

Don was definitely a person who thought outside the box. Come to think of it, I'm not sure he ever knew where the "box" was!

Don Strange of Texas was one of the caterers selected to prepare food for the grand opening of San Antonio's Alamodome in 1993. Subsequently, the company has catered many events there.

I remember when the company was asked to present a proposal for catering the Harley-Davidson Dealer's Conference at the Alamodome in 1996. Don really wanted

this job. So he flew to the company headquarters in Milwaukee with his assistant, Dan Schmidt, and one of his best cooks, Bea Rapelo, to present his proposal along with a few tastings. It was his intention to give the folks from "up north" a taste of Texas smoke, which is the company's signature flavor. They were given an eight-foot table on which to make their presentation. But the only place to create a little fire was outside in the park next door. It was a bitterly cold and rainy day there in Milwaukee, but Don was determined to smoke his renowned chicken and shrimp teriyaki roll-ups, a strip of bacon folded around a shrimp, wrapped in a thin chicken strip, marinated in a teriyaki glaze, and then grilled. So Don and Dan seared them on one of the park's charcoal grills under an umbrella, shivering in the rain, just long enough to give them that smoke flavor, and then finished cooking them in a skillet in the company's kitchen. Bea told Don that that he and Dan looked like a couple of hobos out there cooking on their little fire! But the Harley people were impressed, and the company got the contract.

Then there was the time in 1991 when Don contracted to cater the food for the National Lutheran Youth Conference, held at the restored La Villita in downtown San Antonio. There would be 19,000 hungry kids from all over the world waiting to be fed. I thought surely he'd overloaded his capacity this time. Not only did he pull it off like he'd done such huge jobs hundreds of times before, but he was asked to cater the conference in subsequent years in San Antonio as well as Dallas.

For the 1991 conference, the company transported to the site 25 ice storage bins, 200 portable kitchens, 80 restaurant fryers, 200 twenty-gallon containers of lemonade, and a staff of 475 professionals along with hundreds of local volunteers! The city blocked off the street so the crowd could spill over to St. John's Lutheran Church across from La Villita. There was a famous rock band playing on the front steps of the church, and the kids danced all night. Don had plotted the locations of the various food stations and then rented several hotel rooms overlooking the entire event. The individual stations each had color-coded flags. He had "spotters" with binoculars in the various hotel rooms. When a station needed more food delivered from the supply trucks, the staff member would raise the flag and the spotter would radio a message: "Blue station needs more ground beef for tacos" or "Red station needs more corn dogs." The spotters could also watch for bottlenecks and long lines.

In 2004 the National Lutheran Youth Conference returned to La Villita, only this time there were 35,000 kids attending! Don was asked yet again to cater the event. The kids were divided into two groups of 13,000 and 22,000 to make it possible to get them all fed. This time Don had separate tents for each food, with big signs on each tent stating what type of food was inside.

Two events that were very special to Don were commemorative parties at two of Texas's oldest and most famous ranches—the YO Ranch and the King Ranch.

In 1980, Don Strange of Texas was asked to cater the 100th anniversary of the legendary YO Ranch, located west of Kerrville just outside Mountain Home. The ranch was owned by Charles Schreiner III, whose grandfather had acquired it a century ago and who is best known for his efforts to bring the Texas longhorn cattle breed back from the brink of extinction. The black-tie affair for 3,500 guests was planned a full year in advance. Don remembered the party well.

"On April 15, the day before the party, it was in the nineties. But on the morning of the event, the weather began to head south. It never really got warm in the morning. By afternoon the temperature was falling. As guests began arriving in every conveyance from helicopters to pickups to limos, it began to rain. The ranch headquarters was eight miles from the entrance gate. Eight miles of rain-soaked road was the only entrance for the 3,500 guests. The traffic heading to the ranch house was bumper to bumper for hours, and there were many "emergencies" along the way. (Those were eliminated in later years by the positioning of portable toilets along the road!)

"As the party was getting into full swing, the rain turned to hail and sleet, and it was freezing cold. Imagine

women dressed in elegant gowns scrambling through the mud to get under the food tents. And food there was! There were whole sides of beef hung on big grilling racks to be served with barbecue sauce on pan de campo, gorditas and quesadillas, satay, venison crepes, grilled beef tenderloins with our signature sauces, and chicken teriyaki. Lots of smoke and great aromas. There were bars set up everywhere. Charlie Schreiner III rode into the great hall of the ranch's main lodge on Ranger, his giant pet longhorn steer, parting the crowd in its wake with its four-foot-long horns. There was dancing and drinking all night, with every kind of liquor imaginable. At midnight, Charlie demonstrated his authentic Gatling gun. If anyone thought the party was winding down, that certainly rattled it back to full swing! About 2 a.m. our crew began to serve breakfast, which included omelets made from chicken and ostrich eggs from the ranch. It was quite a sight as the guests began to file through the breakfast tent in their bedraggled formal attire.

"By the time we finally got packed up to leave, the road was slushy with hail. As our caravan headed down the road to the gate, the headlights spotlighted the most beautiful Colorado-style snow we'd ever seen. Only in Texas could it be 90 degrees one day and snowing like it was Colorado the next!"

Our son Brian recalls the YO Ranch party well as the most grandiose party that he'd worked on with his dad. Now, Brian was not the most disciplined student, and his eighth-grade earth sciences teacher at the time had mentioned to him that she'd love to work with Don at one of his events. Brian figured it might benefit his grade average if he could make this happen, so he discussed it with Don, who said that would be fine. Don actually suggested that they take her to the YO Ranch party to really impress her. Of course, when the weather went south, the entire staff was miserable, wet, and freezing, including the poor teacher, who told Don she couldn't see how he could possibly do this for a living! Brian was really worried, but he was relieved the next month when he did, in fact, get to be a ninth grader!

The memorable party at the famous King Ranch, near Kingsville, took place in 2003, when Don Strange of Texas was invited by the owning families to cater the ranch's 150th anniversary. The party consisted of five separate events—breakfasts, lunches, and an evening party for 1,000 to 1,500 guests. Beef was served at each meal in homage to the cattle-ranching industry from which the King Ranch derived its fame. There was plenty of wild game (nilgai) from the ranch, grilled quail, gorditas, pan de campo, and other traditional South Texas foods.

Catering parties and meetings attended by thousands of guests became Don's forte. In August of 2001 the company catered the International Rotarians Convention at the Don Strange Ranch for 7,500 Rotarians from all over the world. Don recounted that when the guests arrived, it was a sight he'd never forget. I remember when he called me from the ranch.

"Can you imagine 250 buses pulling into the ranch, and the people from those 250 buses walking across the dam? I asked myself what we had gotten into, and with my caterer's mind I began to crunch numbers in my head to be certain we were going to have enough food! We've got everything for a real Texas barbecue—six sides of beef, six huge barbecue pits piled high with sausage, and all the trimmings. We've got four bands and a full rodeo with five rodeo events, which we're presenting twice to be sure everyone who'd like to see it gets to attend. And we've set up four circus tents to provide plenty of shade. This will be a party to remember."

In 2002 Don Strange of Texas catered a USAA company picnic for 10,000 employees and their families at the company's facilities in San Antonio. It was a great picnic with barbecued beef sandwiches, roasted corn on the cob, grilled chicken, and funnel cakes. A different food was served at each station, so there weren't huge lines of people waiting to get a plate of food. They could graze around, eating in a leisurely manner.

In 2004 Walt Disney Studios filmed a second version of the iconic movie *The Alamo*, this time starring Billy Bob Thornton as Davy Crockett. Like the original, the Disney version premiered in San Antonio, but this time at the Majestic Theater downtown. Don Strange of Texas was contacted by Disney's marketing arm, Buena Vista Marketing Group, and asked to cater the premiere party for the cast, crew, and invited guests—a total of 1,700 people—after the screening. The theme was to be "Authentic Texas and Spanish Colonial Cuisines—Reminiscent of the Birth of the Republic of Texas." The party was held at Alamo Plaza, and Don put on an event they'll likely never forget. Houston Street was closed to traffic from the theater to the plaza. Don had a bright yellow carpet laid down the middle of the street, starting in front of the theater and going all the way to the Alamo. He waited outside the theater with Rio Bravo, his favorite Texas longhorn from the Don Strange Ranch, and led the entire party down Houston Street to the plaza, where they were greeted by large mesquite fire pits on each side of the plaza. The plaza was flanked by huge lighted tents with four antique chuck wagons and six more longhorn steers, which were handled by ranch personnel. Don had a real cedar split-rail fence built around the plaza, and a spectacular stage was erected in front of the Alamo for the entertainment. Each food station was built of native flagstone and decorated with live Texas and Mexican cacti. As the guests arrived at the plaza, Don Strange of Texas waiters were passing out prickly pear margaritas and Texas wines. The party had all of the flair of the movie itself!

There was never a dull moment in my life with Don Strange. Some cliffhangers, to be sure, but never without great resolutions, plucked from his psyche at just the right moment!

CHAPTER ONE

Humble Beginnings

Werner Edmond "Joe" Strange, Don's father, began his working career as a delivery driver for Barq's Root Beer. Seeking a job with more stability and security, he took a job in the civil service field, where he worked for many years. But he really wanted to pursue the American Dream of creating a better life for his wife, Edith, and their two sons—Don, born on January 9, 1940, and John, who was six years younger. It was the postwar era, and the country was primed for economic expansion and ripe with opportunities for personal success. So in 1952, two years before he was eligible for retirement, Mr. Strange and his wife borrowed $10,000 from her parents and purchased a small grocery store on Bandera Road in San Antonio. The location of the store was, in 1952, a bit remote. In fact, it was the last store between San Antonio and Bandera, but Mr. Strange felt that its distance from the center of San Antonio would be a plus. It would be a natural location for catching the traffic headed for the recreational areas outside the city as well as the neighborhoods on the fringes of town. His decision to open early and stay open late also added to the store's customers.

Don with his mom and dad in Florida, 1946. Don in his third-grade school picture.

Opposite: Strange's Grocery on Bandera Road; 1950s Humble Oil road map of San Antonio.

Don was twelve years old when his parents bought the store. He always said that was the year he went to work in the food business and he never stopped!

The store was attached to a large house that was built in 1910, allowing the family to live and operate the store in one location. Now, neither of Don's parents knew the first thing about the grocery business, but that didn't stop them from barging ahead full throttle with the limited amount of money they had. They must have shared Gandhi's philosophy: "If I have the belief that I can do it, I shall surely acquire the capacity to do it even if I may not have it at the beginning."

They named the store Strange's Grocery, and Mrs. Strange took over its operation. Mr. Strange did the maintenance on the building and machinery. That kept him busy. One of their earliest goals was to carry the best-quality meats. Mrs. Strange learned how to break down whole sides of beef into popular cuts. She kept the meat counter stocked with a choice selection that began to attract discerning customers.

Strange's Grocery was one of the old-fashioned mom-and-pop grocery stores that carried just about everything you needed. Mr. and Mrs. Strange specialized in catering to the needs of area families. They sold animal feed and hay, which they delivered. They sold gasoline, which they pumped from ancient pumps with tanks that had to be refilled every three days. Mr. Strange originally operated as a Humble Oil station but later switched to Mobil. He was also a very good mechanic, so he added a bay and began to do auto repair. The automotive side of the business became quite profitable.

Salesmen began to encourage the Stranges to offer barbecue, using their high-quality meats, as a way to expand their profits. So they added a barbecue pit and began to cook and sell sliced and chopped barbecued beef. They slow-smoked big inside beef rounds, and Mr. Strange concocted his own signature barbecue sauce. If she had time, Mrs. Strange would make pinto beans and potato salad to sell with the meat. Eventually, they hired Garfield Mitchell, an

Don in his early college years (above) and high school (right).

accomplished pit master, to take over the barbecuing. The success of the store, however, brought personal sacrifices. As the store began to grow, adding more cooked meats and an expanded line of grocery items, Mr. Strange would enlarge it, taking in bits of their attached home a room at a time! Strange's Grocery became a full-service country store. As the store expanded, not only did the family lose parts of their living space, they also sacrificed some sleep. The store opened at 7 a.m. and closed at 11 p.m., so the family stayed up late cleaning, stocking shelves, and doing whatever it took to be ready to open again at 7 a.m. the next morning.

Over the years, a bona fide neighborhood began to grow up around the store, bringing competition, so Mr. Strange added a line of used cars to increase revenue. The new neighborhood was called Inspiration Hills, and it became known as an elegant place to live in San Antonio.

Strange's Grocery was open seven days a week. Even on Sunday evenings, the Stranges served their popular barbecue. Neighborhood residents probably had every intention of cooking dinner at home on Sundays, but once the aromas began to waft from that barbecue pit around 4 p.m., they would begin to line up at the store. One very rainy day a regular customer called to inquire if it would be possible for Mr. Strange to deliver some barbecue to her house. He gladly obliged. Soon more customers began to request delivery of the barbecue to their homes, regardless of the weather. The Stranges were inching toward being in the catering business!

There was a house on a half-acre lot on the corner adjacent to the grocery store's property. In 1956 the chef of the Gondola Hotel in San Antonio bought the house and began an extensive remodeling project to turn it into a restaurant, which he named the Broiler and planned to open when he retired from the hotel. Sadly, the chef died just when the building was finished. Mr. and Mrs. Strange bought the Broiler, but their first evening netted only $15 in profit, and they quickly abandoned the notion of being restaurateurs, realizing that they knew less about the restaurant business than they had known about the grocery business! They added on to the building in 1959, renaming it Strange's Private Party House and Catering Service (soon shorted to Strange's Party House). Now they had a location for doing on-premise catering. It was the beginning of a new era in the Strange family's legacy in the food business, which today has spanned over fifty-eight years and four generations.

Strange's Grocery Smoked Beef Rump

★

I remember the delicious cuts of beef that Mr. Strange used to smoke over indirect heat at Strange's Grocery. The smoking meat would create such tantalizing aromas for blocks around. And the customers agreed that the finished product was well worth the mouth-watering wait. Mr. Strange would slice the meat thin and sell it by the pound. Mrs. Strange would chop the tougher pieces, toss the meat with the store's signature barbecue sauce, and then sell chopped beef sandwiches. Mrs. Strange referred to the cut of beef as the "butt," presumably a boneless beef rump cut from the bottom round. If you're looking for a delicious cut of beef to slow-smoke, you can't go wrong with this recipe. The rump has a great flavor, and it's less fatty and much less complicated to slice than the brisket. Allow about 6 to 8 ounces per person, or more if your audience consists of serious Texas beef eaters.

Serves 12 to 15

To make the rub, combine all ingredients in a bowl and toss with a fork to blend well. Massage the rub into the meat on all sides, coating well; reserve any leftover rub. Refrigerate the meat overnight, uncovered. A tacky surface, or pellicle, will form, assuring that the smoke's flavor will adhere to the meat.

When you're ready to smoke the meat, build a hardwood* charcoal fire in a pit with a separate firebox, or build the fire in one side of a regular barbecue pit that has a lid. When the fire has burned down to a temperature of 200 to 225 degrees inside the pit, place the meat on the grill rack. If using a regular pit, place the meat on the side of the grill opposite the fire so that it is not directly over the coals. Combine the reserved rub with enough vegetable oil to make a thin paste. Baste the meat occasionally with the paste. For optimum tenderness, cook the meat to an internal temperature of 140 to 145 degrees (medium), or about 4 to 6 hours. (You will need to rekindle the fire as it dies down to maintain a temperature of 200 to 225 degrees inside the pit.)

When the meat is done, transfer it to a large cutting board, cover loosely with foil, and let rest for a full 15 minutes before slicing. The resting period will allow the juices of the meat to redistribute throughout the entire cut.

Slice the meat in thin slices, cutting across the grain on the bias; serve as desired.

*THE CHOICE OF WOOD CHARCOAL is a personal one. Generally a combination of hickory, an assertive flavor, and oak, a milder flavor, is a good choice for beef. If you'd like to experiment with flavors, applewood imparts a delicate, well-rounded smoke flavor, while cherry and pecan lend a fragrant nuttiness. Mesquite can be either delicately sweet or overwhelmingly assertive, depending on how much is used. It not recommended for extended cooking times as it is a resinous wood and can give the meat a turpentine-like flavor. If you'd like to get some of that Texas mesquite flavor in the meat, add some about halfway through the cooking process when you have to rekindle the fire. Use 1 part mesquite to 3 parts of your other main wood.

1 beef rump roast, 5 to 6 pounds

Beef Rub (see recipe below)

Vegetable oil

Beef Rub

⅓ cup brown sugar

⅓ cup kosher salt

½ cup ground black pepper

¼ cup paprika

¼ cup ground cumin

1 tablespoon smoked paprika

⅓ cup chili powder

¼ cup whole coriander seeds, toasted and ground

⅓ cup granulated garlic

Mrs. Strange's Potato Salad

★

2 pounds potatoes, peeled and cut into bite-size dice

½ cup finely chopped bell pepper

½ cup finely chopped celery

2 tablespoons minced, drained pimiento

2 tablespoons sweet pickle relish

1¼ cups real mayonnaise, or more as needed

2 teaspoons ballpark-style mustard

Kosher salt and freshly ground black pepper to taste

When Mr. and Mrs. Strange began cooking barbecue to sell at Strange's Grocery, Mrs. Strange would make up big batches of her tasty potato salad. She would sell it at the meat counter so customers would have a good side to go with the barbecue. It was always a popular dish and still appears on menus for casual events because of its wide appeal.

Serves 10 to 12

Place diced potatoes in a heavy-bottomed 6-quart pot. Add cold water to cover. Bring the potatoes to a boil over medium heat. Lower heat to a simmer and cook for about 20 minutes, or until potatoes are tender. Drain into a colander and set aside to cool.

In a large bowl, combine the bell pepper, celery, pimiento, pickle relish, mayonnaise and mustard. Stir to blend well.

When potatoes are cool, stir them into the dressing. Season with salt and pepper. Cover and refrigerate until ready to serve.

Ranchero Beans

★

2 dried ancho chiles, stems and seeds removed

1 pound dry pinto beans

1 pound fresh pico de gallo

½ pound applewood-smoked bacon, cut into ½-inch pieces

6 quarts chicken stock, or more as needed

3 large garlic cloves, minced

Kosher salt to taste

Pinto beans are a Texas staple that folks never seem to get their fill of. They are *soooo* good you could make a meal of a bowl of them. Mrs. Strange cooked pinto beans to go with the barbecue sold at Strange's Grocery.

Serves 8 to 10

Place the chiles in a saucepan and cover with water. Bring to a boil over high heat and simmer 3 to 4 minutes. Set aside and allow to cool slightly, about 15 minutes. Place the chiles in the blender and add about ⅓ cup of the cooking water. Puree until thick and smooth. Set aside.

Pick through the beans to remove any pebbles or bits of dirt. Wash the beans in a colander, then transfer to a heavy-bottomed 6-quart soup pot or Dutch oven. Add the ancho puree and all remaining ingredients except salt.* Fill the pan with enough chicken stock to cover the beans by about 2 inches. Cook, stirring occasionally, until beans are very tender, about 1½ hours. If you like a thickened, gravylike consistency, scoop out 1½ cups of the beans with a slotted spoon and puree in the food processor. Return to pot and stir to blend. Cook an additional 15 minutes to thicken the beans. Season to taste with salt. Serve hot.

*IF YOU ADD SALT to the beans before they become soft, they will remain hard and never cook down to form a thickened bean gravy.

Mr. Strange's Barbecue Sauce

1 cup ketchup

2¾ cups tomato sauce

2 tablespoons medium-hot chili powder

¾ teaspoon cayenne pepper

2 tablespoons plus 1½ teaspoons black
   pepper

1¾ cups water

2 tablespoons granulated garlic

½ teaspoon kosher salt

2 tablespoons plus 1½ teaspoons
   Worcestershire sauce

1 cup firmly packed light brown sugar

2 tablespoons plus 1½ teaspoons
   honey

1 tablespoon liquid smoke

¼ pound (1 stick) plus 5 tablespoons
   unsalted butter

Mr. Strange created the barbecue sauce for the barbecued meats at Strange's Grocery. It has always been a favorite with clients. The recipe makes a good-sized batch, but the sauce will keep in the refrigerator for about two weeks. Better yet, share some with your friends!

Makes 5 cups

Combine all ingredients in a heavy-bottomed 3-quart saucepan over medium heat. Stir the sauce until the butter has melted, then reduce heat and simmer for 1 hour, or until the sauce is the consistency of ketchup. Remove from heat and cool completely. Transfer to a storage container with a tight-fitting lid and refrigerate.

CHAPTER TWO

The Strange's Party House Years

Parties . . .
CATERING AND
CUSTOM BAKING!
TURKEYS AND HAMS BAKED
FOR YOU, FOR THE HOLIDAYS!
**STRANGE'S
PARTY HOUSE**
1513 BANDERA HIGHWAY
GE 4-2331

Don (at microphone) with some of his fraternity brothers from San Antonio College at the Party House. (Hopefully he was talking and not singing!)

Don was nineteen years old when Mr. and Mrs. Strange opened Strange's Party House in 1959, the same year he graduated from Jefferson High. He had already been working at the family's grocery store and barbecue stand since he was twelve. Over the years of serving customers at the grocery, Don learned valuable lessons from his parents about treating people fairly and offering the highest quality of service and food possible. This foundation made his transition into the catering business smooth, but he also learned that there was much more to the business than there appeared to be. Even at such a young age, Don's character led him to be a person who never backed away from a challenge, and he jumped headfirst into the catering business, perfecting his talents with each new event.

Don and I were married in September of 1961, a year after we met at San Antonio College, where he was a sophomore and I was a freshman. We had gone to different high schools but had mutual friends at SAC. On a particular weekend, a friend of mine had a date with Don to go to a fraternity party at the Party House. The boy she had been dating was free, so she fixed me up with him. I

wanted a date with Don, and she knew it. She said they were not a serious couple. So off we go to the party, and all night we were plotting in the girl's restroom about how to switch dates. What we didn't know was that the boys, with Don as their ringleader, had put a tape recorder on the roof of the Party House, with the microphone hidden in a vent of the restroom. After the party, the guys took their dates home and went back and played the restroom entertainment. I seemed to be loud and clear and in there all evening. Apparently, it didn't scare Don off because we started dating right after that. So the Party House played a role as matchmaker in a way!

Mr. Strange had been plotting various uses for the facility and had hit upon what he thought would be an immensely popular idea. He proposed serving fixed-price dinners each Sunday featuring a set menu, which would consist of a salad, entrée, two side dishes, and a simple dessert, plus iced tea. The menu would change every week, but the fixed price was to be 99 cents! He called it the Sunday Supper Club. Mr. Strange hired waiters who had been trained as railroad Pullman-car waiters with all of the traditions of fine dining service. The tables were covered with linen cloths and napkins; water glasses were set at each place. The first of the dinners was scheduled for the Sunday

after our wedding on Saturday! Mr. Strange advertised the dinners in the San Antonio newspapers and with flyers.

Thankfully, Don and I left for a short honeymoon. On the day of that first Sunday Supper Club, San Antonio responded, and I mean the entire city responded! Whole families with children, groups of friends, and singles began to line up outside the doors early in the morning. Traffic on Bandera Road came to a standstill from all of the cars trying to find parking spaces. Eventually, the city police had to direct traffic around the knot of vehicles trying to park. Mr. Strange had no idea what he had gotten himself into. All of the unfortunate relatives who were still around after our wedding were pressed into service cooking, filling plates, washing dishes, and bussing tables. Needless to say, the concept was quite successful, but it was so much work and the crowds were so large that the Sunday Supper Club continued for only five or six weeks. When the dinners ceased, it was the end of "open to the public" service at Strange's Party House.

After we married, Don continued to work with his dad in the catering operation while juggling part-time studies at local colleges—San Antonio College, Trinity, and St. Mary's. I worked with Mrs. Strange at the grocery store. Don decided he wanted to be a full-time student without the distractions of the catering business, so we moved to Austin and he enrolled at the University of Texas. I got a job working at the Capitol, and we managed to make ends meet. Don, however, was an average academic student, and he eventually realized that the validation of his talents would not come within the halls of academia—and he sorely missed the food business. So we moved back to San Antonio, where he plunged into the family catering business with a passion.

In 1963 Don landed a catering opportunity that really excited him. It offered him the chance to break into upscale catering. His family doctor, Charles Hooper, asked him to cater the annual banquet of the Bexar Country Medical Society at its facility. In doing so, Dr. Hooper broke the tradition of using a few select, well-established San Antonio caterers, even though many of the other doctors felt that Don was not qualified. Don knew that he must do a stellar job. As a centerpiece for the event, he made a huge Jello mold in the shape of a caduceus, the insignia of the medical profession. Don recalled how impressive it was. But before the beginning of the party, Dr. Hooper came to see how the preparations were going. Don was anxious to show off the centerpiece, but when they approached the table where it had been placed, Don noticed that Dr. Hooper was studying the caduceus very seriously. It seems that Don had unknowingly copied the version used by the veterinary medical profession! It was the first of many "learning opportunities" that were quickly scraped into the trash and replaced with something from the reserves of Don's great ability to think on his feet. The party was a smashing success, and the doctors were quite impressed with the innovative flair and unique foods offered by "the new kid in town." I think it may have been when I coined the phrase that is a caterer's mantra—"Do it, or rig it!"

Mr. and Mrs. Strange leased out the grocery store operation in 1964 to concentrate their time and resources totally on the catering operation. Eventually Don was running the operation, both on-premise at Strange's Party House and off-premise. He began to infuse the business with his particular, often quirky brand of creative genius. By working diligently, Don built the company into the hottest catering ticket in San Antonio.

Our first son, Brian, was born on July 7, 1966, followed in eighteen months by Matt, on January 24, 1968. In 1970, when I was expecting our third son, Jason, I went to visit my ob-gyn, Don Krause. During my visit, Dr. Krause mentioned, "I saw your husband's ad for 'gourmet catering' in the paper. What does that mean?" Well, I hadn't a clue what it meant and told him that I'd have to get back to him on that! Before that ad, the company had done mainly barbecue dinners, as did most of the catering companies in San Antonio. But Don was itching to get away from the

Promotional glass from the Party House.

traditional forms of catering and try out some of the ideas that were hatching in his creative mind. Dr. Krause and his wife, Neal, became Don's first "gourmet catering" clients when they scheduled a party for other doctors at their home. The menu consisted of lamb curry, a poached salmon dish, and roasted beef tenderloin, served buffet style, with someone serving the salmon and slicing the beef. There was a cheese station and several regal desserts. The requested menu sparked the beginning of Don's extensive cookbook collection, which was augmented each time he had to learn a new dish or technique. The event was a huge success as well as a huge leap out of the box for Don. He had graduated from the small events at Strange's Party House and into the realm of off-premise catering, which offered the endless possibilities for innovation that Don yearned for.

Mr. Strange had begun to explore other avenues for off-premise catering while Don concentrated on the gourmet end of the business. By 1960, they had bought a vintage stainless steel travel trailer and refitted it as a mobile kitchen. The company had begun to do simple events—mainly municipal functions or private events in park settings—from the trailer. Don recalled that it was a pretty slick kitchen on wheels. One particular event, however, was a particularly vivid one in his memory. Mr. Strange had been hired to cater an event for 600 in the basement of the Municipal Auditorium in San Antonio. They loaded the trailer with the food and several five-gallon tanks of water for making the iced tea and drove it into the basement of the auditorium. When the event was over and all of the water and food gone, they loaded up their equipment to leave. What they hadn't calculated, however, was the fact that the food for 600, plus the heavy tanks of water, had put a great deal of weight on the tires. When the food and water were gone, the tires, without the burden of weight, were considerably more inflated. The trailer was now stuck in the basement, wedged against the ceiling! They had to let all of the air out of tires to get the trailer out, and then, once they were out of the basement, have the tires reinflated for the drive back to the commissary. Another lesson learned.

HemisFair brought the first big infusion of outside culture to modern San Antonio, followed by the building of the University of Texas Health Science Center in the city. The opening of the medical school brought well-traveled, cultured doctors from all over. They sought a higher standard of catering than what had existed previously in San Antonio. One of the new doctors affiliated with the

school, Leo Cuello, a thoracic surgeon, had attended that party at Dr. Krause's home. He called Don to talk to him about doing a party at his home, mentioning that he had previously used a couple of other caterers in town. But he told Don that he was so impressed with the fact that Don had created an event with delightful food—and not a deviled egg in sight! Dr. Cuello wanted to serve oysters on the half shell, which would be arranged on ice and shucked at the party. Don had never dealt with an oyster in its shell. So off we went to the Kangaroo Court restaurant in downtown San Antonio, where Don knew they served oysters on the half shell. He ordered a bucket of oysters, which came with an oyster knife. Our waiter showed him how to open a couple, and then Don tackled the rest. By the time he had reached the bottom of the bucket, he could shuck an oyster with the best of them! He taught the company's staff how to shuck oysters, and another party was a success.

At Dr. Cuello's party, Don had also served his roasted beef tenderloin, which impressed one of the guests, Arthur McFee, who was head of the surgery department at the medical school. Dr. McFee inquired about having Don cater a party for forty guests at his home in Olmos Park,

One of the three banquet rooms at the Party House set for a dinner.

$1 Turkey Dinner $1
With chef salad dressing, giblet gravy, cranberry sauce, candied yams, green peas, hot rolls and butter, coffee or tea.
STRANGE'S
1513 Bandera Rd. · GE4-2331

Party House Affords Best Parties

Anyone who struggles and strains to stage an impressive private party by his own efforts nowadays is almost as far behind the times as a housewife who churns butter for her own family.

Strange's Private Party House and catering service can arrange and serve any kind of meal, of any nationality, with all the appropriate window dressing and do it better, and probably for far less cost, than is possible for any individual or small group.

The Party House, located at 1509-13 Bandera rd at Quill dr., is functionally designed and exclusively dedicated to production of private parties of all kinds. It has two beautifully decorated, completely separate serving areas. Each of these, in turn, consists of a large banquet hall and an adjoining reception and cocktail area.

The party house system was conceived and launched five years ago by W. E. "Joe"

STRANGE'S PRIVATE PARTY HOUSE (TOP); HAWAIIAN ROOM (BOTTOM)
Popular service designed to meet every conceivable catering need.

serving the beef tenderloin. Only he wanted it served with béarnaise sauce! Don had never heard of béarnaise sauce, and being the honest person he was, he told Dr. McFee he didn't know how to make it. The doctor really liked Don and told him that was no problem: "Make an appointment with my wife Iris, and she will teach you how to make béarnaise sauce; then you will do the party." Don learned how to make the sauce and catered the party, which was for all of the department heads at the medical school. Each new party led to another party, and Don quickly gained a reputation as one of the finest caterers in San Antonio.

Don was contacted by one of San Antonio's most prominent attorneys, Jessie Oppenheimer, who asked him to cater a Christmas party in his offices, the first of many in years to come. At the first party, Don met John Leeper, who was the director of the McNay Art Museum. John commented that he'd heard Don was catering more parties than any other caterer in San Antonio. The museum had been using a longtime San Antonio caterer, to whom John had been very loyal, but she had recently announced that she was getting too old for the business and wished to retire. So Don began to cater lavish events at the museum, sautéing oysters over gas burners right under the Picassos and serving fresh steamed mussels among the sculptures. Today, of course, food and beverages are not even allowed in the exhibit rooms, much less being cooked in them! Through the museum events Don gained an entrée to the arts community, which led to ever more requests for parties in the homes of the patrons.

Don began to create innovative dishes like his acclaimed oysters Ernie. He was the first caterer to serve French-boned, grilled rib lamb chops, which guests held by the meatless bones, as finger foods. But Don still felt that his skills and general knowledge of food were limited. He decided that he needed to travel and learn more about the types of food that were being served on the east and west coasts to further expand the company's menus.

So in 1974 we made a trip to San Francisco, where we ate our way through the city's restaurants. Don discovered the Magic Pan Créperie, and we ate there twice in one day. He was fascinated with the flexibility of crepes and introduced them to San Antonio through his parties, serving both savory and dessert crepes.

The next year, Don and I made a trip to New York City. John Leeper insisted that we go to the Palace restaurant in Manhattan. We made reservations for dinner, priced at $100 per person, an extraordinary amount of money for a meal at the time! (Beluga caviar could be included for an additional charge.) The restaurant didn't even have a sign outside. The caviar was served from a little trolley that was wheeled around the dining room. Don loved the concept. The tables in the restaurant were arranged so that each was cloaked in privacy. We had never even dreamed a place like this existed. We didn't have wine, although the sommelier brought us the large, multi-paged wine list. The only wine we had ever tried was Mogen David, and, besides, we were totally intimidated by both the wine list and the sommelier. I ordered a whiskey sour, simply because it was the only cocktail I'd ever heard of! Ours eyes were opened to truly gourmet food, and Don's mind raced with the possibilities such food offered. After all, he had recently jumped from very basic barbecue to "gourmet catering" without even knowing what it was!

At the Palace, Don was introduced to the concept of tableside cart cooking. He was impressed as he watched elegantly clad waiters prepare Caesar salad in huge bowls from the carts. But he was especially fascinated with entrées like steak Diane, actually cooked in front of him in a shiny

copper sauté pan, then elegantly arranged on his plate with the side dishes and sauced with a flourish. Then there were the fabulous flamed desserts created tableside.

From these travel experiences in the mid-1970s, Don learned a great deal about new foods, new techniques, and new serving ideas. With each new bit of knowledge, he developed more confidence in what he was doing. While not as elegant and certainly not as pricey as the Palace, Don's catering was not far off from the style and range of menu items offered there. He added on-premise cooking stations, where guests were served meats, salads, appetizers, and desserts that had been prepared right in front of them. He began to set up omelet stations at his brunches, where guests could choose the fillings for their omelet and

watch as it was prepared. Don literally revolutionized catering in San Antonio. And, yes, he included caviar in many dishes!

Over the years Mr. Strange added on to the Strange's Party House property on Bandera. When the original version of *The Alamo*, starring John Wayne, was filmed in Texas in 1960, its premiere was held at the now historic Woodlawn Theater. San Antonio's chamber of commerce organized a four-day celebration, including a breakfast catered by the San Antonio Restaurant Association, and Mr. Strange was involved in planning and staging the event. In the process of tidying up the area around the theater in preparation for the premiere, the old Pig Stand restaurant next door was sold. Mr. Strange bought the building, had it cut in half, and moved it to the company's compound on Bandera Road, where he turned it into a commissary complete with a small kitchen.

But by the early 1970s the Party House building was used for perhaps only five or six on-premise events per year. Eventually it just became too much of a job to keep the place going, since the major focus had shifted to off-premise events, so the Stranges rented the spaces out to other businesses—there was the Beef and Bourbon restaurant for

A "frontier breakfast" is served by members of the San Antonio Restaurant Association as part of *The Alamo's* premiere celebration. Joe Strange serves Richard Boone (opposite, left) and Linda Cristal (this page); he looks on as John Wayne takes a plate (opposite, right).

Her parents were dirt farmers, and they certainly set the pace. Even though she was now ninety, this would be new to her. But remarkably, with a few changes to her room, she carried on business as usual. In the place of the hospital bed, two recliners were brought from her home. (Because of a bad back, she slept better in a recliner.) A fax machine was installed so that she could be in close communication with the office and receive daily reports. Someone from the office would bundle up all the mail and bring it over for her to open. Even if a letter was marked "personal" and addressed to somebody else, she would still open it and then send it back for distribution. She said you never knew when there would be a check inside, and she wasn't going to take any chances.

Don would talk to her every day, and she would bring him up to date on the gossip. Using a walker, she strolled all over the place to see what was going on. There was a larger room down her hall that she really wanted to move into, so she checked on the man living there to see how he was faring. Then she would bring him up to date on the goings-on—oh, how she loved it. The man down the hall outlived her, but she stayed closely involved in the company right up until her death in 2005 at the age of ninety-two.

In 1986 the company, which had still been operating under the name Strange's Party House, Inc., became Don Strange of Texas, Inc., to take advantage of a statewide initiative to support and promote Texas businesses.

My mother, Mary Singleton, had taken early retirement from her job at USAA but soon became bored. She went to work for Don and his mother in 1975, starting in the office, but Mrs. Strange thought she'd be more valuable in the kitchen operations. Eventually, Mother did all of the ordering for events and scheduled and supervised the permanent kitchen staff of seven, adding more part-time workers as needed for larger events. She was also responsible for developing many of the dishes that remain client favorites today, such as the company's signature Hot Mustard Sauce and the corn pudding, which is served with barbecue rather

a while, then a Japanese restaurant, a motorcycle shop, and a printing shop. In 1972 Mr. Strange passed away. In dire need of space for the expanding company and no longer needing the income, or headaches, from the leased spaces, Don and Mrs. Strange turned the entire space into a commissary kitchen, offices, and warehouse for the growing array of equipment, serving pieces, linens, and props that the company was amassing. After Mr. Strange's death, Don and his mother operated the company, with Don as the creative arm and Mrs. Strange taking care of the operation's finances with the same grit she had always possessed.

When it became necessary for her to move to an assisted-living facility, we were a bit concerned. We didn't know how she would take to a more sedentary existence. For Mrs. Strange, work was her life—it was all she knew.

than the usual sides. Mother started the practice of serving handmade breads and desserts at all company events, a practice still rare in San Antonio catering today. Mother had always been a wonderful home cook. I have delicious memories of a childhood filled with great comfort foods. She had never cooked in large quantities, however, nor was she used to cooking foods that were being called "gourmet" back then, so the job was a great challenge. But Mother rose to the challenge as if she'd been doing it all her life. Her biggest test came the day that Don brought her a menu for serving 35,000 teenagers for the International Lutheran Youth Conference! But she sourced all the food and supervised its preparation, helping to make the event happen. Mother retired from the company in 1989, after fourteen years of helping it grow.

Ours sons, Brian, Matt, and Jason, followed in their father's footsteps, with each starting to work for the company by the time they were from six to eleven or twelve, during the years of Strange's Party House. And they were all paid the going rate for the jobs they performed. Brian, our oldest, began to do whatever was necessary. By the time he was twelve, he knew how to tend bar. He didn't know beans about liquor, but he made the best martini around, and his presentation skills, like his dad's, were pure flair. He was fast and kept the lines moving. I remember a gray-hair-producing moment that occurred when Brian was fourteen. He had gone with his dad and the crew to do a party in Waxahachie. It was back when those big, clunky mobile phones had first been introduced. They were a godsend to the business, as Don could have personal contact with the various crews wherever they went. I had one at the house so that I could keep up with Don! It was in the wee hours of the night and I knew that the event would be over, but I hadn't heard from Don, so I called on the mobile phone. To my surprise, Brian answered. He told me they were on the road headed home. When I asked where his dad was, he replied, "He's asleep." Brian was driving the truck and pulling an equipment trailer! It was neither my first nor my last moment of temporary hysteria.

Brian went off to college and, following graduation, did a stint in the rock concert promotion business in Dallas. After a year in this high-pressure environment, he was convinced that he really didn't want to be a rock concert promoter, so he joined the company operations in the sales department. He had, however, learned a great deal about promoting events, which proved to be a valuable asset to the company.

I have a particularly vivid memory of Brian after one party. It was the Cattle Baron's Ball, held in September of 1990 at the Alamo—yes, the real-life Alamo in San Antonio. It was a very elegant affair for 1,800 guests, with Willie Nelson as the entertainer. After the guests had left, Brian and I were sitting on a rock wall, anticipating the monumental process of cleaning up and packing up that would soon begin. Brian spoke softly in the late-night quiet: "This is the part that really sucks." That night, in addition to the cleanup, the longhorn steers that Don had taken to the party decided they liked being at the Alamo and steadfastly refused to be loaded onto the trailer for the trip back to the ranch! We were all so exasperated with them that they almost got to stay there! Eventually Brian became the general manager of the company, and after Don's death, the CEO.

Matt, our middle son, recalls realizing in elementary school that his family was a bit "different" from the families of his schoolmates. His dad worked very late into the night, often not getting home from out-of-town events until the next day. And then there were all those famous people—politicians, celebrity chefs, wealthy business moguls—with whom his dad associated and who came to the house for parties: people like James Beard and Craig Claiborne, the Dixie Chicks, who played for an event at the ranch before they ever cut their first CD, and many more. Once, there was a project in Matt's home economics class for which the kids were all supposed to bring an apron from home. The other kids brought one of their mothers' aprons, some quite frilly with ruffles and appliqués. Don gave Matt a real chef's apron signed by one of the big-name chefs who had been to the house! The teacher was quite impressed. When he began to travel with his dad to out-of-town events, Matt mostly remembers the hard work and late hours. Back then, when a party was over, they packed up everything and drove back to San Antonio—from wherever they were, no matter what time it was! So Matt recalls many nights of sleeping on the floor of the company van on the way home, often pulling into San Antonio as the sun was rising.

After graduating from Hardin Simmons University in 1990, Matt joined the company. He worked with his grandmother, who had earned a reputation as a "steel magnolia" in business dealings, learning the firm's business aspects. After Mrs. Strange's death, Matt took over as the company's business manager as well as the events supervisor. Regardless of a person's "day job" at the company, everyone works at events! When Matt decided to spread his wings and explore new career opportunities away from the company, we supported him. Don was very proud to know that Matt had inherited his entrepreneurial spirit, which led to the founding of his home health care business, Assure Home Healthcare, Inc. But he still remains close to the business and is often called upon to answer various questions.

Jason, our youngest, got his first paycheck from the company when he was six years old. He helped his grandmother Mary make dinner rolls. For reasons he can't explain today, he feared that his older brothers would take his check, so he hid it by pinning it inside the shade of his bedside lamp, next to the light bulb. Well, the light bulb burned up his check, and he was afraid to tell anyone. When the check never cleared the bank, Don asked him what he had done with it. Jason broke down in tears and explained what had happened. He had no idea that a check could be replaced.

Jason worked his way into larger jobs and eventually began to travel with Don to out-of-town events. When he was twelve, he went with Don to cater a party at a horse auction at the Ruidoso Downs Race Track in Ruidoso, New

Left to right: Matt, Brian, Edith Strange, Jason, and Don.

Mexico. Company policy requires every company vehicle to be equipped with a tow chain. Don always figured that Murphy's Law ("if anything can go wrong, it will") haunted the catering business, and it was the norm, more often than not, that one vehicle on any given job would break down. This job was no exception. When they were all packed up and ready to make the drive home, the refrigerated truck, the largest vehicle they had taken, broke down. So Don got out the chain and hooked up the truck to the company van. Even as young as he was, the memory stuck in Jason's mind as a real Keystone Cops adventure. "I remember there was a really steep pass that you had to climb to get out of Ruidoso. When we started to climb the pass pulling that big truck, the front of the van came completely off the ground! Dad just kept yelling for them to give it more gas and keep going! By sheer will, I think, he made the little van pull that big truck over the pass and all the way back to San Antonio!"

The Don Strange Cheese Pineapple

★

2 cups (8 ounces) grated Cheddar
    cheese

2 cups (8 ounces) grated Swiss cheese

¼ cup mayonnaise

¼ cup Dijon-style mustard

½ teaspoon cayenne pepper

½ teaspoon granulated garlic

½ teaspoon kosher salt

1½ to 2 cups whole green pimento-stuffed
    olives, sliced into ¼-inch rounds

Leafy top cut from a fresh pineapple

Crackers of choice

From the early days of catering, the company featured an assortment of cheeses on its finger-food menu. To use the surplus of cheeses that were never put on the tables at catered events, Don created this cheese "pineapple." It was requested so often that soon cheese was being purchased specifically to make the creation. The bonus is that you have fresh pineapple to enjoy after your party!

Serves about 10 to 15

Combine the cheeses in a medium bowl. In a separate bowl, mix together the mayonnaise, mustard, cayenne pepper, granulated garlic, and salt, blending well. Stir the mayonnaise mixture into the cheeses, combining thoroughly. Form the cheese mixture into a pineapple shape, with a flat bottom so it will stand upright with stability. Place on an attractive serving platter. Refrigerate for about 4 hours, or until firm.

    Using a sharp, thin-bladed knife and beginning at the top of the pineapple shape, make a series of shallow cuts about 1¼ to 1½ inches apart on the bias across all sides. Then make another series of the cuts from the opposite direction to make a cross-hatch pattern (see photo). Gently press an olive slice into each diamond formed by the cuts. Place the leafy top from the fresh pineapple on top of the cheese shape. Serve with crackers of your choice.

Fried Cheese Balls

★

This is one of the dishes that Don served in the early days at Strange's Party House. As with all good dishes, we still get requests for these tasty little nibbles. Often Don just liked to bring them out again, and whenever he did, they were always a hit.

Makes about 30 cheese balls

Melt the butter in a heavy-bottomed 2-quart saucepan over medium heat. When the butter has melted, add the flour all at once and whisk to form a smooth roux. Whisk in the milk and adobo sauce; cook, whisking, until smooth and thick. Add salt and pepper. Remove pan from heat and whisk in the cheese, green onion, and cilantro. Continue to whisk until cheese has melted and mixture is smooth. Using a rubber spatula, turn the mixture out into a bowl and refrigerate until well chilled.

Shape the chilled mixture into 30 small balls. Place the cracker crumbs in a shallow baking dish and the beaten egg mixture in a separate bowl. Dip the cheese balls first in the cracker crumbs, coating well all over and shaking off excess. Then dip into the egg wash and once again in the cracker crumbs, coating well and shaking off excess. Place the breaded balls on a parchment paper–lined baking sheet. Cover with plastic wrap and refrigerate for up to 24 hours.

To cook the cheese balls, heat the oil to a temperature of 360 degrees. Fry quickly in small batches, turning often, until the crust is golden brown and crisp, about 1 minute. (The balls shouldn't touch, or they will stick together; they must be cooked quickly, or they will split.) Place the fried balls on a wire cooling rack set over a baking sheet to drain. Repeat with remaining balls, making sure that the oil returns to 360 degrees before beginning each batch. Let cool for at least 5 minutes before serving. Serve warm.

4 tablespoons unsalted butter

½ cup all-purpose flour

1 cup milk

1½ teaspoons adobo sauce from canned chipotle chiles

½ teaspoon kosher salt

Freshly ground black pepper to taste

2 cups (8 ounces) shredded sharp Cheddar cheese

1 large green onion, minced

2 teaspoons minced cilantro

6 cups fine cracker crumbs

2 eggs, well beaten and whisked into 2 cups milk

Canola oil for deep-frying

Dill Dip with Crudités

★

2 (8-ounce) packages cream cheese, softened and cut into 1-inch cubes

2 cups real mayonnaise

1 cup sour cream

Dash of Tabasco sauce

1 teaspoon dried dill weed

1 tablespoon minced parsley, preferably flat-leaf

1 tablespoon chopped chives

1 teaspoon Worcestershire sauce

1 tablespoon freshly squeezed lemon juice

1 teaspoon granulated garlic

1 teaspoon kosher salt

Raw vegetables, cut into bite-size pieces, such as broccoli, cherry tomatoes, carrot sticks, julienne strips of red and green bell pepper, celery sticks, cauliflower florettes, halved white mushrooms

One of the most popular stations at any party is the dip station. Great conversations commence around the dips as people munch, sip, and catch up on old friendships or good gossip. This remains one of the company's most popular dips and goes back to the days of Strange's Party House. It's terrific when served with bite-size pieces of raw vegetables.

Makes about 5 cups

Combine all ingredients except raw vegetables in work bowl of food processor fitted with steel blade. Process until smooth. Turn out into storage bowl with tight-fitting lid and refrigerate until ready to serve.

To serve, place an attractive serving bowl in the center of a large platter. Secure the bowl to the platter with a rolled piece of masking tape or duct tape so that it doesn't scoot around on the platter. Turn the dip out into the bowl. Arrange the vegetables around the dip as desired.

Dried Beef Dip

★

2 (8-ounce) packages cream cheese, softened

¼ cup milk

2 (2½-ounce) jars dried beef, finely chopped

½ cup finely chopped green bell pepper

¼ cup finely chopped green onion and tops

½ teaspoon granulated garlic

1 cup sour cream

½ cup plus ¼ cup chopped pecans

¼ cup real mayonnaise

4 tablespoons (½ stick) butter

Melba toast or toasted French bread rounds

Party guests really love this hearty dip with its beefy, nutty taste. Serve it in the casserole directly from the oven, or transfer it to a chafing dish if you want to keep it hot. Add the pecan topping after turning the dip out into the chafing dish if you choose the latter serving method.

Makes about 4 cups

Preheat oven to 300 degrees. Combine cream cheese, milk, dried beef, bell pepper, green onion, garlic, sour cream, and ½ cup of the pecans in a medium bowl; stir to blend well. Turn the mixture out into a 2-quart casserole dish suitable for serving. Bake in preheated oven until hot and bubbly, about 30 minutes. While the dip is cooking, melt the butter in a heavy-bottomed 8-inch skillet over medium heat. Add the remaining ¼ cup of chopped pecans and sauté until lightly browned and aromatic. When the dip is done, scatter the pecans over the top. Serve either hot or cold with Melba toast or toasted French bread rounds.

Grilled Lamb Cocktail Meatballs in Sweet and Sour Sauce

★

2 tablespoons medium-grain bulgur wheat, soaked in 1 cup warm water for 30 minutes, or until soft, then well drained

1 egg, well beaten

1 pound ground lamb

2 large garlic cloves, minced

1 small onion, minced and drained in a fine strainer

1 teaspoon freshly ground black pepper

1 teaspoon kosher salt

1 teaspoon ground cumin

1 teaspoon smoked paprika

2 tablespoons minced cilantro

Olive oil

Sweet and Sour Sauce

¼ cup olive oil

1 medium onion, finely chopped

2 large garlic cloves, minced

1 medium green bell pepper, finely chopped

1 (5-ounce) can tomato paste

1 (46-ounce) can pineapple juice, 3 tablespoons reserved

1 cup freshly squeezed lemon juice

1 teaspoon Oriental chili paste with garlic (available in the Asian section of most upscale supermarkets)

1¼ cups light brown sugar

2 tablespoons cornstarch, blended with reserved 3 tablespoons of pineapple juice

Kosher salt and freshly ground black pepper to taste

The cocktail meatball, or "Swedish" meatball, so named for unknown reasons, is one of the most often requested items in a caterer's repertoire. Our party planners are accustomed to hearing from clients, "And could we have some of those little meatballs in the sauce?" Company policy has always been that even if a client requests a timeworn dish, make it the best the client has ever tasted—something exciting, like it's brand new to the planet. The company's cocktail meatballs are from ground lamb, which turns them into an outside-the-box version.

Makes about 24 small (1-inch) meatballs

Combine the drained bulgur wheat and beaten egg in a large bowl, blending well. Add remaining ingredients except olive oil and blend together with your hands to form a smooth, well-blended mixture. Form into 24 small (1-inch) meatballs and thread onto bamboo skewers that have been soaked in water for 1 hour. Brush the meatballs with olive oil. Refrigerate until firm.

Make the Sweet and Sour Sauce. Heat olive oil in a heavy-bottomed, deep-sided 12-inch skillet over medium heat. Sauté the onion, garlic, and bell pepper until onion is wilted and transparent, about 5 minutes. Add the tomato paste and stir to blend well. Cook, stirring often, until the tomato paste is darkened and thick, about 5 minutes. Add the pineapple and lemon juices, chili paste with garlic, and brown sugar. Cook, stirring frequently, until the sugar has dissolved. Simmer on medium-low heat for 15 minutes. Bring to a boil and add the cornstarch mixture. Cook, stirring constantly, until the sauce thickens, about 2 minutes. Add salt and pepper. Keep hot over low heat; or cool and refrigerate, covered. Reheat when ready to use.

When ready to serve the dish, heat a gas grill to medium heat, or build a hardwood charcoal fire in a barbecue pit and allow it to burn down until the coals are glowing red and covered by a layer of white ash, about 20 to 30 minutes. Position the grill rack 6 inches above the heat source. Grill the meatballs for about 5 minutes per side, turning once. Do not overcook.

Slide the meatballs from the skewers into the hot Sweet and Sour Sauce in a chafing dish. Serve with toothpicks.

Chicken and Shrimp Teriyaki Roll-ups

⭐

Don created this dish in the 1970s and originally called it Shrimp Teriyaki. It became such a favorite with clients that it was served at just about every event until Don tired of it and created Grilled White Wings. Shrimp Teriyaki was served to James Beard at our 1976 reception in his honor and was one of the dishes that he praised.

Makes about 12 roll-ups

Place the chicken breasts between two sheets of plastic wrap. Using a meat pounder or dowel-type rolling pin, pound the breasts to a thickness of about ⅜ inch and a width of about 6 to 8 inches. Take care not to tear the meat! Cut each breast into 2-inch-wide strips. Place a shrimp at the end of each breast strip closest to you. Roll the breast into a tight roll, enclosing the shrimp. Wrap each roll in a bacon slice and thread onto a bamboo skewer, three per skewer.

      Place the roll-ups, seam sides down, in a single layer in a non-aluminum baking dish. Pour a liberal amount of the teriyaki sauce over the breasts. Cover with plastic wrap and refrigerate overnight or for at least 8 hours, turning often in the marinade.

      When you're ready to grill the roll-ups, heat a gas grill to medium heat, or build a hardwood charcoal fire in a barbecue pit and allow it to burn down until the coals are glowing red and covered by a layer of white ash, about 20 to 30 minutes. Place the grill rack 6 inches above the heat source. Remove the roll-ups from the marinade and grill, turning often, until cooked through and browned, about 10 to 15 minutes. Serve hot.

4 (8-ounce) boneless, skinless chicken breast halves

12 medium (16–30 count) shrimp, peeled and deveined

12 slices smoked bacon

Bottled teriyaki sauce

Creole Green Beans

⭐

In the early days of Strange's Party House, Mrs. Strange created the dishes and often did most of the cooking. The type of dishes the company served back then were good homemade comfort foods, like these tasty green beans. This one has remained a favorite for many, many years, although no one knows what Creole ties exist to the dish!

Serves 8

Preheat oven to 350 degrees. Fry the bacon slices until crisp; reserve the drippings. Drain the bacon on absorbent paper towels and crumble into small bits. Combine the bacon and reserved drippings in a 2-quart casserole dish. Add the drained green beans. In a separate bowl combine the ketchup, brown sugar, and chopped onion, stirring until the sugar is well blended. Pour the ketchup mixture into the casserole dish and stir to blend. Bake in preheated oven for 30 minutes, or until lightly browned and bubbly.

4 slices bacon

2 (15-ounce) cans green beans, drained

1 cup ketchup

1 cup light brown sugar

1 medium onion, chopped

Sautéed Oysters with Ernie Sauce

⋆

This is one of the most popular dishes in the Don Strange of Texas repertoire. It's a must-try for all oyster lovers. The sauce can be spooned onto the oysters or served on the side for dipping.

Makes 24 half-shell servings

Drain the oysters, reserving ¼ cup of the oyster liquor; pat oysters dry with absorbent paper towels and set aside.

Prepare the Ernie Sauce. Melt the butter in a heavy-bottomed 3-quart saucepan over medium heat. When the butter is sizzling, add the flour all at once, stirring vigorously to blend. Cook, stirring constantly, for 3 to 4 minutes. Combine all remaining ingredients and add to the butter roux, whisking to incorporate. Bring the mixture to a boil to thicken, then reduce heat and cook for 5 minutes. Keep warm while preparing the oysters.

Dredge each oyster in the seasoned flour and shake off excess. Melt the butter in a heavy-bottomed 14-inch skillet over medium-high heat. Add the oysters. Cook, stirring gently, just until the oysters begin to curl at the edges, about 3 to 4 minutes. Take care not to overcook them. They should still be quite soft.

Arrange the oyster shells on individual plates. Using a slotted spoon, place an oyster in each shell. Spoon some of the Ernie Sauce over each oyster or pass the sauce separately; serve at once.

*DISCARD THE FLAT HALF OF EACH OYSTER SHELL, saving the curved half. Scrub the shells thoroughly with a brush, then place them in the top rack of the dishwasher. Run the dishwasher on the normal cycle. After being washed following each use, the shells can be stored in a covered container and reused.

24 shucked oysters, shells scrubbed and reserved* (see "Purchasing and Shucking Oysters" on page 53)

4 cups all-purpose flour, seasoned with 2 tablespoons finely ground black pepper and 2 tablespoons kosher salt

½ pound (2 sticks) unsalted butter

Ernie Sauce

¼ pound (1 stick) unsalted butter

3 tablespoons all-purpose flour

¼ cup freshly squeezed lemon juice

2 tablespoons Worcestershire sauce

½ cup A-1 Steak Sauce

¼ cup reserved oyster liquor

¼ cup dry red wine

Strange's Party House Scalloped Potatoes

2 tablespoons butter

1 medium onion, chopped

3 garlic cloves, minced

½ teaspoon minced fresh thyme

Kosher salt

Freshly ground black pepper

2 cups whipping cream

½ teaspoon freshly grated nutmeg*

3 russet potatoes (about 1¾ pounds), peeled and sliced very thin

1 cup (4 ounces) shredded Cheddar cheese

Scalloped potatoes is a staple dish in a caterer's repertoire. Some versions are pretty bland and boring; others demonstrate a lot of creativity and actually taste very good. This dish was served in the early days both at Strange's Party House and at off-premise events. It's definitely in the creative category of scalloped potato recipes! When Don and I got married, Mr. and Mrs. Strange prepared a huge buffet reception for us, and this was one of the dishes they prepared. He never told me, but I'm sure Don was pressed into service to help cook the food!

Serves 6 to 8

Preheat oven to 350 degrees. Spray a 2-quart gratin dish with nonstick vegetable spray and set aside. Melt the butter in a heavy-bottomed, deep-sided 12-inch sauté pan. When butter foam subsides, add the onion, garlic, and thyme. Season to taste with salt and pepper. Cook, stirring often, until onion is wilted and transparent, about 8 minutes. Add the cream and bring it to a rolling boil. Reduce heat to a bare simmer and cook the mixture for about 3 to 4 minutes. Stir in the nutmeg and adjust seasonings, if desired. Turn off the heat and add the potatoes to the pan, stirring them gently into the cream mixture. Allow the mixture to sit for 5 minutes.

Turn half of the potato mixture out into the prepared dish; scatter half of the cheese evenly over the potato mixture. Pour the remaining potato-cream mixture into the dish and top with the remaining half of the cheese. Bake in preheated oven until potatoes are very tender and the top is lightly browned, about 45 minutes to 1 hour. Let the potatoes sit for 10 minutes before serving.

*THE FLAVOR OF NUTMEG deteriorates very quickly once it has been grated, so it is best to buy whole nutmeg pods and grate it as needed. There are many types of nutmeg graters on the market.

CHAPTER THREE

HemisFair San Antonio

A twenty-eight-year-old Don at an event in the United States Pavilion at HemisFair.

Many longtime residents regard the selection of San Antonio as the site for the 1968 World's Fair as a turning point in the city's modern history. Don always said that it was the turning point in the company's history as well as his personal awakening to the vast world of food and wine that existed beyond Texas—even beyond the United States. Don was twenty-eight when HemisFair opened, bringing visitors from around the globe to San Antonio. Along with the vast influx of visitors came the demand for trendy, upscale foods, the likes of which had not been served in the city prior to the fair. Don had such charisma and a vision of how he wanted to grow the business. He knew that capitalizing on the wealth of knowledge that had descended on the city was an excellent way to help accomplish his goals.

In the catering business in San Antonio in 1968, there were three or four companies that were doing barbecue dinners. Then HemisFair came, and a level of excitement began to ripple through the city as the complex rose from the ground. The city's downtown was transformed

45

with the creation of HemisFair Park, the enhancement of the San Antonio River into the present-day River Walk, and the building of the many hotels on its banks. One of the most noteworthy construction projects leading up to HemisFair was the "assembling" of the Hilton Palacio del Rio. I say "assembling" because that's precisely what they did to construct the hotel—they assembled it. The site, located in a choice spot on the river, was prepared, then the offices, restaurants, bars, parking, and other venues on the ground level were completed. The individual rooms were built as freestanding modules elsewhere, right down to the décor, bath fixtures, and window coverings—a finished hotel room ready to check into! The modules were brought to the site and lifted by cranes into place, stacked on top of each other, and bolted into place, creating an instant hotel. It was a much-talked-about innovation in commercial construction. Don was bowled over by such a unique concept and actually took our son Brian to watch the day they assembled the hotel, even though he was only eighteen months old. By the time the fair opened, downtown San Antonio had been turned into a haven for the thousands of visitors that converged on the city.

The company began to get requests from many of the directors of the foreign pavilions to cater various events. Don was particularly impressed by the Spanish Pavilion, where he catered many events. Each week the Spaniards would feature a different sherry producer at their site and would pair Don's menu items with the sherries. Because he was such an eager student, they loved teaching Don all about sherry. He learned about the importance of proper glassware and serving protocol. These evening events would be lavish affairs, with flamenco dancers and fabulous music. The Spaniards were masters of hospitality and shared their traditions with Don. He became fascinated with the concept of the "little bites," or *tapas,* which they asked him to prepare. He began planning private parties featuring the little bites as appetizers, eons before tapas became a major food trend in the United States. Don noticed that the Spaniards

were using the serving-station concept. He had been experimenting with the idea at a few of the company's parties for a while. In the Spanish Pavilion they would stretch rustic boards across two vintage wooden wine barrels to make serving bars for the sherry tastings. Don copied the barrel serving station, and hosts loved these unique, casual concepts that Don was introducing to their parties.

Don and his dad became friends with two cooks from India who had built a giant tandoori oven at the Indian Pavilion. They served tandoori chicken prepared in the oven every day of the fair. Don loved the exotic spices and flavors of this dish, flavors that he had never experienced. He would often wander the fair just tasting foods and flavors from faraway places. He would experiment with each flavor that appealed to him, creating new dishes or adding zesty flavors to existing ones in his repertoire.

During the fair each country's pavilion would celebrate a major event in its history on its anniversary date. Don recalls being hired by the pavilion of a very small Central American country to cater its independence-day celebration. The budget was miniscule—$100—so all it would cover was to have Don provide stemware and personnel to serve some very inexpensive champagne. But Don, of course, treated each and every job with the same respect and decorated the pavilion with his usual flourish. There was a parade and a little band playing the country's national anthem, and then the signal was given to begin serving the champagne. I can only imagine Don's horror as he watched the staff trying to open the chilled bottles. The corks, every single one of them, broke off at the neck. He said it was one his greatest acts of thinking on his feet to hide what was happening and get that bubbly opened and poured!

On the Fourth of July, Don was hired to provide bar service for the grand celebration at the United States Pavilion. Sponsored by American Airlines, the event was spectacular, and a truly fitting tribute to the host country. President Lyndon Baines Johnson, a multi-generation Texan, was scheduled to visit the pavilion for the celebration. Don and his staff had set up bars and beverage tables everywhere. During a lengthy briefing on the day's protocol by the Secret Service, they were told that there were to be absolutely no photographs taken during the president's visit, nor attempts to make personal contact. When LBJ arrived and strolled through the pavilion, flanked by Secret Service agents, one of Don's staff members, Waymon Lawson, stepped from behind a table and began to snap pictures. Don froze as he realized that the Secret Service agents were poised to jump at Waymon. He had visions of the whole team being hauled out of the pavilion in shackles! LBJ, however, stopped and said, "Why, hello sir! Here, let me stop and pose so that you can get a good picture." And Waymon snapped away to his heart's delight! Don said a sigh of relief had never felt so good before—or after.

I had no idea how the whole advent of Hemis-Fair would change us all. When we had the grocery store, Strange's Party House, and the catering events, it always seemed that if one of them was making money, the other two were losing it! We were always trying to make it, but never quite doing so. So, with my eighteen-month-old and a newborn baby, I'd listen to Don's stories about the happenings at HemisFair, but it was another world from changing diapers and making formula. Don told me that the company was doing well, but we were both so used to thinking of good times as only temporary that we certainly weren't going to count on this run of business as a permanent thing.

After all, HemisFair would only last a year—and then what would happen?

On the last day of the fair, all of the vendors were allowed to have a booth to advertise their services. Don and Mr. Strange set up their booth and told anyone who'd listen about the company and what they offered. At the end of the day, the two guys from India came by to ask Mr. Strange if he had any work for them. They'd decided they wanted to stay in Texas! Mr. Strange didn't, but years later Don was catering a large wedding at the Fort Worth Country Club. To his surprise, he discovered that one of the guys was the head chef at the club!

After the fair closed, there was an influx of people relocating to San Antonio. Many were fairgoers who had fallen in love with the city. Many saw the city as a growing entity and, therefore, a good place to relocate a business or open a new one, as the expanding population demanded an increasing variety of services. The University of Texas Health Science Center was built, bringing doctors and auxiliary personnel from around the country. The River Walk had established San Antonio as a very desirable tourist destination with its luxury hotels, shops, and many restaurants. As a result, not only did business continue at the Hemis-Fair pace, but it began to increase. And Don, having seen a glimpse of the world in his own backyard, became a man on a mission—a mission to take his catering to a new level of innovation and excellence.

Marinated Artichokes

⋆

6 whole artichokes

Juice of 2 lemons, halves reserved

3 tablespoons red wine vinegar

10 whole black peppercorns

½ teaspoon salt

Lettuce leaves

Marinade

1 quart apple cider vinegar

½ cup extra-virgin olive oil

1 tablespoon minced garlic

1 cup (4 ounces) finely grated Parmesan cheese

2 teaspoons kosher salt

1 tablespoon freshly ground black pepper

Don loved the great presentation that these majestic whole artichokes make when standing tall on a big colorful platter. He began serving them in the early days of off-premise catering, and they're still much in demand today. They're presented at the raw vegetable station at most parties.

Serves 6

Begin by preparing the marinade. Combine all ingredients in blender and blend until smooth. Set aside while cooking the artichokes. Whisk again before using.

Prepare the artichokes. Using a sharp knife, trim off the stems so the artichokes rest firmly on their bottoms and do not tip over. Using a serrated knife, slice 1 inch off the top of each artichoke. Rub the cut surfaces with a lemon half to prevent discoloring. Pull off any small or discolored leaves at the bottom of the artichokes. Using kitchen shears, trim the sharp points from each leaf. Hold the trimmed artichoke under cold running water until the leaves separate. Using your fingers, pull out the purplish prickly leaves down in the center of the artichokes. Then, using a small spoon, scrape out and discard the hairy choke. Press the cone of leaves back together.

Set the artichokes on their bottoms in a saucepan large enough to hold them all in a single layer, or use two saucepans. Add the lemon juice, red wine vinegar, peppercorns, and salt; then add cold water to cover the artichokes. Bring to a boil, reduce heat, and simmer, covered, until the leaves pull off easily and the heart in the center is tender when tested with a sharp knife, about 15 to 20 minutes.

When the artichokes are done, remove from the pan and drain, upside down, in a colander. Arrange artichokes on their bottoms in a single layer in a deep-sided baking dish. Pour the marinade evenly over the artichokes and refrigerate until well chilled, spooning marinade over them frequently. Serve chilled on a bed of lettuce leaves.

Texas Gulf Coast Crab Cakes with Rémoulade Sauce

Don's crab cakes have long been one of the company's most frequently requested dishes. Be sure to use lump crabmeat and don't mix too vigorously. You should still have plenty of nice, juicy lumps of crabmeat in the mixture. Both the crab cakes and the sauce can be made ahead of time and refrigerated.

Makes 18 crab cakes

Make the Rémoulade Sauce. Combine all ingredients in work bowl of food processor fitted with steel blade. Process until smooth and well blended. Transfer to storage container with tight-fitting lid and refrigerate until ready to use.

To make the crab cakes, pick through the crabmeat to remove any bits of shell and cartilage. Combine the two types of crabmeat in a large bowl; taking care not to break up the lumps; set aside. In a separate bowl, whisk together the sour cream, mustard, green onions, parsley, and eggs until well blended. Pour the mixture into the crabmeat and add the bread crumbs. Mix well, but stir gently, taking care to break up the lumps of crabmeat as little as possible. Season with salt and pepper.

Using your hands, firmly pat the mixture into 18 crab cakes. Place the seasoned panko bread crumbs in a shallow baking dish. Press both sides of each crab cake into the crumbs, coating well and shaking off excess. If preparing the crab cakes in advance, place on a parchment-lined baking sheet, cover with plastic wrap, and refrigerate for up to 24 hours.

When ready to cook the crab cakes, preheat oven to 300 degrees. Heat the canola oil in a heavy-bottomed 12-inch skillet over medium heat. Working in batches of 4 to 6 cakes, sauté the crab cakes in a single layer, without crowding, until golden brown on both sides, turning once. Transfer to a baking sheet and place in warm oven. Repeat with remaining crab cakes.

To serve, drizzle a portion of the Rémoulade Sauce over each cake. Garnish with minced parsley and a lemon twist, if desired.

1 pound jumbo lump crabmeat

1 pound regular lump crabmeat

1 cup sour cream

⅓ cup Dijon-style mustard

1 cup thinly sliced green onions and tops

¼ cup minced fresh parsley, preferably flat-leaf

4 eggs, beaten

3 cups fresh bread crumbs, or more as needed

Kosher salt and freshly ground black pepper to taste

4 cups panko (Japanese-style) bread crumbs, seasoned with 2 tablespoons kosher salt and 1 tablespoon black pepper

⅓ cup canola oil

Minced parsley and lemon twists as garnish, if desired

Rémoulade Sauce

2 cups real mayonnaise

¼ cup Creole mustard, or substitute another whole-grain mustard

3 green onions and tops, roughly chopped

1½ tablespoons minced fresh parsley, preferably flat-leaf

2 anchovy fillets, roughly chopped

2 tablespoons capers, drained

2 tablespoons freshly squeezed lemon juice

2 tablespoons dry sherry

1 tablespoon Worcestershire sauce

½ teaspoon cayenne pepper

½ teaspoon kosher salt, or to taste

Pinch of finely ground black pepper

Shrimp Ceviche

★

Ceviche, prepared using sweet Texas Gulf shrimp, is hard to beat when served in the summer. It's such a cooling, refreshing dish, yet it embodies the real taste of a Texas summer.

Serves 10

Place the shrimp in a nonreactive bowl. Add the lemon juice and Tabasco, tossing to coat well. Cover and refrigerate until the shrimp have turned opaque throughout, about 3 hours. Toss the shrimp in the lemon mixture frequently.

Combine the tomatoes, onion, cilantro, chiles, cloves, oregano, ketchup, salt, and pepper in a medium bowl and stir to blend well. Turn mixture out into the bowl of shrimp and stir to combine thoroughly.

To serve, line 10 large martini glasses with a portion of the shredded romaine leaves. Spoon a portion of the shrimp mixture into each glass; garnish glass rim with a lime wedge.

2 pounds peeled and deveined cocktail (70–90 count) shrimp, uncooked

2 tablespoons freshly squeezed lemon juice

1 tablespoon Tabasco sauce

2 cups tiny-diced Roma tomatoes

1 cup tiny-diced white onion

½ cup minced cilantro

2 tablespoons minced serrano chiles

3 large garlic cloves, minced

1½ teaspoons minced Mexican oregano

1 cup ketchup

Kosher salt and freshly ground black pepper to taste

Shredded romaine lettuce leaves

Lime wedges for garnishing

Oysters Rockefeller

★

Rock salt

24 shucked oysters on the half shell (see "Purchasing and Shucking Oysters" on opposite page)

1 (10-ounce) package frozen chopped spinach, thawed

6 tablespoons butter

1 bunch watercress, chopped

¼ cup minced flat-leaf parsley

5 green onions and tops, finely chopped

¼ cup finely minced celery

¾ teaspoon kosher salt

½ teaspoon freshly ground black pepper

½ teaspoon dried marjoram

½ teaspoon dried basil

½ teaspoon cayenne pepper, or to taste

2 tablespoons Pernod or anisette liqueur

1 cup whipping cream

⅔ cup unseasoned bread crumbs mixed with ⅓ cup finely grated Romano cheese

Baked oysters on the half shell make a stunning presentation at any party. Don's version of Oysters Rockefeller is a party favorite with customers. The addition of peppery watercress and a touch of Pernod, or another anise-flavored liqueur, takes the flavor of the classic spinach topping totally over the top.

Makes 24 half-shell servings

Preheat oven to 400 degrees. Line a heavy-duty rimmed baking sheet with rock salt. Nest the oysters in the half shell in the rock salt; set aside while preparing the topping.

Place the spinach in a wire strainer and press firmly to remove all moisture; set aside. Melt the butter in a heavy-bottomed 12-inch skillet over medium heat. Add the spinach, watercress, parsley, green onions, and celery. Sauté until the vegetables are wilted, about 3 minutes. Add the seasonings, Pernod, and whipping cream, stirring to blend well. Bring the mixture to a boil and cook, stirring often, until thickened, about 4 minutes. Remove from heat.

Place an even layer of the spinach topping on each oyster, then scatter some of the bread crumb mixture over each. Bake in preheated oven until topping is lightly browned, the filling is bubbly, and the oysters are just barely cooked, about 8 to 10 minutes. Serve hot.

HERE'S HOW YOU DO IT
Purchasing and Shucking Oysters:

Despite the old adage about eating oysters only in months ending with an r, oysters are edible year-round, although they have more flavor during spawning season, which occurs in the cold-weather months. Oysters are a valuable source of protein, vitamins, and minerals. And, here's the best part. They're very low in fat. A 3-ounce serving, or about 6 oysters, has only 58 calories and 46 milligrams of cholesterol. They're also an excellent source of iron, zinc, and vitamin B_2, as well as a good source of phosphorus.

When buying oysters in their shells, pick up a few of them. They should be cold and dirty or sandy, as though freshly plucked from the oyster bed and not overwashed. (Washing can cause the shell to open.) Smell the oysters. They should smell like the ocean, with a briny, fresh smell. Each oyster should feel heavy for its size, meaning that it has retained a lot of moisture.

When you purchase oysters in their shells, keep them cold. If you keep them on ice, be sure to place the ice on a perforated pan or in a colander so the melting ice will drain. If oysters are immersed in fresh water, they will die. They will keep in the refrigerator for up to five days. If a shell is wide open, tap it. If it closes, the oyster is still alive; if it doesn't close, the oyster is dead and must be discarded.

To shuck an oyster, always wear heavy gloves. Scrub the shell with a stiff brush and rinse right before opening. Holding the shell in one hand and the sturdy, specially designed oyster knife in the other, insert the knife at the hinge and twist. Run the blade all the way around to pry the oyster open. Cut the oyster muscle where it fastens to the inside of the shell to free the oyster.

If you don't intend to use the oyster liquor inside the shells, reserve and freeze it for use in sauces or soups. The liquor, prized by chefs, has a marvelous, slightly marine flavor that can add a nuance of the sea to many dishes.

Chicken Bisteeya

★

These delicious sweet and savory rolls, with origins in Morocco, make great party foods. They can be assembled and frozen, then baked frozen when you need them. Don first served them back in the 1980s, and they still have a dedicated following at parties today. They're as addictive as potato chips—you can't eat just one!

Makes 24 rolls

Combine the almonds, granulated sugar, and cinnamon in work bowl of food processor fitted with steel blade. Process until the mixture is the consistency of cornmeal; set aside.

Combine the saffron and hot water in a small bowl. Let stand for 10 minutes.

Melt 3 tablespoons of the butter in a heavy-bottomed 5-quart soup pot over medium-high heat. Sauté the onion and garlic, stirring often, until the onion is golden brown, about 4 to 5 minutes. Reduce heat to medium and add the ginger, turmeric, cumin, and pepper. Cook, stirring, for 3 minutes. Add the chicken pieces, chicken stock, and saffron mixture. Simmer, covered, until chicken is very tender and cooked through, about 30 to 35 minutes. Turn chicken pieces once while cooking. Remove chicken from pot and set aside to cool. Reserve pan juices. When chicken is cool enough to handle, remove meat from bones; discard skin and bones. Shred the chicken using your fingers.

Reduce the reserved liquid in the pan to 2 cups. Reduce the heat to medium and add the beaten eggs in a slow, steady stream while whisking. Cook until eggs are curdled and set. Quickly add cilantro, parsley, and lemon juice. Stir in the shredded chicken and season to taste with salt and pepper. Remove pan from heat and pour the mixture through a fine strainer. Let the chicken mixture drain, undisturbed, for 1 hour.

Melt the remaining butter in a small saucepan. Cut the phyllo dough sheets in half lengthwise. Stack them together and cover with parchment paper. Place a slightly damp kitchen towel over the top.

Working with one cut piece of dough at a time, brush the surface of the dough lightly with melted butter and scatter some of the almond mixture over the length of the sheet. Repeat with another piece of dough, buttering and sugaring it and aligning it on top of the first half so that the edges are even.

With the small edge toward you, place ¼ cup of the chicken mixture about 2 inches from the bottom of the pastry. Spread it slightly over the dough, leaving a 1-inch border at each side. Fold the bottom of the pastry up over the filling and then fold the borders in over the filling on each side. Roll the pastry tightly into an egg-roll shape, continuing until you reach the top of the pastry. Butter the edge flap and press it down on the roll. Place seam side down on a baking sheet. Repeat with remaining dough and chicken mixture to make 24 rolls. Refrigerate for 1 hour. (The rolls can also be frozen at this point; cover them with 2 or 3 layers of plastic wrap, then foil.)

When ready to cook the bisteeya, preheat oven to 425 degrees. Place the baking sheet in preheated oven and bake until pastry is browned and puffed, about 15 to 20 minutes. Remove to a wire cooling rack and cool slightly. Place confectioner's sugar in a fine strainer and dust some over each bisteeya. Sprinkle a pinch of cinnamon over each roll. Serve warm.

⅔ cup sliced, skin-on almonds

¼ cup granulated sugar

1 teaspoon ground cinnamon

¼ teaspoon crumbled saffron threads

3 tablespoons hot water

6 ounces (1½ sticks) unsalted butter

1 medium onion, chopped fine

2 large garlic cloves, sliced thin

¾ teaspoon ground ginger

¼ teaspoon ground turmeric

½ teaspoon ground cumin

½ teaspoon freshly ground black pepper

1 (3-pound) chicken, cut into 8 pieces

2 cups chicken stock

5 eggs, beaten

3 tablespoons minced cilantro

3 tablespoons minced parsley, preferably flat-leaf

1 tablespoon freshly squeezed lemon juice

Kosher salt and freshly ground black pepper to taste

24 sheets phyllo pastry

Confectioner's sugar and ground cinnamon for dusting

Dauphine Potatoes

★

5 medium russet potatoes, about 2¼ pounds, peeled and cut into 1-inch cubes

½ teaspoon cayenne pepper

2 tablespoons finely chopped chives

1½ teaspoons kosher salt

1 teaspoon freshly ground black pepper

⅔ cup milk

¼ pound (1 stick) plus 2 tablespoons butter

6 eggs

1 teaspoon freshly grated nutmeg

1 cup water

1 cup all-purpose flour

Canola oil for deep frying heated to 350 degrees

Don added this tasty potato dish to the menu for seated dinners in the late 1970s. The crispy little morsels were piled onto a serving platter and passed separately from the entrée for a very showy presentation. Clients have always loved them. You'll never want another French fry after you taste these crispy-shelled little bites with their creamy, buttery centers!

Serves 8 to 10

Place the diced potatoes in a heavy-bottomed 4-quart saucepan. Add cold water to cover and boil until the potatoes are very tender, about 20 to 25 minutes. Drain the potatoes and transfer to a large bowl. Mash well and season with cayenne pepper, chives, salt, and black pepper. Add the milk and 2 tablespoons of the butter. Beat 2 of the eggs in a separate bowl and add the nutmeg. Add the beaten eggs to the potatoes.* Set aside.

Combine the water and remaining stick of butter in a heavy-bottomed 2-quart saucepan and bring to a rolling boil. Vigorously whisk in the flour and remove pan from heat. Continue to whisk the mixture until it comes together in a satiny mixture and begins to leave the side of the pan. Add the remaining eggs, one at a time, whisking vigorously and blending well after each addition. Stir the flour mixture into the potatoes, incorporating thoroughly. The potatoes may be made ahead of time up to this point and refrigerated for 24 hours.

Just before serving, preheat oven to 225 degrees. Place a wire cooling rack over a baking sheet. Drop the potato mixture by rounded teaspoonfuls into the preheated oil. Do not crowd the potato balls. Fry until golden brown, about 3 minutes. Remove the puffed potatoes using a slotted spoon and place them on the wire rack. Keep warm in preheated low oven while frying the remaining batches, or the potatoes will become greasy.

*THE POTATO MIXTURE can be "customized" to the entrée by adding finely minced onion, minced bell pepper, crabmeat, minced boiled shrimp, parsley, chives, and other seasonings.

CHAPTER FOUR

The Halcyon Days of the Texas Oil Boom

"**W**henever you are asked if you can do a job, tell 'em, 'Certainly I can!'—then get busy and find out how to do it." This well-known advice from Theodore Roosevelt, another of America's more colorful and ambitious men, was surely familiar to Don Strange because this was the way he operated: first getting the job, then figuring out how to pull it off. By the late 1970s, Strange's Party House had established a firm reputation as a quality catering company under Don's stewardship. There were weddings and elegant private parties, barbecue galas, and Mexican fiesta–style events, each one bringing a new challenge to Don. And he met each new challenge with a heightened level of innovation, making every event more spectacular than the previous one. Bookings came at a steady pace. The company provided employment to about twenty people, and business was growing.

Then the oil boom exploded in Texas. It was a boom to rival the actual discovery of oil in the state in the early 1900s. Suddenly there were overnight millionaires as money gushed from the ground. "Black gold" they called it. The newly rich oil barons became the defining class of high

Don's Uncle Merle.

society in Texas. Even Hollywood took note of the new life-style developing from the wealth flowing in the state with the creation of the long-running TV series *Dallas*. Every Friday night America tuned in to catch the latest scandal in the lives of the oil-rich Ewing family at their grand Southfork Ranch. The oil barons, eager to show off their newfound wealth, combined with the older established clientele to suddenly overwhelm Strange's Party House with business.

There were requests for huge events, and the company was doing parties seven days a week. Often there were multiple bookings for the same dates. And the parties weren't just in San Antonio but all over the state. One holiday season the company did twelve parties in one day. It became a routine for Don to be in Houston or another Texas city on Friday night, catering the grand opening of some high-rise building, and in West Texas the next day, doing an oil company's barbecue. I remember the chaos before Don was able to hire enough staff to pull off near-simultaneous events all over the state. He bought trucks and vans to carry food and equipment. He hired buses to

transport staff to the huge events, which often required staffs of forty or fifty. I think he rarely slept. He would charter private aircraft to get himself and his key people from one event to the next, often in the middle of the night in order to be at the location of the next event to begin setting up and grilling the next morning. He said he was able to sleep on the planes! Looking back, Don said that chartering private aircraft was the only way the company was able to handle the hundreds of events that were scheduled during those days.

One weekend the company catered an event for 700 people to celebrate the opening of a new building in Laredo on a Friday night. There was a noon luncheon for 50 scheduled at Iron Mountain Ranch outside Marathon the next day. One caravan of the company's supply trucks was on the road to Marathon as Don was heading to Laredo with another. He had chartered a King Air to be waiting at the Laredo airport after the evening event there. Don

and his key party managers got on the plane as the Laredo crew headed back to San Antonio in the trucks. The plane landed at the private airstrip at the ranch in the middle of the night. A Suburban with the keys in it was waiting for Don and his group to drive to the ranch headquarters, which was five miles from the airstrip. He got two hours of sleep that night on the plane, then headed straight to the area where the crew from San Antonio was setting up pits to start cooking for the party at noon.

The owner of Iron Mountain Ranch was very pleased with the party and hired Don to cater the opening of his new offices in a bank building in Midland. The oilman's offices constituted the entire seventeenth floor of the building. Applying his station concept, Don used different offices as the various food stations! It was a spectacular event with grilled beef tenderloin served in the oilman's office. Oysters were sautéed on-site in the offices of a family member, and many more dishes were served in other offices, even in the hallways where people mingled. The following week a family member called to tell Don how much everyone had enjoyed the event and to thank him for making it such a success. He said the sautéed oysters were one of the most delicious dishes he had ever tasted. "But," he wondered, "do you have any solution for getting the smell of oysters out of that office?"

The cattle business was flourishing right along with the oil industry, as oil was discovered on many of the old ranches. The ranching families around the state began to enhance their ranch properties. With the proliferation of the ranches came the demand for ever more exotic breeds of cattle, many of which were being imported from foreign countries. Dallas carpet magnate L. D. Brinkman, who popularized the Brangus breed, is credited with introducing the concept of the upscale cattle auction when he hosted the first one, which he asked Don to cater.

The ranch-sponsored cattle auction became a grand social event. Ranchers would arrive by every conveyance, from limousines to private jets and helicopters, to attend the auctions, where a single bull might fetch a million dollars. After the auction the party would begin, and Don was often the man behind the party. He had developed a method for slow-smoking an entire side of beef in a special rack that he designed and had fabricated solely for the company's use. The "Don Strange side of beef" became a much-requested item at ranch barbecues. Budgets were large, sometimes nonexistent, at these events.

There were so many legendary events involving celebrities and, well, Texas legends during those days. Don catered a cattle auction at the Pyramid Ranch near Tyler. No expense was spared for this event. A special stage had been erected for the entertainment, which turned out to be Fats Domino! The auction arena was designed and built just like a movie theater. There were over a hundred private planes parked at the ranch's landing strip. Don said it was a spectacular sight to see.

Three huge tents were set up for the party before the auction. One was for the food. The host requested that the catering staff wear black slacks and red tails, which Don had to source from a band uniform supplier. The food service began at 10 a.m. with Bloody Marys and sautéed oysters, to be followed by a grand buffet at noon. The other two tents were for luxury retailer Neiman Marcus, one for fur sales, the other, jewelry. The day turned very cold, with

rain and accompanying thunder and lightning. Don said that Neiman Marcus sold a lot of those fur coats that day!

The rain continued to get worse, and the lightning was so intense that it seemed like thousands of flashbulbs were going off every few minutes. Fats Domino wouldn't go on stage because there was so much electronic equipment set up for his performance. So Don's crew had to wait to serve the buffet. Finally the lightning abated, and Fats performed to a delighted audience. Then the crew was given five minutes' notice to serve the buffet. They began to scramble in every direction, and Don said he began to panic because he and two of the cooks had to leave as soon as the buffet was served to join another crew setting up for a bank opening in

Houston that night. He was running to tend to some detail when he pulled a tendon in his leg. He supervised the buffet, dragging his leg behind him! Most people would've just gone home, but not Don Strange. After the buffet, he got on the plane that was waiting for him, flew to Houston, and supervised the event for the bank opening, all the while in agony, dragging his leg. Not until he returned home would he see a doctor.

With all the successes of the cattle auctions, the well-established Hereford breeding families decided to enter the arena. After a couple of sales that were rather conservative in nature, one family decided to try hosting an auction. Their first sale was a good one, with Don's food and a popular country and western band. Six months later they called Don to plan the food for another sale, only this time they wanted the event to be outrageously lavish. They not only completely refurbished their ranch headquarters but arranged to have Donnie and Marie Osmond as the entertainment. The Osmonds presented a spectacular show, the guests were awed by the food and its presentation, but the sale was a flop.

The company catered the opening of a new building for the Homart Corporation in Dallas. It was a five-story building with a lobby on each floor. Ray Charles and his band performed in the main lobby. Don prepared food with a different theme for each floor, using the station concept for serving. One floor was devoted to Texas food like barbecued beef and roasted pig, another to Asian foods, and so on. The setup for the event was, understandably, extensive and lasted until 2 a.m. The hotel rooms that Don had reserved for himself and the staff had been given to others since they hadn't been claimed earlier, so the entire crew slept on couches in the building's many lobbies.

Don catered private business parties for Dallas real estate developer Trammel Crow at his home. The "parties" would include six or seven busloads of guests! Most of these parties were Mexican-themed dinners using the station concept. Then Don was asked to cater the opening of Trammel Crow's Las Colinas in Dallas. There was a meeting at the corporate office to plan the event. Don told me that he had been introduced to a man by the name of Stanley Marcus but that he didn't know who the man was. Don was never known for either name-dropping or celebrity worship. To Don, all of his clients were celebrities.

The directive to Don from the Las Colinas staff was that they wanted the guests to be totally in awe of the uniqueness of the event. Don raised a huge white tent next to the Las Colinas fountain, which featured life-size bronze

horses at full gallop. Don said the horses were so lifelike that they seemed on the verge of charging out of the water! Centered inside the tent was Don's forty-foot antique mirror-backed lighted bar that he had transported to Dallas. On both sides of the bar he set up colorful and elaborately decorated food stations. At one station a whole side of beef was slowly smoking over glowing coals; at another, staff members hand-patted gorditas, which they then grilled and topped with refried beans, guacamole, cheese, and pico de gallo. At yet another station, the staff sliced avocados in half, serving them with bowls of various fillings, plus there were many more stations. On the opposite side of the fountain was another white tent equipped with bleacher seating and elegant chandeliers. Inside this tent the Dallas Symphony Orchestra played. Don described the scene as an awesome testament to the unique blend of opposite cultures in Texas—a side of beef slowly smoking and ladies patting out gorditas to the strains of classical music.

Each year in the early 1980s Don did a large Christmas party for a San Antonio doctor who would invite the local hospital staff. There was always a huge spread of finger foods, including thin-sliced grilled beef tenderloin, cheeses, a variety of sandwich condiments, and small rounds of rye bread and French bread at a station where guests could put together sandwiches. But the signature item of this doctor's parties was the piña coladas. The doctor loved them and spared no expense to have an unlimited supply for his annual party. At the time, Don had a bartender by the name of Washington, who was very good but never got ruffled over details. Washington always called the piña coladas "Pinaladas," despite Don's best efforts at teaching him how to pronounce the name of the drink. But it didn't seem to matter, as the guests would ask for them by Washington's name—Pinaladas. The party was always a great success, and generally a pretty raucous event. But one year the party just seemed like it wasn't getting off the ground. The atmosphere was way too quiet and subdued. The doctor came to Don in somewhat of a panic, asking if he could tell what was wrong. Don had noticed that Washington was not acting quite like himself that day, so he went to check on the situation at the bar. There he discovered the problem. There was no rum. Washington had neglected to bring the rum in from the van and had been making the Pinaladas with no booze. Don got the rum, and the party was soon as cacophonous as ever.

Exxon had a huge oil field in South Texas. When one of the wells would hit pay dirt, company executives would call Don to throw a little "celebration party." Celebration parties were scheduled by all the ancillary industries involved in the production of oil, too—the drilling

companies, the operating companies, the tool companies, and more. I'm sure he forgot more events than he remembered. But Don never forgot some of the real-life J. R. Ewings he met along the way, including Larry Hagman himself. These were indeed halcyon times.

Sometimes it seemed that for every successful event, there was a near disaster. Don often said that the fellow credited with Murphy's Law must've been a caterer. He would often joke about writing a book about some of the calamities and said he'd call it something like *If You Only Knew What Happened before Your Party*! Looking back on them, he could laugh, but I had to thank the Man Upstairs for seeing him through each potentially bad situation.

On one occasion, the company had scheduled a large event in San Antonio on a Friday evening and another large event in Corpus Christi on Saturday. Don knew that the San Antonio party would last very late into the night, so he had another crew load the food and equipment trucks for the Corpus Christi event and arranged a time to meet them at the company's Bandera Road commissary. When Don and the Corpus crew convened to head south, they discovered that someone had driven through the gates at the company headquarters and stolen the van filled with the food for the Corpus event! But Don, ever the quick thinker, sent part of the crew with the equipment on to Corpus to start the setup and then got enough cooks back into the kitchen to replicate the food for the event. He chartered a plane, and he and the remaining crew loaded the food into another truck and drove to the airport, where they loaded it all onto the plane and flew to Corpus. By then, the equipment truck had arrived at the location of the Corpus party and unloaded, so they met Don at the airport and unloaded the food from the plane onto the truck, drove to the event site, and started cooking. The host never knew that the party almost didn't happen. And, yes, the other truck was found near Loop 1604, undamaged.

On one particularly busy night, there were several events scheduled. The kitchen was running behind with the food order for one party, but Don needed to get to the site to begin setting up. So he left one of his managers to oversee the remaining food prep and the loading of the truck. The manager, however, was scheduled to be at another event, so he turned the task over to yet another staff member. The food was finished in plenty of time and loaded onto the truck, but the driver got very lost trying to find the party. Don couldn't leave the setup, so he called me to go find the truck and guide the crew to the party. I did, and the party started on time and went off without a hitch, although I think Don aged a year waiting for that food and then scrambling to get it in place at the serving stations.

Di-Anna Arias, the company's director of sales and marketing, recalls another cliffhanger. On a Friday shortly after noon, my cousin Melinda Martin, who has worked for the company for since 1977, answered a phone call from the manager of a new nursing home. The woman calling was concerned that she hadn't been notified what time the crew would arrive to set up for the nursing home's grand opening at 5 p.m. Melinda went to the event schedule book but didn't find the party listed! Not wanting to convey this problem to the woman, she finessed the call, getting details of what food was ordered and the name of the company sales rep who had booked the party. Melinda immediately went to Di-Anna about the predicament. Di-Anna discovered that, sure enough, one of the sales staff had indeed scheduled the party but neglected to put it on the schedule; therefore, it hadn't gone through the proper sequence of steps used by the company to prepare food, equipment, and staff for parties. Di-Anna knew that other events had been scheduled for later that same evening, many of which had ordered the same foods, so she raced to the kitchen and commandeered some of the foods for the later parties, instructing the cooks to start new batches for those parties. She rounded up enough staff to serve the nursing home party and to load all of the equipment and food. Then she and Melinda grabbed props and serving pieces to create a lovely setting and dashed to the location to set up the party, which began promptly at 5 p.m. Whew!

By far the biggest disaster happened in 1980, when the company was scheduled to do a large event in Houston for a regular client. I knew that Don was always willing to risk life and limb to see that every party was perfect. I'd seen him get hurt many times and just keep on going because that's what he had to do to make an event successful. But this time he used up several of those proverbial

nine lives! That's probably when I began to believe that success is often lunacy that works. He had retrofitted several of the company's vans to run on propane because it was more economical than gasoline. For this particular event he was serving steamship rounds of beef, only the timing was so tight that he wasn't going to be able to cook them on-site. They would have to be roasted until almost done and finished in Houston—and that was against his policy of always cooking meats at the event so that he could season them as they cooked and slice them fresh at their peak moment of perfection.

The success of running the vans on tanks of propane spawned the idea in Don's mind that perhaps he could put two residential-type gas stoves in one of the vans and hook them up to two propane tanks. And that's just what he did. Then he seasoned the two beef rounds and put them in large roasting pans in the mobile ovens; he and Lee, one of his waiters at the time, headed to Houston with the caravan of other company vehicles. Lee drove the van so that Don would be free to tend to the meat. The meat was roasting marvelously, he said, but the one thing he hadn't taken into account in his grand plan was that roasting such huge cuts of beef creates a *lot* of melted fat. About the time they were rolling into Katy on I-10, just outside of Houston, the fat began to slosh out of the roasting pans and onto the open-flame burners of the stoves. Don was resting in the passenger seat when Lee smelled smoke. Glancing to his right, he noticed flames shooting up the side of the van where Don had hung his dress clothes for the party. Don said he was jolted awake when Lee started yelling, "Mr. Don, your clothes are on fire!" Lee hurriedly pulled off the side of the road, leaped out of the van, and started running. But Don's first concern was not getting himself out of the van, now visibly on fire, but saving the meat. He managed to get one of the huge pans out of the oven by pulling it out the back doors of the van. When he tried to climb back in to get the other roast, the flames, which by now had filled the van, were too intense. He dragged the red-hot roasting pan with the one roast away from the van. Don's van was in the middle of the caravan, so of course the other company trucks pulled off the highway, too.

Several passersby who saw the van on fire called the police, who arrived right ahead of the fire department. The women from the staff were hysterical there on the side of the road, and Don was pacing frantically. Just as a police officer came to talk to him, one of the propane tanks blew up. Don said the officer looked relieved when he said, "Well, we've got that out of the way." Of course, Don had to tell him "No, actually, there are two more tanks."

After the other two tanks blew and the fire department put out the fire, Don loaded his saved roast onto the refrigerated truck, and the crew headed into Houston. As they began to set up the tables, someone knocked over a lighted candle and caught one of the tablecloths on fire. The women began to scream, and Don said he really thought they were going to mutiny. He poured water on the tablecloth, putting out the fire, and eventually managed to calm everyone down. Once he was satisfied that everything was set up perfectly and the one roast would be ample for the party, he dashed out to get some clothes to wear, returning in time to greet the host, perfectly attired and at ease. The host never knew what had happened, and the party was a smashing success. The compliments on the taste of the perfectly roasted steamship round were glowing.

The oil boom was certainly an extended adventure of many facets. But then there's that old saying about all good things coming to an end. When the oil boom ended abruptly in the early 1980s, the Texas economy hit rock bottom within a few short months. Events were being cancelled left and right. Companies and individuals who had always given special-event parties on a regular basis weren't rescheduling. And there were no new bookings. What's more, Don had catered a lavish affair for a family

that apparently ran out of money shortly afterward, and he never got paid. The company had geared up during the boom, buying trucks and loads of equipment. There was a huge staff. Plus, we had recently bought a ranch. And we had two sons in college and one in private school.

At the beginning of the downturn, Don catered a fund-raiser for the Midland Symphony. The gala was held in the grand atrium of a new twelve-story bank building in Midland. A CPA at the party pointed out to Don several famous paintings hanging in the bank's lobby. He told Don that most of them had been on the walls of his clients' homes two weeks before.

I don't know how he did it or how we survived, but Don rethought the whole scope of the company and developed new sources of business. Weddings saved the day. Don always said they're the bread and butter of any catering operation. A wedding is one event that doesn't seem to depend on the economy. People will continue to fall in love and get married. From its early days the company had been known for doing beautiful weddings, and now we had the ranch to offer as an attractive wedding venue, so weddings became a big portion of our business.

Don developed a rapport with the planners of community galas and fund-raisers, which led to several lucrative events. He made it a point to get to know all of the folks at the San Antonio Convention and Visitors Bureau. San Antonio was becoming a popular destination for conventions, which offered additional opportunities for catering jobs. By concentrating on local events, cutting staff, which was very painful for Don, selling off unneeded equipment, and tightening our personal belts, our family and the company managed to survive the black days of the oil bust. Don remarked that one thing he could say about the whole era—boom and bust—was that he learned a lot!

Spinach Quesadillas

★

1¼ cups (6 ounces) shredded Monterey Jack cheese

1 (10-ounce) package frozen chopped spinach, cooked, drained, and pressed to remove all water

Half of a medium green bell pepper, cut into ¼-inch dice

2 green onions and tops, finely chopped

1½ teaspoons granulated garlic

½ teaspoon ground cumin

¾ teaspoon kosher salt, or to taste

6 (8-inch) flour tortillas

Don Strange of Texas has always been known for great Tex-Mex dishes. To Don, the quesadilla offered endless possibilities. The ingredients for the filling are limited only by the cook's creativity. They can be customized to harmonize with other dishes on the menu or merely to please your guests! This tasty spinach filling has always been popular.

Makes 18 wedges

Combine all ingredients except tortillas in a medium bowl. Toss to blend well.

Working with one tortilla at a time, place an equal portion of the spinach mixture across the bottom half of each tortilla. Fold the top portion of the tortillas over the filling to enclose. Press with the palms of your hands to compress the quesadillas.

Spray a large skillet or flat griddle with nonstick cooking spray and heat to medium-hot. Cook the quesadillas on one side until very lightly browned and the cheese is melting, about 2 minutes. Turn and cook the other side, about 2 minutes. Repeat until all quesadillas have been cooked. Cut each quesadilla into 3 wedges. Serve warm.

Stuffed Avocado Halves

★

10 unpeeled avocados, halved and seeded

Suggested Stuffings

Assorted salad dressings, such as Green Goddess, French, blue cheese, ranch, Thousand Island, or your choice

Pico de Gallo (see page 70)

Shredded cheeses, such as Monterey Jack, Cheddar, or your choice

Sour cream

Caviar

Bacon bits

The hostess for a party that Don catered many years ago gave him the inspiration for this dish, a version of which she had seen at an avocado plantation in Mexico. It quickly became a much-requested favorite among the company's repertoire. The unpeeled avocado halves are served at an avocado bar, piled on platters or wooden dough bowls and served with an array of stuffings. Be sure to use the black, bumpy-skinned Haas avocados for this dish; select those that are moderately ripe (not overly soft) so the flesh can easily be scooped out with a spoon. The variety of stuffings is limited only by your imagination. During cooler months you could offer chili or carne guisada with complementary condiments.

Serves 10 to 15

To serve, arrange the avocado halves on a serving platter, wooden dough bowl, or other serving piece. Arrange the various stuffings and condiments in colorful bowls around the avocado halves.

Picadillo Dip

★

Picadillo is a very traditional Mexican condiment. It is often used as a stuffing for chiles rellenos or empanadas as well as a filling for quesadillas. Don created this version to use as a hot dip served in a chafing dish with a basket of corn tortilla chips alongside.

Makes about 7 cups

Heat the canola oil in a heavy-bottomed 12-inch skillet over medium heat. Add the ground beef and cook, stirring often to break up any lumps of meat, just until it is cooked through and no pink remains, about 5 to 6 minutes. Stir in the bell peppers, onion, and garlic. Cook, stirring frequently, until the onion is very wilted and transparent, about 8 minutes. Add all remaining ingredients except salt and pepper. Cook, stirring often, until the mixture thickens and the potatoes are soft, about 15 to 20 minutes. Add salt and pepper. Taste for seasoning and adjust as needed. Serve hot in a Crock-Pot or chafing dish with corn tortilla chips.

¼ cup canola oil

8 ounces lean ground beef

2 medium green bell peppers, cut into ¼-inch dice

1 medium onion, cut into ¼-inch dice

3 large garlic cloves, minced

2 medium potatoes, about 11 ounces, cut into ½-inch cubes

¼ cup golden raisins

¼ cup sliced, skin-on almonds

1½ teaspoons ground cumin

2 large tomatoes, skins and seeds removed, diced

1 (28-ounce) can crushed tomatoes

1 teaspoon kosher salt, or to taste

1 teaspoon freshly ground black pepper, or to taste

Corn tortilla chips

Gorditas

★

2 cups masa harina, or more as needed

¼ cup all-purpose flour

2 teaspoons baking powder

½ teaspoon kosher salt

¼ cup lard or solid shortening

1½ cups warm water, or more as needed

¼ cup canola oil

2 cups hot Refried Beans (see page 71)

Maggie's Guacamole (see page 156)

1 pound shredded Cheddar cheese

Pico de Gallo (see recipe below)

Pico de Gallo

6 Roma tomatoes, cut into ¼-inch dice

⅔ cup red onion, cut into ¼-inch dice

3 or 4 serrano chiles, seeds and veins removed, minced

½ cup chopped cilantro leaves and tender top stems

Juice of ½ large lime

Kosher salt to taste*

Gorditas were one of Don's favorites ever since the early days, and the company still serves them at just about every party—at special stations where they're cooked in front of the guests and topped with various toppings. They never seem to go out of fashion. Gorditas were served at receptions for both James Beard and Craig Claiborne at our home. Neither of these distinguished food personalities had ever tasted real Tex-Mex foods, and both were quite enamored with the fresh new flavors.

Makes 14 gorditas

Prepare the Pico de Gallo. Combine all ingredients in a nonreactive bowl. Toss to blend well. Season with salt. Refrigerate, tightly covered, until ready to serve.

Heat a flat griddle to about 375 degrees. Combine the masa harina, all-purpose flour, baking powder, and salt, tossing to blend well. Add the lard, water, and canola oil. Knead until all ingredients are well blended and the dough forms a ball. Divide dough into 14 balls, about 2½ ounces each, or the size of a golf ball. Keep the balls covered with a clean dish towel.

Using a rolling pin, a tortilla press, or your hands, roll each ball between 2 plastic bags to form a 5-inch-diameter disk about ¼-inch thick. Place the disks on the preheated griddle in batches and cook until lightly browned, about 2 minutes per side.

Top the warm masa cakes with equal portions of the refried beans and guacamole, then scatter a portion of the shredded cheese over the beans. Top each gordita with a portion of the Pico de Gallo and serve at once.

*IN A GOOD PICO DE GALLO, salt is the ingredient that creates harmony among the ingredients and makes them do a little two-step in your mouth. So don't be stingy with the salt.

Refried Beans

★

Mexican-style refried beans are a very versatile dish in the world of catering. When cooked right, they're very tasty. They can be served as a side dish with just about any meat, and they make a good topping for a variety of casual foods like chalupas and gorditas. The company always serves them as a condiment with fajitas.

Serves 6 to 8

Combine the beans and their liquid, onion, and garlic in a large saucepan over medium heat. Cook, stirring occasionally, until the mixture has thickened and the onions are very soft, about 30 minutes. Remove pan from the heat and mash the beans until fairly smooth. (If you like your refried beans completely smooth, you can puree them in the food processor to desired degree of smoothness.)

Heat the bacon drippings or lard in a heavy-bottomed 12-inch skillet, preferably cast-iron, over medium heat. Add the mashed beans to the hot fat and cook, stirring often, until the mixture is very thick and creamy and the beans have absorbed the drippings. Do not allow the beans to stick to the bottom of the skillet. Serve hot, topping each portion with some of the shredded cheese and a scattering of green onions.

3 (15-ounce) cans pinto beans and their liquid

1 large onion, chopped

1½ teaspoons minced garlic

⅓ cup bacon drippings or lard

1¼ cups (5 ounces) shredded Colby cheese

⅓ cup sliced green onions

Elizabeth Taylor Chili

This recipe, which party guests have loved for many years, came from the recipe files of my mother, Mary Singleton. The recipe originated at the long-shuttered Los Angeles restaurant Chasen's, which was once the hot spot of movie stars and studio moguls. The legend goes that Elizabeth Taylor loved this chili so much that she had it shipped to her in Rome when she was filming the epic *Cleopatra*. Thereafter, the restaurant called it Elizabeth Taylor Chili. In the beginning, the company would serve it at parties during cooler weather. Then at a large event many years ago the weather turned suddenly cold, so the chili was served as a filling for the popular stuffed avocado halves in addition to the customary cold fillings. The guests appreciated the hearty hot chili so much that it became a staple condiment for avocado halves in the winter!

Serves 10 to 12

Cook the beans according to directions on package; stir in the cumin and tomatoes, blending well. Keep warm over low heat.

In a heavy-bottomed, deep-sided 14-inch skillet, heat the canola oil until hot. Add the chili meat and ground pork. Cook, stirring often, until meats are lightly browned, about 10 minutes. Add the chili powder and black pepper, stirring to blend well. Pour off fat and set meat aside. Melt the butter in a separate heavy-bottomed 12-inch skillet; add the onions, garlic, bell peppers, and parsley and cook until onions are wilted and transparent, about 8 to 10 minutes. Stir the vegetables and meats into the beans, blending well. Simmer for 1 hour. Serve hot.

1 pound dried pinto beans

½ teaspoon cumin seed

½ teaspoon ground cumin

2⅔ (15-ounce) cans diced tomatoes and their liquid (5 cups)

¼ cup canola oil

4 pounds chili meat

1 pound ground pork

½ cup chili powder

1 teaspoon black pepper

¼ pound (1 stick) butter

2 onions, chopped

4 medium garlic cloves, minced

2 medium green bell peppers, chopped

1 bunch parsley, chopped

Opposite: Elizabeth Taylor Chili with Don Strange Jalapeño Corn Bread.

Spinach Soufflé Crepes

⭐

2 tablespoons unsalted butter, melted

2 tablespoons dry bread crumbs

24 ounces fresh spinach, chopped

1 small onion, finely chopped

⅔ cup water

4 tablespoons unsalted butter

3½ tablespoons all-purpose flour

½ teaspoon kosher salt

¼ teaspoon cayenne pepper

4 eggs, separated, yolks beaten and whites reserved at room temperature

Juice of 1 medium lemon

1 cup (4 ounces) shredded Monterey Jack cheese

¼ teaspoon cream of tartar

10 ready-made crepes, warmed

This dish was a big hit with clients. The crepes were always served at a special station where they were assembled, plated, and handed to guests. They also make a great side dish for a seated dinner, served with a simple grilled or broiled meat dish.

Makes 12 crepes

Preheat oven to 350 degrees. Grease a 3-quart round casserole dish with the melted butter; coat bottom and sides of dish with bread crumbs and shake out excess. Set aside. Place the spinach and onion in a heavy-bottomed 2-quart saucepan and add the water. Cover and cook over medium-high heat until spinach is wilted and cooked through, about 10 minutes; set aside. Melt the butter in a small saucepan over medium heat. Add the flour, salt, and cayenne pepper; stir to blend well. Cook, stirring constantly, for 2 to 3 minutes; remove from heat. Add the flour mixture to the undrained spinach, blending well. Cook just to thicken. Remove from heat and quickly stir in the egg yolks, lemon juice, and cheese. Blend well and set aside.

Combine the egg whites with cream of tartar in an oil-free bowl and beat at high speed until medium-stiff peaks form. Add the spinach mixture to the beaten whites and fold together gently until well mixed. Turn mixture out into prepared casserole dish, taking care not to jostle the mixture and deflate the egg whites. Set the casserole dish in a larger dish and place on middle rack of preheated oven. Add hot water to the larger dish to come halfway up the sides of the casserole dish. Bake until soufflé is puffed and set, about 50 minutes. It should not jiggle when the dish is gently shaken.

To serve, spoon a portion of the soufflé along the center of each warm crepe. Fold the sides over to cover the filling. Place on serving plates with seam side down.

HERE'S HOW YOU DO IT

Making Crepes: Crepes were a favorite medium of Don's for serving food and making it look great on a plate. You can fill a crepe with just about anything. Fold it over, put it on a plate seam side down, drizzle a little sauce on it (even if the sauce is store-bought or made from a mix), garnish it with some herb or mint leaves, or a shrimp, or a berry, depending on what's inside the crepe, and you've got yourself a very elegant presentation.

If you're going to make your own crepes, it's wise to invest in a dedicated French crepe pan—one that you'll use only for making crepes. Once the pan is well seasoned with butter, never wash it in water. After you're done with a crepe-making session, simply wipe it out thoroughly with paper towels and put it away. (Once it's well seasoned, nothing will stick.)

Much like breakfast pancakes, the first batch or two never turns out a great-looking crepe. But don't give up—the pan must re-season itself, especially if it hasn't been used in a while, and then you'll be flipping out crepes like greased lightning!

Chilled Poached Salmon with Avocado Mayonnaise

★

This poached salmon dish makes a beautiful presentation when the salmon is served on a large platter and garnished with lime and lemon slices. Serving such an elegant dish as catered fare (and with a flavored, homemade mayonnaise) caused quite a sensation back when Don first began to serve it. The mayonnaise is served in a separate bowl placed beside the salmon. It's a great party dish for home cooks, too, as it can be prepared ahead of time!

Serves 8 to 10 as a buffet dish

Trim any ragged edges from the salmon and remove any small bones that you feel along the edge of the fillet, using tweezers or small needle-nose pliers; refrigerate while making the poaching broth.

Combine all ingredients for the court bouillon in a large pot and bring to a rolling boil. Boil for 5 minutes, reduce heat, cover, and simmer for 1 hour. Strain the court bouillon through a fine strainer, pressing down on vegetables to remove all of the liquid. Discard vegetables.

Pour the strained court bouillon into a deep-sided oval roasting pan large enough for the salmon to lay flat. Bring to a simmer. Place the salmon on a double thickness of aluminum foil large enough to extend above the rim of the pot. Lower the fish into the simmering court bouillon and simmer until flesh is no longer translucent, about 8 to 12 minutes. Remove the fish by grasping the sides of the foil and lifting it from the court bouillon. Cut away excess foil and transfer the fish to a wire rack set over a baking sheet; refrigerate until well chilled.

Meanwhile, make the Avocado Mayonnaise. Combine avocado, green onions, cilantro, and orange zest in work bowl of food processor fitted with steel blade. Process until smooth. Add the lemon and orange juices, mustard, egg yolks, and salt; process until smooth and yolks are thickened, about 2 minutes. With machine running, add the olive oil in a slow, steady stream through the feed tube until all has been added. Process an additional 15 seconds to form a smooth emulsion. Transfer to a storage container with tight-fitting lid and refrigerate until ready to serve.

When the fish is well chilled, slide it onto a large serving platter with the aid of a long metal spatula. Garnish with lime and lemon slices. Serve with a separate bowl of the Avocado Mayonnaise. Provide a small spatula so that guests can cut portions of the fish.

1 wild-caught salmon fillet, about 4 pounds, skinned (see "Buying Fresh Fish [and Making Sure They're Fresh]" on page 146)

Lime and lemon slices as garnish

Court Bouillon

2 cups dry white wine

½ cup white wine vinegar

2 large leeks, root ends and green tops removed, washed well, and sliced (see "Using Leeks" on page 76)

2 carrots, scraped and sliced thin

2 large garlic cloves, peeled and smashed

1 celery stalk, roughly chopped

2 fresh thyme sprigs

2 fresh tarragon sprigs

12 whole black peppercorns

1 bay leaf

6 sprigs parsley

2 teaspoons kosher salt

6 cups seafood stock or bottled clam juice (see "Making Seafood Stock" on page 140)

Avocado Mayonnaise

1 medium avocado, peeled, seeded, and cut into chunks

2 green onions and tops, roughly chopped

¼ cup firmly packed cilantro leaves and tender top stems

1 heaping teaspoon orange zest

2 tablespoons freshly squeezed lemon juice

2 tablespoons freshly squeezed orange juice

2 teaspoons Dijon-style mustard

2 egg yolks

1½ teaspoons kosher salt

1½ cups extra-virgin olive oil

Crab-Stuffed Artichoke Bottoms

★

2 (14-ounce) cans artichoke bottoms

¼ cup olive oil

1 cup real mayonnaise

⅓ cup sour cream

2 tablespoons whole-grain mustard

¼ cup whipping cream

2 teaspoons freshly squeezed lemon juice

1 heaping tablespoon drained capers

1 tablespoon minced cilantro

3 green onions and tops, sliced thin

1½ teaspoons curry powder, or to taste

¼ teaspoon cayenne pepper

Kosher salt to taste

1 pound lump crabmeat

These delicious, dazzling little hors d'oeuvres were served to James Beard at a 1976 reception in his honor. Everyone loved them, and Mr. Beard wrote about them later in one of his syndicated newspaper columns. They make great finger food at a party or an elegant first course to a seated meal. If you use them as a first course, serve two per person on a bed of lettuce leaves or spring mix salad.

Serves 10 to 12

Drain the artichoke bottoms and pat dry using absorbent paper towels; set aside. Heat the olive oil in a heavy-bottomed 12-inch skillet over medium heat. Sauté the artichoke bottoms in the oil until they are just beginning to brown, about 6 minutes. Drain on absorbent paper towels and set aside to cool.

Combine all remaining ingredients except crabmeat in a medium bowl. Whisk to blend well. Carefully pick through the crabmeat to remove bits of shell. Gently fold in the crabmeat, taking care not to break up the luscious lumps, but making sure that all of the crabmeat is covered with dressing.

Fill each artichoke bottom with a portion of the crabmeat and serve as desired.

HERE'S HOW YOU DO IT

Using Leeks: Leeks, a delicious member of the *Allium* genus, are often overlooked by home cooks. When you're looking for a delicate onionlike taste in a dish—without onion's pronounced, front-of-the-mouth hit—try leeks. Their taste is very subtle and can often provide just the needed note to round out the flavor of a dish.

When using leeks, always wash them well. Cut off and discard the root ends and the upper green portions. Slice the white portions in half lengthwise through the center. Run the leeks under cold, running water, fanning out the layers to remove imbedded dirt.

Grilled Beef Tenderloin with Henry Bain Sauce

★

Don Strange of Texas is known for fine grilled and pit-roasted meats, and this grilled tenderloin is now its signature dish. Don served beef tenderloin instead of the more common brisket because the tenderloin is the leanest, tenderest cut of meat on a steer, and that translates to an immensely flavorful, juicy, tender serving of barbecue. Don had no idea where he first tasted Henry Bain Sauce, but we recently learned that it was created at the historic Pendennis Club in Louisville, Kentucky, where Henry Bain was the head waiter. The original version of the sauce contained Kentucky bourbon whiskey, but it can be omitted. The grilled tenderloin can be served chilled and sliced thin, with thin-sliced party rye bread and various sandwich spreads so that guests can make their own sandwiches.

Serves 10 to 12

Make the Henry Bain Sauce by placing all ingredients in a blender and processing until smooth and well blended. Refrigerate until ready to serve. Serve at room temperature. Any unused portions of the sauce can be refrigerated for up to two weeks.

To grill the tenderloin, season the meat all over with salt and a liberal amount of black pepper, actually rubbing the pepper into the meat. Using cotton butcher's twine, tie the tenderloin at 2-inch intervals to maintain the round shape and uniform thickness. Place the meat on a parchment-lined baking sheet and set aside to dry-marinate at room temperature for 1 hour.

Build a hardwood charcoal fire in a barbecue pit and allow it to burn down until the coals are glowing red and covered by a layer of white ash, about 20 to 30 minutes. Place the grill rack 6 inches above the coals. Glaze the tenderloin all over with olive oil. Place the meat over the hottest part of the fire to sear it, turning often with chef's tongs (searing the meat gives it a nice caramelized brown color and seals in the juices). Finish grilling on medium-low heat.*

When the meat is done to the desired stage, transfer to a cutting board, cover loosely with foil, and allow to rest for about 10 minutes to redistribute the juices. Slice into ½-inch-thick slices. Serve hot with Henry Bain Sauce.

*TOTAL COOKING TIME will vary according to the exact weight of the meat, but generally, for medium-rare, the doneness level for optimum taste and tenderness, figure about 16 minutes of grilling time per pound. Be sure to use an instant-read meat thermometer to determine the internal temperature.

Here's handy guide for calculating the degree of doneness in grilled or roasted meats:

Rare: 120–125°F

Medium-rare: 130–135°F

Medium: 140–145°F

Medium-well done: 150°F

Well done: above 155°F

1 whole beef tenderloin, 4½ to 5 pounds, trimmed of fat and silverskin (see "Trimming a Whole Beef Tenderloin" on page 80)

Kosher salt and freshly ground black pepper to taste

Olive oil

Henry Bain Sauce

2 cups Major Grey's chutney

1¾ cups ketchup

1¼ cups A-1 Steak Sauce

1¼ cups Worcestershire sauce

⅔ cup good-quality bourbon whiskey (optional)

2 teaspoons Tabasco sauce

Opposite: Grilled Beef Tenderloin with Henry Bain Sauce and Dauphine Potatoes.

HERE'S HOW YOU DO IT

Trimming a Whole Beef Tenderloin: Many home cooks are daunted by the prospect of trimming a whole beef tenderloin. But take a deep breath, and take your time—it's easy to do.

Remove all surface fat and membranes using your fingers. Next, remove the "chain," a long piece of fat and tendons running the length of the tenderloin. Start at the narrow end of the tenderloin and, using your fingers, separate the chain from the meat. When you get to the top, or butt end, of the tenderloin, use a sharp boning knife to make long, feathered cuts to remove the chain. Discard the chain (or render it slowly, along with the other waxy fat you remove, to produce some nice beef fat). Next, remove the silverskin, the thick, silvery fat that covers portions of the tenderloin on both sides. Shimmy your knife under a ½-inch-wide portion of silverskin at a time. Use your free hand to hold the silverskin taut; slide the knife down the length of the silverskin with the blade always angled up toward the silverskin, not on the meat. Repeat until all silverskin has been removed. Next, remove the large piece of meat attached to the large butt end of the meat. Save this piece for later use (it's perfect for making Steak Diane). Cut off the bottom 2 inches of the tenderloin, which are thin and would burn before the rest of the meat is cooked. Save this piece also. You should now have a well-trimmed, solid 12- to 13-inch-long cut of meat!

If you'd like to have a little supply of pure beef fat (for frying some delicious, real *pommes frites*, or French fries), place all of the tenderloin trimmings in a saucepan on very low heat. Cook, turning often, until the trimmings are very brown and crisp and all the fat has been rendered, about 4 to 5 hours. Be sure to render the trimmings over very low heat so that they do not cook too quickly, which will give the fat a charred taste.

Don Strange Jalapeño Corn Bread

⭐

This corn bread is pretty legendary. The secret to making corn bread with a nice crispy crust is to cook it in a cast-iron skillet. Grease the skillet liberally with bacon drippings and place it in the preheating oven while you make the batter. You'll have a crispy crust with a hint of bacon flavor. And who wouldn't love that, especially when served with barbecued meats?

Serves 8 to 10

Preheat oven to 425 degrees. Grease a 12-inch cast-iron skillet liberally with bacon drippings and place in the oven. In a large bowl combine the cornmeal, flour, sugar, baking powder, salt, and dehydrated onion. Whisk or stir with a fork to blend well. Add the eggs, milk, bacon drippings, corn, jalapeños, and cheese; stir to combine thoroughly. Do not over beat the dough.

Remove the skillet from the oven and place on a heat-proof surface. Pour the batter into the skillet and return to the oven. Bake for 20 minutes, or until a wooden pick inserted in the center of the cornbread comes out clean. Turn out onto a cooling rack to cool slightly before cutting into wedges. Serve hot.

2 cups cornmeal, preferably stone-ground

1 cup sifted all-purpose flour

¼ cup sugar

2 teaspoons baking powder

¾ teaspoon salt

¼ cup dehydrated onion

2 eggs, beaten

1 cup milk

¼ cup bacon drippings

½ cup frozen whole-kernel corn, thawed

2 jalapeños, seeds and veins removed, minced

1 cup (4 ounces) shredded Cheddar cheese

Sopapillas with Leche Quemada

★

3 cups unbleached all-purpose flour

2 teaspoons baking powder

1 teaspoon salt

5 tablespoons lard, or solid vegetable shortening

About 1¼ cups warm water

Canola oil for deep-frying, heated to 350 degrees

Cinnamon-sugar for dusting

Leche Quemada

2 cups sweetened condensed milk

¼ teaspoon cinnamon

2 teaspoons Mexican vanilla

½ cup sugar

4 tablespoons unsalted butter, cut into 1-inch cubes

⅔ cup whipping cream

Don served these wonderful, eat-with-your-fingers dessert treats at an intimate party for forty people, hosted by Texas carpet magnate L. D. Brinkman at his ranch in Kerrville, Texas. You can bet that whenever and wherever these little sinfully delicious puffy pastries are served at a party, there will be plenty of oohs and aahs. They're quite addictive on their own, but Don raised the bar of pleasure about ten notches higher by serving them with Leche Quemada, a Mexican burnt-milk caramel. Don would always have his cooks fry the sopapillas in front of the guests. It's such an experience to watch the pastries puff in the hot oil. When they're done, they're dusted with cinnamon sugar and served hot, with the Leche Quemada for dipping. Just really decadent!

Makes 26 sopapillas

Make the Leche Quemada. Combine the condensed milk, cinnamon, and vanilla in a bowl and set aside. Melt the sugar in a heavy-bottomed 6-quart saucepan over medium-high heat. (The large pan size is necessary to prevent overflow when liquid is added to the hot caramel.) Cook until it has formed a rich, dark caramel, or a candy thermometer registers about 320 degrees. Add the milk mixture to the caramel all at once. (The mixture will spit and bubble furiously, and the caramel will harden. Take care that none of this very hot mixture splashes on you.) Lower the heat and stir the mixture until it is smooth and the caramel has melted. Remove from heat and cool to lukewarm. Whisk the butter into the lukewarm sauce until well blended. Rapidly whisk in the whipping cream. Serve warm.

To make the sopapillas, mix all dry ingredients in a large bowl, tossing to blend well. Using a fork or pastry cutter, or just your hands, cut in the lard until the mixture resembles coarse meal.

Add the warm water a little at a time, mixing after each addition, until the dough is soft but not sticky.

Turn the dough out onto a lightly floured work surface and knead for a few minutes. Form the dough into a disk and cover with a clean kitchen towel. Let it rest for 10 minutes. Arrange a wire cooling rack over a baking sheet; set aside.

Lightly flour work surface and roll the dough out into a large rectangle about ⅜-inch thick. Cut the dough into small rectangles about 4 inches by 2½ inches. Fry a few pieces at a time, without crowding, until they are golden brown and puffed, about 2 minutes per side; turn once. Remove the sopapillas to the prepared cooling rack. Dust both sides with the cinnamon-sugar mixture immediately. Repeat with the remaining dough pieces, maintaining the oil temperature at 350 degrees.

Serve the sopapillas hot with the Leche Quemada for dipping.

CHAPTER FIVE

Innovations in Catering

By the time Don and I were married in 1961, he had been working in the food business for nine years. But it wasn't until after a year's stint at the University of Texas in Austin, during which he realized that his greatest talents wouldn't be recognized in a classroom, that his creative flair in the food business began to blossom. In retrospect, I've come to believe that he acquired his sense of innovation from his dad, who was a visionary. Mr. Strange had taken the great leap of faith to quit his job and open the original grocery store, which was the company's genesis, in a remote location with borrowed money, with no knowledge of the grocery business. But Don took his father's ideas to a much higher level than Mr. Strange had ever dreamed of.

Don had no formal food training whatsoever. He always said he was trained by the "seat-of-the-pants" method. Early in his career he realized that imagination was the key element to innovation. Make events fun; create action; make a big splash—those were Don's hallmarks. You can hire good people to cook the dishes you dream up, but not everyone can create magical settings that are unique to each event. Yet Don could. His food is not complex, but it's

At a time when catering in San Antonio meant a very predictable Texas-style barbecue dinner—smoked, sliced brisket, maybe some sausage, potato salad, pinto beans, coleslaw, loaves of white bread, barbecue sauce (with hamburger dills and sliced onions, if it was an upscale affair), and some sort of sheet cake for dessert—Don was dreaming up ways to be unpredictable. He began to realize that there was a rich heritage of food right under his nose in San Antonio. The city's culinary heritage was not built on cowboy barbecue but rather on the *norteño* foods that had been evolving in the city since way before Texas became a state.

By tapping into that vast repertoire of north-of-the-border Mexican cooking, he created a style of catering that was unheard of at the time. He fused the mystique of Texas history and culture with a style of cuisine that remains unsurpassed today. Don began to serve dishes like gorditas and quesadillas at parties. And not only did he serve them, but he created the concept of on-site cooking and serving stations. The cooks would pat out the masa dough and cook the gorditas on a special cast-iron cooker that Don had designed (he later named it the Texas Grill Pardner); then they would top them with traditional toppings and hand them to the guests freshly made. The same method was used to make the quesadillas; corn and flour tortillas were placed on the special grill, topped with various fillings and cheese, then folded and toasted just to melt the cheese—all in front of the guests. Having noticed the colorful, two-wheeled carts of street vendors in Mexico, he envisioned using similar, moveable carts as food cooking and serving

made from scratch, using fresh ingredients, and it's good! When he met with potential clients, he would listen to them, paying attention to what they said and what they implied. He had an uncanny ability to actually match a party to the host's personality! Don started a company tradition of adding a *surprise* at each event. Perhaps he would serve an incredible dish that wasn't on the menu (or the bill) or bring an elaborate prop that would add a note of flair and excitement to the party. It would always be something that was fresh, out-of-the-box, and spectacular.

stations at parties. He had an uncle, Merle Strange, who was retired and looking for something to do at the time, so Don drew up a plan and hired him to make about fifty of the carts. Each was designed with a canvas top that could be changed to coordinate with the color theme of the event. The carts were accents at parties as well as an alternative to buffet-style service. Some of the carts were fitted with stainless steel inserts so they could be filled with ice and used to serve chilled boiled shrimp or oysters on the half shell, which would be mounded on top of the ice with bowls of cocktail sauce nested among them. Imagine being at a party and nibbling away at a whole cartful of tasty boiled shrimp or freshly shucked oysters.

Don found the inspiration for some of his most successful ideas simply by listening to people. Guacamole was a popular topping for the gorditas, so there were always many cases of avocados in the kitchen. Don was delighted when he catered an event for a woman who told him about going to a party at an avocado plantation in Mexico. She said that at this party the host had served what he called "avocados on the half shell." It was simply unpeeled, seeded avocado halves piled on a platter and surrounded by various dips and dressings, which guests would spoon into the seed cavity. Don thought it was such a unique idea that he served the dish at the woman's party. He surrounded the avocado halves with bowls of sour cream, various salad dressings, cheeses, caviar, and condiments like chopped bacon and chives.

At one of the cattle auctions Don catered, the weather turned miserably cold, so the staff served the avocado halves with hot chili, grated cheese, and sour cream. They could be adapted to the season! Stuffed avocado halves became one of the company's signature dishes, and today we've added the popular shrimp ceviche as a filling. When he catered the 1976 Cattle Baron's Ball in Dallas, Don filled a vintage farm wagon with ice and covered the ice with a mountain of avocado halves. The toppings and condiments, including caviar, were in bowls nested in the ice among the hundreds of avocado halves. Don had

learned over the years to position the most spectacular items right inside the door of an event, so the avocado-filled wagon was placed where it would be the first thing the guests saw as they entered the party tent. Even Don, who was always hesitant to applaud himself, said it was, indeed, a spectacular sight. When the company catered the Go Western Gala, which opens the annual rodeo season in San Antonio, a newspaper article about the party described the avocado station as "More avocados than anyone had ever seen in one place!"

The company began to amass a supply of colorful props, decorative accessories, colorful fabrics, Mexican serving pieces, and sometimes even bizarre items that Don used to create elaborate settings for parties. Don Strange events became known not only for great food but for the pure aura of showmanship that pervaded them. He began to hire artists like Bob Dale, a popular cartoonist for a San Antonio newspaper and a freelance artist, to paint settings for events and eventually to create life-size Styrofoam building fronts and paint them to fit specific themes. Once he made an elaborate church façade of Styrofoam. Don created an "environment" for each party.

One of the things that Mr. Strange had taught him was to use "smoke and aroma" to draw people. Back in the days of Strange's Grocery, Mr. Strange would get the fire going to cook his meats. When the fire began to produce a good head of smoke, he'd throw some thick-sliced onions on the grill. The combined smell of the wood smoke and the aroma of those grilling onions, slowly caramelizing, would draw people like a magnet! Don wanted to break out of the smoked brisket mode, yet still serve a Texas barbecue, and he envisioned a spit on which he could smoke an entire side of beef! "How impressive would that be?" he wondered, "And just think of *that* aroma!"

The first attempts with the side of beef resulted in disaster, as the meat literally fell apart and into the fire when it was almost done. Don said it was not a pretty sight! But he still believed the concept had a lot of merit, so he designed and had fabricated a special wire sling suspended from an iron pole to hold the beef above the fire pit. It worked like a charm. Today the smoked side of beef is a standard item at parties at the Don Strange Ranch.

Don began to serve roasted beef tenderloin at parties early in the company's history, although it was unheard of to serve such an expensive cut of meat at catered functions! He would slice the tenderloin right in front of the guests and serve it with various sauces. Such an elegant,

gourmet dish was immediately embraced by clients. After mastering classic béarnaise sauce, Don gave it his own spin by adding jalapeños. Hosts and their guests went wild over the tenderloin topped with this creamy, herb-laced version of the classic sauce, with its nice little kick of chile. Not long after he started serving the beef tenderloin, he hired Dan Schmidt, who had worked for us at the house while he was in high school, mowing the lawn, babysitting, and doing odd jobs. Dan got into the rhythm of Don's style very quickly. One day when Don was planning a party, Dan suggested that maybe he should *grill* the tenderloins, not roast them, in keeping with the idea of enticing people with good, smoky aromas. Today grilled beef tenderloin with Jalapeño Béarnaise Sauce is one of the company's major signature dishes. And Dan has been with the company since 1977!

By the early 1970s the company was doing well, catering events all over the state. Don wanted to raise the bar to an even higher level, however, and to see what was happening in the food world outside of Texas. On our trips to New York and San Francisco, we tried every kind of food from the finest restaurants to diners and the small cafés favored by locals. We even tried street food on San

Design sketch for the Cantina set by Bob Dale.

Francisco's waterfront. He discovered crepes and introduced them to San Antonio—crepes as a main dish, as a side dish, and dessert crepes. Don's crepes took the city by storm, and soon local restaurants were serving them. At the Hyatt Hotel in San Francisco he was fascinated by the omelet stations at brunch. I don't know how many omelets he ate that day, going back again and again, to custom-order different fillings and watch as the chefs sautéed his omelet right in front of him. The custom omelet station became a fixture at every Don Strange brunch—and a first for San Antonio.

After visiting New York City and watching in awe as entrées and spectacular desserts were cooked tableside over attractive alcohol-fired burners, Don could hardly wait to get home so that he could duplicate these new dishes and service methods. As soon as we got back to San Antonio, he found a source for alcohol burners, and steak Diane became part of the company's growing menu. He would create a station equipped with four or five of the burners. The steak would be precut, with all of the ingredients for the sauce at hand. Each cook would prepare four or five portions in their sauté pans, serving the guests scratch-made steak Diane right from the pan! Don was right. Folks were

agog over each new cutting-edge innovation, and hosts lined up to have Don cater their events.

From the Old San Francisco Steakhouse Don borrowed an idea that the company has used all these years. Instead of bringing a plastic basket of saltine crackers and margarine to the tables as guests were seated, the San Francisco waiters brought large wooden platters with a huge chunk of cheese and a big knife, along with some good-quality wafers and breads. Chunks, wedges, and whole rounds of cheese became standard party fare, served at a separate cheese station, of course. The Cheese Table, as Don called it, was one of those *Wow!* features that always made a big splash. He laughingly described one party at which he had piled so much cheese on a table that it collapsed just before the guests arrived. What a scramble it was to salvage the cheese station in time, albeit with a little less cheese! One of the most popular items Don ever added to the menu was the large wedge of Stilton cheese surrounded by wedges of several varieties of apples.

In the early 1970s Don hired a part-time waiter who had worked as a cook at Lackland Air Force Base. He told Don about a new chef at the base who was serving some sort of whole fried jalapeño chile. He brought some to Don to taste. He ate two or three of them, loved them, and then deconstructed the remaining chiles to figure out how to make them. He reached two conclusions. First, the secret was the stuffing, and he knew he could make a better one using shredded cheese that would melt and become creamy but not runny. He experimented with several types of cheese. Cream cheese melted too quickly; Cheddar became too runny. He settled on Muenster cheese because it didn't ooze out of the jalapeños when it melted. Second, whole pickled jalapeños would not be quite as incendiary in taste as fresh ones—spicy, but not so hot that people couldn't eat them. Through experimentation, he discovered that the concept worked best if the chiles were stuffed, breaded and frozen, and then fried in the frozen state (at their own station, of course). The crust was perfectly browned, the cheese perfectly melted. From the very first time he served

them, the fried jalapeño station was the center of attention. Today, of course, they've been commercialized around the globe. Don would always chuckle when an eager new food sales rep would come to sell him a great new finger-food innovation—frozen, of course—called Jalapeño Poppers.

Don is credited with commercializing the fajita, nowadays a mainstay at Tex-Mex restaurants around the country and a favorite at backyard cookouts. In the mid-1970s the International Bank of Commerce in Laredo built a stunning new building, and Don was called about catering a party for 1,200 guests. He went to Laredo to look at the building and plan the event with the bankers. They wanted to have serving stations scattered around the lobby, some in the parking garage, and some outside in the landscaped courtyard. One of the bankers asked Don if he had ever cooked fajitas. Well, he'd never even heard of them! So the banker told him to stop at a certain little café and order them before making the trip home. He discovered that they were quite good. He asked the owner of the café what kind of meat was used. "Skirt steak" was the reply. Don was unfamiliar with this cut, so when he got back to San Antonio he contacted his meat supplier to find out what it was. The meat rep told him that it was a somewhat tough and

scraggly piece of meat that lies across the belly of the beef in strips, like a belt—hence the name *fajita* (*faja* is Spanish for "belt"). He also told Don that most skirt steak was used for ground meat, and the rest sent to Mexico. But Don asked that they get some for him, and he began to experiment with the dish, trying various marinades and cooking methods. Eventually he settled on running the meat through the tenderizer, marinating it, and grilling it quickly to get a good sear on the outside. In the interim, the value of the peso crashed, and the bank party was cancelled. But what a serendipitous happening!

As Don began to serve the fajitas at small parties, it was like a stampede. People started calling to book parties with "that new fajitas dish." It seemed people couldn't get enough of them. Noted food writer and TV food personality Craig Claiborne and his coauthor and costar, Chef Pierre Franey, came to San Antonio for a celebrity chef cooking class. Don and I hosted a party for the two at our home. Don decided to serve the fajitas, as he figured it would surely be a dish they had never tried. Mr. Claiborne

Opposite, left: Mel
Tillis with saloon
girls at *The Best Little
Whorehouse in Texas*
opening.
Left: Staff member
Joe Rodriguez grilling
at McNay Museum
event.

arrived first and began to graze around the party, discovering the fajitas about the time Chef Franey arrived. "Come over here, Pierre! You've got to try these things!" Mr. Claiborne called from across the room. Neither of them had ever heard of fajitas, and what's more, they had never seen a flour tortilla. When he left San Antonio Mr. Claiborne had procured a package of tortillas that Don told him he could freeze until later. Don's meat supplier soon began to keep a large stock of choice skirt steak for Don. Eventually he added chicken and shrimp to the fajita mix at the request of clients, although he never considered them really authentic fajitas. The rest, as they say, is history.

When Don began to cater private parties at the McNay Art Museum in San Antonio, he was challenged to provide upscale menu items to the discerning, world-traveled patrons in attendance. He would serve his popular sautéed oysters with Ernie sauce, a dish he created by dusting the oysters with flour and quickly sautéing in butter, then placing them back in the shells and topping them with a sauce made from a recipe long secreted in the bayous of Louisiana. He also devised a spectacular method for serving mussels steamed in their shells. He designed a serpentine-shaped table that was lined with mirrors; a stainless steel pan in the same serpentine shape fit into a stainless

frame, elevated slightly over the mirrored table. The staff would set up the table in the midst of the museum's sculpture exhibits and fill the stainless pan with a small amount of water. The chilled, unopened mussels were placed in the water, and dozens of votive candles in clear glass holders were set on the mirrored surface of the table under the pan. About 15 minutes before the guests arrived, the candles would be lit. They would warm the water just enough to cause the mussels to open. It was a spectacular sight, with the reflection of the candles on the mirror and glinting on the shiny pan. The whole table had a very magical sort of look. Guests were amazed that they could just walk up and eat fresh mussels from this lovely display while gazing at the sculptures.

One of Don's earliest signature dishes was one he called shrimp teriyaki. The dish consisted of a strip of bacon wrapped around a shrimp, then folded into a thin strip of chicken breast and secured by a wooden pick. The bundles were marinated in teriyaki sauce, then grilled in front of eager guests who had been lured to the station by the delicious aroma. The dish was served for years, until Don tired

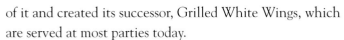

of it and created its successor, Grilled White Wings, which are served at most parties today.

Grilled White Wings, as Don named the dish, were originally devised for a luncheon that the company catered at the YO Ranch in 1984. It was given for Monaco's Prince Rainier and his son, Prince Albert, who had come to New York to attend a fund-raising event for the Princess Grace Foundation. During his visit, the prince had mentioned that he'd like to do some hunting in Texas. So a hunt was arranged on the 50,000-acre ranch. The luncheon was an intimate affair for only fourteen guests. Don wanted to create a very innovative dish, yet one that would serve as a representative "taste of Texas." It was the first time that the company had ever served bona fide royalty, and Don was clearly terrified about protocol. He created the Grilled White Wings as the main dish of the luncheon. It consisted of doves stuffed with a jalapeño and cheese, then wrapped in a slice of bacon and grilled. When the food was served, the staff was so intently focused on the proper serving order that they simply forgot to serve Charlie Schreiner III, the host. Don always said that Charlie never minced words, so he wasn't surprised when Charlie just hollered across the

table to one of the waitstaff: "Hey, am I going to get any food?" A ripple of laughter circled the table as a plate was rushed to Charlie. The prince and his son loved the dish, delighted with its spicy chile filling.

Don knew that dove, being a native game bird, could not be sold, and he really wanted to turn the dish into a replacement finger food for the shrimp teriyaki, so he substituted chicken breast in the final version of the dish. It evolved into a thin strip of chicken breast laid on an applewood-smoked bacon slice, topped with a cube of Monterey Jack cheese and a slice of pickled jalapeño, rolled up, pinwheel-style, then secured with a wooden pick, marinated in a white-wine marinade, and grilled on-site. Grilled White Wings are one of the company's most-requested hors d'oeuvres.

Don's food innovations set trends that have been emulated by caterers everywhere, but some of his greatest ideas in catering involved his presentations. Don's parties were pure theater. At every party he would develop a theme with the host, then set about to create a "set," much like a movie company does when filming a movie. He would create "rooms" that were so real you could become totally immersed in the era or the theme. Sometimes he created "towns," complete with life-size building facades made of Styrofoam and painted by local artists to reflect the era or mood of the party's theme.

He used table props that mirrored the host's theme or the corporation's business. When the company was hired to cater a corporate party with a Harley-Davidson theme, Don used shiny chrome Harley motorcycle parts as serving pieces and props. Tortilla chips were served in Harley hubcaps. Harley chrome gears were used as napkin rings. A small Harley engine powered the margarita machine. Bar stools were from Harley motorcycle seats. The tables were overlaid with leather studded to resemble Harley jackets. It was pure Harley and pure Texas, Don Strange style.

Don was hired by Bill and Darolyn Worth, owners of a San Antonio limestone quarrying business, to cater a party at their home. They wanted a Fifties theme, so Don gave them the Fifties in spades. He created a set that smacked of diners and drive-in burger joints. He had dozens of huge advertising signs painted with wording like "Don's Burger Shack—Crispy Fries," "Foot-Long Coneys and Chili Dogs," "Soft-Serve Ice Cream—Waffle Cones," "Burger Baskets with Onion Rings," and "Malts and Shakes," each painted with 1950s-era images of burgers and fries, malts and shakes, or onion rings in plastic baskets lined with deli paper. He positioned the signs around the party. Don built a retro stainless steel–topped soda counter, where guests could sit on spinning chrome seats and order shakes, malts, and slices of pies. His Aunt Helen, who was dressed in a Fifties-style diner waitress uniform, complete with the little paper hat, manned the soda counter. Other waitresses were dressed in short poodle skirts with white sweaters and red scarves tied around their necks. They wore roller skates, wheeling around the party serving cocktails from small round trays they held aloft. (Don had them "rehearse" often to pull off this feat!)

My cousin Melinda recalled one of the years that Don catered the Go Western Gala, the preview to the San Antonio Rodeo, at the old Municipal Auditorium. He created a Gay Nineties theme for the event and borrowed an idea that he remembered from our visit to the Old San Francisco Steakhouse, which is designed to replicate a grand saloon of the 1890s. Melinda described the elaborate setting Don created, saying that it looked just like a fancy saloon from that period. All the staff was dressed in Gay Nineties apparel, with the serving girls attired in elaborate

sequined gowns and feathered hats. Over each end of the grandiose bar he had taken to the party, "saloon girls" were swinging on swings that were hung from dramatically long velvet ropes. Melinda, who was pressed into swing duty, said they had to use ladders to get to the swings, but the effect was pure theater as they swung out over the guests.

One of the most popular party themes for events was Texan or Southwestern. When the company catered a Texas-themed party, Don went to great lengths to create a rustic Texas ambiance, right down to split-rail or barbed-wire fences. He would use authentic chuck wagons as serving stations, positioning his grills full of meat strategically so that the tantalizing aroma of the grilling beef and Grilled White Wings would waft over the guests. Soon the company became known for its unique Cactus Cake Table. The beautiful cakes, which really do look like live cacti, right down to the thorns and blooms, are made by the Sweet Designs Bake Shop in San Antonio in all sizes and in various cactus shapes. The effect of a table full of these cakes, arranged on limestone rocks at various heights and interspersed with native grasses, Texas accessories, and other native plants,

is quite spectacular. Don Strange of Texas is the exclusive agent for the cakes, which are wildly popular at parties.

Over the company's long history Don was constantly asked for the recipes for various dishes that he would serve, and he was always generous in sharing them. In fact, it was his directive that the recipes for the company's most popular dishes should be included in this book! But more than wanting recipes, people would want to know if they could just buy a dozen of this dish, or two dozen of another, or a bottle or two of a sauce or condiment. He always hated to tell people that the kitchen simply was too busy to do such tiny batches of one or two items.

Never being one to pass up a trip to New York City, I went with Don to help him with a fund-raiser for the Meals on Wheels program. Sponsored by the James Beard Foundation, the event was held at Rockefeller Center during the first week of June, one of the busiest times for caterers. Don, of course, wanted to do something that would represent the company's unique style, but at the same time, it had to be something that would be quick and easy and not put a strain on the already busy kitchen. He decided to

together as fast as we could, and people just kept coming. I looked up once and got a little weak in the knees when I couldn't even see the end of the line at our spot! It was longer than any of the others. And then people who'd been through the line once began to come up and ask where they could buy the cranberry-jalapeño chutney! We did the event the next year, only then we topped the tenderloin with the company's Jalapeño Béarnaise Sauce. Same scenario. "Where can we buy that sauce?"

When we returned home after the second year, I told Don that we really must get serious about bottling those sauces. I'd been trying to persuade him to bottle his barbecue sauce for over ten years, but we had no idea how to get such a venture off the ground. I would start, hit a roadblock, and quit. But I kept harping on the need to put our private label on the company's popular sauces and condiments. The New York event convinced me that it would be another way to add revenue—with something we were already doing!

Don was solidly behind the idea, but he had enough on his plate at any given time, so it was agreed that I would be in charge of this venture. Somewhere along the line it

do miniature whole wheat tortillas, topped with thin-sliced grilled beef tenderloin and his signature cranberry-jalapeño chutney. At the time, no one was doing whole wheat tortillas, much less miniature ones.

We loaded up our stuff and traveled to New York. As we were setting up to begin serving, Don looked around and commented that we were in grand company, with most of the other participants being luminaries in the culinary world. Culinary celebrities were the only celebrities he ever seemed to notice. He'd spotted Stephan Pyles and Mario Batali, to name just two. We were putting our little tortillas

was decided that we would also produce some of the company's signature meat dishes and a few of the most popular small sweets. Our kitchen was already making Grilled White Wings, Christmas Bacon, Texas Two-Bite Pecan Tarts, Double-Barrel Brownies, and Kendall Creek Honey Bars in large volume, so it seemed only natural to add these signature company dishes, with a proven track record of popularity, to the offerings. With age, I've learned that what things seem to be today is not what they will be tomorrow, and if you overreact to everything you'll be overreacting most of the time! So I approached this new challenge as I'd seen Don approach thousands of challenges over the years. He was very goal-oriented, and from him I learned that everything is possible. We were fortunate enough to live to see so many of our dreams fulfilled that I knew I could pull off this venture. This was my dream.

But it's been quite a learning process. At the time I started working on the project in earnest, the e-commerce field was just getting started. Don had hired Frank Moore to work in the office. Thank goodness, I've had Frank to help execute my vision. He's been the nuts-and-bolts person in the project, setting up the online shopping carts, handling paperwork, arranging for shipping, packing boxes, and so

on. Frank and I hoped that Don would stay out of it, but every now and then he would worm his way in! Of course, because the products would bear his name, we let him know what was going on. Before Don's death, we had set up the Don Strange Market Place website, found a very reputable food manufacturer that we trusted to produce the sauces and condiments, designed the labels, and set up production formats for the meat and dessert items that would be made in the company's commissary kitchen.

One of Don's greatest innovations for both cooking and serving party foods was the Texas Grill Pardner. Don designed the original version of the grill many years ago for on-site preparation of quesadillas, gorditas, and many other dishes. People attending Don's parties would always comment on the uniqueness of the grill. So I hammered on the need to include the Texas Grill Pardner with the Market Place offerings because it's such a unique tool for both cooking foods and keeping them warm. Customers who have purchased the grill love it. To Don, designing it was just answering the need for another specific gizmo.

Sometimes, though, problems arose when the fruits of Don's creativity fell upon poor souls who didn't know, love, and understand him like we did. One such instance

happened when we were vacationing in the Tuscany region of Italy and had rented a large home with four other couples. On one of our outings we visited a local butcher shop that had been recommended to us for its unusual items for sale. The owner of the shop was very friendly and interested in showing all that he had to offer. Don got caught up in the moment and decided that we needed to buy a whole lamb. When he told the butcher what he wanted, the poor man was sure he had misunderstood what this crazy, bigger-than-life Texan had asked for. After several translations, he said he would do what he could but that he was going to have to check with his supplier in Florence and let us know. He finally said he would have to get it as quarters. That was fine with Don. For a man who cooked entire sides of beef instead of a few briskets, cooking lamb quarters would be no trouble.

Now, the house where we were staying had no barbecue pit at all, but little things like that didn't deter Don.

So off we go back to the house to make plans for the task at hand. The other couples in our group were made up of physicians, attorneys, and other professionals. Don went into his Huckleberry Finn routine, showing these doctors and lawyers how to dig a hole for the fire. Now he needed a structure to hold this animal. He went to the local hardware store and bought two grills with handles. Putting each handle on the outside with the two grills overlapping made a perfect solid grill. Now for the lid. After scrounging in the dump behind the house, he found the lid from an old Maytag washing machine. Now he had a complete grilling station. His laborers went to work, and when the lamb arrived the next day, the festivities began. As I recall, a large amount of local wine was consumed, and a great time was had by all. To this day, all who were gathered there remember our Maytag barbecue grill. Never say never!

Anyone need a six-foot iron rack to hold a side of beef on a spit?

Fried Stuffed Jalapeños

★

The battered, fried, stuffed jalapeño—which Don named a "bomber"—was one of his early innovations in catering. The cooks would bread and fry the chiles on-site at a special station set up just for that one item. They were wildly popular as a delicious oddity in the beginning. Nowadays, of course, everyone has copied them, and they've become well commercialized. While there are a plethora of different fillings, clients continue to love Don's original version filled with mild, creamy Muenster cheese, which provides the perfect foil to the heat of the jalapeño.

Makes 15 stuffed jalapeños

Make a slit in the side of each jalapeño using a sharp knife. Taking care not to tear the chile, use your index finger to scrape out the seeds; discard seeds. Pat the chiles *very dry* using absorbent paper towels. (They must be very dry, or the batter will not adhere.)

Stuff 2 tablespoons of the shredded cheese into the cavity of each chile; set aside. Combine the flour, cornmeal, and salt in a medium bowl, tossing to blend well. Place the evaporated milk and egg mixture in a separate bowl. Press the edges of the slit in the chiles together. Dip a chile in the milk and egg mixture, coating well, then into the cornmeal mixture, pressing the breading onto the chile and coating well. Shake off excess. Place the breaded chile on a parchment-lined baking sheet. Repeat with the remaining chiles. Cover the tray and freeze the bombers until solidly frozen, about 6 hours.

Working with batches of 5 or so, fry the frozen bombers in the preheated oil, without crowding, until golden brown, about 3 minutes. (Test the first one to be sure the cheese is melted and hot.) Drain on a wire cooling rack set over a baking sheet. Serve warm.

1 (12-ounce) jar whole pickled jalapeños, well drained (15 jalapeños)

1¾ cups (7 ounces) shredded Muenster cheese

½ cup all-purpose flour

2 cups yellow cornmeal

2 teaspoons kosher salt

1 (14-ounce) can evaporated milk, beaten with 1 egg

Canola oil for deep-frying, heated to 350 degrees

Lunchbox Salad with Lemon and Honey Vinaigrette

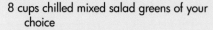

8 cups chilled mixed salad greens of your choice

1 small Haas avocado, peeled and sliced thin

1 cup sliced strawberries

1 cup whole raspberries

1 metal, dome-shaped lunchbox, lined with parchment paper (extending above the edge of the lunchbox)

Lemon and Honey Vinaigrette

1 teaspoon minced lemon zest

¼ cup freshly squeezed lemon juice

¼ teaspoon kosher salt

2 tablespoons honey

1 teaspoon Dijon-style mustard

1 tablespoon finely chopped shallots

½ cup extra-virgin olive oil

Freshly ground black pepper to taste

When Don was asked to cater the luncheon for the grand opening of San Antonio's Alamodome, he wanted—being Don—to serve a dish that would be a striking example of his out-of-the-box thinking. When he hit upon the idea of serving a colorful salad in an industrial-style lunchbox, many of the staff members thought perhaps he'd gone too far with the concept by using a real box. But the lunchboxes caused an audible stir of oohs and aahs, and the guests loved both the idea and the salad! To make the salad a bit heartier, you can add a grilled chicken breast, fan-sliced and arranged in the center.

Makes one salad

Begin by making the vinaigrette. Combine all ingredients except olive oil and black pepper in work bowl of food processor fitted with steel blade. Process until smooth. With processor running, add the olive oil in a slow, steady stream through the feed tube. Add black pepper and process to blend. Transfer to a storage container with tight-sealing lid and refrigerate until ready to use.

To assemble the salad, toss together the greens, avocado slices, strawberries, and raspberries, reserving a few avocado slices, strawberry slices, and raspberries for garnish. Turn the salad mix out into the parchment-lined lunchbox and drizzle the desired amount of vinaigrette over the top (see "Dressing Green Salads" on page 122). Garnish with the reserved fruits. Serve at once.

Grilled White Wings

★

Grilled White Wings, which Don created for a luncheon honoring Monaco's Prince Rainier and his son at Charlie Schreiner's YO Ranch, have become a staple finger food at Don Strange of Texas parties. They're so popular that we decided to add them to the Don Strange Market Place products.

Makes 24 roll-ups

Using a sharp, thin-bladed knife, cut each chicken breast in half horizontally. Using a flat meat pounder, pound each breast half into a piece about 8 inches wide and 5 inches long, taking care not to tear the meat. Cut each half into six strips about 1 inch wide. (The chicken strips should match the width of the bacon slices.) Set aside.

Place a half strip of bacon on work surface. Line up a chicken strip even with the end of the bacon strip nearest you. Place a cube of cheese in the center of the chicken strip, then top the cheese with a jalapeño slice. Beginning at the end nearest you, roll the bacon tightly with the chicken, cheese, and chile, forming a tight roll. Stick a skewer through the roll at the end of the bacon slice. Repeat with remaining ingredients, allowing 3 roll-ups per skewer spaced ½ inch apart. Arrange the skewers in a single layer in a nonreactive baking dish. Set aside.

Whisk together the wine and canola oil; season with salt and pepper. Pour the mixture over the skewered roll-ups, cover the dish with plastic wrap, and set aside to marinate at room temperature for 1 hour, but no longer.

Heat a gas grill to medium heat, or build a hardwood charcoal fire in a barbecue pit and allow it to burn down until the coals are glowing red and covered by a layer of white ash, about 20 to 30 minutes. Remove the skewers from the marinade and grill until chicken is cooked through and bacon is nicely browned, about 11 minutes on each side, turning once. Serve hot.

4 (12-ounce) boneless skinless chicken breast halves

12 good-quality smoked bacon slices, cut in half

Block of Monterey Jack cheese, cut into cubes 1½ inches long and ½ inch thick (about ½ ounce)

24 nacho-sliced pickled jalapeño slices

Thick bamboo skewers, soaked in water for 1 hour

1 cup dry white wine, such as chardonnay

⅔ cup canola oil

Kosher salt and freshly ground black pepper to taste

Beef Fajitas

★

3 pounds beef skirt steak, tenderized

Fajita Marinade (see recipe below)

Refried Beans (see page 71)

Shredded Cheddar cheese

Maggie's Guacamole (see page 156)

Pico de Gallo (see page 70)

Warmed corn and/or flour tortillas

Fajita Marinade

½ cup bottled mole sauce

¼ cup freshly squeezed lime juice

1 teaspoon minced lime zest

½ teaspoon crushed fennel seeds

1 teaspoon freshly ground black pepper

1 teaspoon granulated garlic

2 small serrano chiles, seeds and veins removed, minced

1½ cups vinaigrette-style Italian salad dressing

½ cup clear tequila

After discovering fajitas at a small Mexican café outside of Laredo, Texas, in the mid-1970s, Don upgraded the recipe many times, adding the accompaniments that are served with them today. Don Strange of Texas is generally credited with commercializing the fajita, which is now known and loved all over the country and featured on Mexican restaurant menus everywhere. And, of course, fajitas have become a staple of Texas backyard barbecues. They still remain one of the company's most-requested dishes. We serve the fajitas with refried beans, which are spread on the tortillas first, followed by the meat and the other toppings, as desired. The fajitas can also be served with grilled red and green bell peppers and onions.

Serves 6 to 8

Trim any fat and stray edges of meat from the skirt steak. Place the meat in a single layer in a nonreactive baking dish. Make the marinade by combining all ingredients in a medium bowl and whisking to blend well. (Marinade can be made up to two days ahead and stored in the refrigerator. Shake or whisk well before using.) Pour the marinade over the skirt steak, coating well. Cover with plastic wrap and marinate, refrigerated, for 8 hours.

When ready to cook the fajitas, heat a gas grill to medium heat, or build a hardwood charcoal fire in a barbecue pit and allow it to burn down until the coals are glowing red and covered by a layer of white ash, about 20 to 30 minutes. Remove the skirt steak from the marinade; discard marinade. Grill the meat to medium, about 6 to 8 minutes per side, or to desired level of doneness. (Note that medium is ideal, as skirt steak cooked to well done will be fairly tough.)

Using a sharp knife, slice the skirt steak into thin slices, about ½-inch wide. If the strips are long, slice them in half. Pile the meat on a serving platter and surround it with bowls of the Refried Beans, cheese, guacamole, and Pico de Gallo as garnishes. Place the tortillas in tortilla warmers alongside so that guests can customize their fajitas.

Steak Diane

★

4 center-cut beef tenderloin medallions,
about ¾-inch thick

Kosher salt and freshly ground black
pepper to taste

4 tablespoons unsalted butter

1 large French shallot, minced

1 large garlic clove, minced

½ cup sliced white mushrooms

½ teaspoon minced fresh thyme

⅓ cup Cognac or brandy

2 teaspoons Dijon-style mustard

⅓ cup whipping cream

2 teaspoons Worcestershire sauce

¼ cup veal demi-glace* or reduced veal
stock

Dash of Tabasco sauce

1 tablespoon very thinly sliced green onion
and tops

1 teaspoon minced flat-leaf parsley

Don discovered this classic dish many years ago when we made a trip to New York City and dined at the Palace restaurant. He was intrigued as he watched the tuxedo-clad waiters prepare the steak tableside, flaming it with cognac and a flourish, then topping the medallions of tenderloin with sauce from the pan. While tableside cooking is no longer a hot trend in the restaurant world, it's still a very elegant way to present food. When Emeril Lagasse was planning the reopening of the iconic Delmonico's Restaurant in New Orleans, he decided to bring back the tableside service for which the restaurant and the city were known many years ago. Speed is of the essence in cooking Steak Diane, so it is important to have all of your ingredients measured, prepared, and readily available before beginning the cooking.

Serves 2

Season the beef medallions on both sides with salt and pepper. In a heavy-bottomed 12-inch sauté pan over medium-high heat, melt the butter. When the foam subsides, add the medallions and sear until nicely browned, about 30 seconds per side, turning once. Transfer the medallions to a plate and cover to keep warm.

Add the shallot and garlic to the pan. Sauté, stirring, for about 25 seconds, then add the mushrooms and thyme. Cook, stirring, until mushrooms are limp, about 2 minutes.

Tilt the pan slightly away from you and toward the flame. Add the Cognac and shake so that the flame will ignite it. (If using an electric burner, light the alcohol with a long match or a butane lighter.) Shake the pan gently until the flame subsides, then stir in the mustard, whipping cream, and Worcestershire sauce, blending well. Cook for about 2 minutes over high heat to reduce and thicken the sauce, then add the veal demi-glace and Tabasco, stirring well. Return the medallions to the pan. Cook just to reheat, about 25 seconds. Add the green onions and parsley, stirring to blend.

Transfer the medallions to 2 serving plates. Spoon a portion of the sauce and mushrooms over each portion of meat and serve at once.

*VEAL DEMI-GLACE is a pretty labor-intensive undertaking. It also requires that you begin with a good homemade veal stock, which most home cooks don't have time to make. But don't despair. There's a fabulous product on the market that's a condensed veal demi-glace: More Than Gourmet's Demi-Glace Gold. You simply cook it in boiling water and you have a fine demi-glace. It's available at specialty food markets and most larger H-E-B stores in Texas, where you'll find it in the same section with base pastes, canned broths, and soups. Each 1.5-ounce container makes 1 cup of demi-glace.

Jalapeño Béarnaise Sauce

⋆

This is one of the company's signature sauces, and one that is wildly popular with party guests. Leave it to Don to take a classic sauce and elevate the flavor a notch or two—in this instance, with the jalapeños he loved so much. The sauce is served on medallions of grilled beef tenderloin, a favorite entrée for weddings. Grill the trimmed tenderloin to medium-rare for the best taste and tenderness, then slice it into ½-inch-thick portions. Drizzle the sauce over the slices and enjoy! The company had so many requests for the recipe for this sauce that we included it in the products available through our online Don Strange Market Place.

Makes about 2 cups

Whisk the evaporated milk and sauce mix together in a small, heavy-bottomed saucepan over medium heat until smooth. Add the butter, water, and lemon juice. Bring to a boil while stirring. Reduce heat and stir in the green onions, jalapeños, cayenne, and herbs. Stir until thickened, about 1 minute. Serve hot.

2 cups evaporated milk

2 (0.9-ounce) packages Knorr Hollandaise Sauce Mix

¼ pound (1 stick) butter

¼ cup water

2 tablespoons freshly squeezed lemon juice

1 tablespoon minced green onion

2 medium jalapeños, seeds and veins removed, minced

¼ teaspoon cayenne pepper

1 tablespoon minced parsley

1 tablespoon minced chives

2 tablespoons minced tarragon

Cranberry Pecan Sauce

⋆

This versatile and delicious sauce makes a fabulous topping for many meats—grilled quail, chicken, pork, and turkey. It can transform a fairly ordinary meat into a feast, and it's really easy to prepare. Created many years ago, the sauce has proven to be such a popular condiment that we decided to include it in the Don Strange Market Place line of products.

Makes about 1 quart

Pour the apple jelly into a heavy-bottomed 4-quart saucepan over medium heat and cook until jelly is melted. Stir in the cranberries and cook, stirring often, until cranberries begin to pop and come apart. Add all remaining ingredients and reduce heat to low. Cook, stirring often, until the sauce is thickened and well blended, about 7 minutes. Serve warm.

*IF USING FROZEN cranberries, thaw them first.

1 (18-ounce) jar apple jelly (about 2 cups)

3 cups whole (fresh or frozen) cranberries*

3 medium garlic cloves, minced

¼ teaspoon ground cinnamon

¼ teaspoon ground cloves

¼ teaspoon ground allspice

¼ teaspoon freshly grated nutmeg

¼ teaspoon ground ginger

1 teaspoon crushed red pepper flakes

⅓ cup chopped chives

⅓ cup minced parsley

2½ cups golden raisins

2½ cups chopped pecans

Christmas Bacon

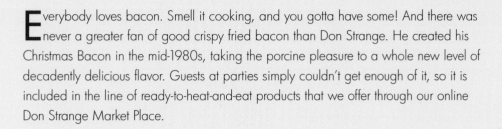

Everybody loves bacon. Smell it cooking, and you gotta have some! And there was never a greater fan of good crispy fried bacon than Don Strange. He created his Christmas Bacon in the mid-1980s, taking the porcine pleasure to a whole new level of decadently delicious flavor. Guests at parties simply couldn't get enough of it, so it is included in the line of ready-to-heat-and-eat products that we offer through our online Don Strange Market Place.

1 pound applewood-smoked, thick-sliced bacon

1⅓ cups firmly packed light brown sugar, or more as needed

Makes about 14 slices

Preheat oven to 350 degrees. Line a large rimmed baking sheet with parchment paper or foil. Place a wire cooling rack inside the baking sheet. Arrange the bacon slices on the rack in a single layer so they don't overlap. Pat about 1½ tablespoons of the brown sugar on each slice, covering it entirely. Bake in the preheated oven until the bacon is crisp and the brown sugar has caramelized on the slices, about 25 to 30 minutes.

Remove from oven and allow bacon to cool slightly. Serve warm.

Red New Potatoes with Chipotle Cream Cheese Stuffing and Caviar

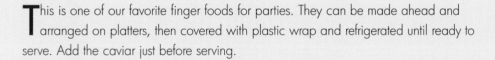

This is one of our favorite finger foods for parties. They can be made ahead and arranged on platters, then covered with plastic wrap and refrigerated until ready to serve. Add the caviar just before serving.

1 jar red lumpfish caviar

20 small (B size) red new potatoes, unpeeled

2 packages (8-ounce) cream cheese, cut into chunks

1 tablespoon real mayonnaise

¼ cup firmly packed cilantro leaves

1 tablespoon minced canned chipotle chiles in adobo sauce

Kosher salt to taste

Makes 40 individual servings

Place the caviar in a fine strainer. Slowly pour 2 quarts of ice-cold water over the caviar, taking care not to break the eggs. (This will remove the fishy taste and sticky texture from the caviar.) Allow to drip completely dry, then place in a small bowl, cover, and refrigerate until ready to use.

Place the whole potatoes in a heavy-bottomed 4-quart saucepan and add cold water to cover. Bring to a boil over medium heat, cover, and cook briskly until potatoes are tender when pierced with a metal skewer, about 13 minutes. Drain into a colander and allow to sit until cool enough to handle. Cut each potato in half; scoop out about 1 tablespoon of the potato flesh using a melon baller, taking care not to tear or puncture the skin. Cut a very thin slice from the bottom of each potato half so they will sit flat without falling over. Refrigerate the potato shells until chilled. Store the potato flesh in the refrigerator for another use.

Meanwhile, combine the cream cheese, mayonnaise, cilantro leaves, and chipotle chiles in work bowl of food processor fitted with steel blade. Process until smooth. Add salt to taste and process to blend. Transfer the mixture to a pastry bag fitted with plain tip.

Pipe a dollop of the cream cheese mixture into the hollowed portion of each chilled potato shell. Just before serving, add a dash of the caviar to the center of each potato.

Corn Pudding

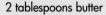

2 tablespoons butter

1 medium onion, chopped

1 cup sour cream

2 cups cream-style corn

3 eggs, beaten

1 (6-ounce) package Pioneer Brand corn muffin mix

2 cups (8 ounces) shredded Cheddar cheese

When Don and his parents began to cater large parties serving their popular barbecue, Don wanted to serve side dishes that were also noteworthy, rather than the same old menu of coleslaw, potato salad, and pinto beans. He settled on Corn Pudding, which no one else served with barbecue, and it became one of the company's signature barbecue side dishes in the 1980s. It's still served with barbecue today. Hard to beat a good side dish!

Serves 8

Preheat oven to 350 degrees. Grease a 13-by-9-inch baking dish; set aside. Melt the butter in a heavy-bottomed 10-inch skillet over medium heat. Add the onion and sauté until it is wilted and transparent, about 5 minutes. Do not allow it to brown. Remove from heat and blend the onions and sour cream in a bowl, mixing well; set aside.

In a separate large bowl combine the creamed corn, eggs, and muffin mix. Turn out into the prepared baking dish. Spoon the onion mixture evenly around the baking dish in dollops. Scatter the shredded cheese over the top and bake in preheated oven until a wooden pick inserted in the center comes out clean, about 45 minutes. Cut into squares and serve hot.

Variation: Cornshuck Pudding

Serves 12

For a striking presentation at a formal seated dinner, serve Corn Pudding in corn shuck "bowls," which are made by lining a large muffin tin or popover tin with corn shucks.

Soak 12 corn shucks in a large bowl of lukewarm water for about 45 minutes, then drain and pat dry. Instead of a baking dish, use a muffin tin with 12 large (2½-inch-diameter) cups; spray each cup with nonstick vegetable spray. Push a softened corn shuck down into each cup, letting the ends extend upward. Set aside and make the Corn Pudding as directed in the recipe.

To bake the individual puddings, spoon equal portions of the corn batter into the muffin cups. Spoon equal portions of the sour cream mixture into the center of each cup. Scatter the shredded cheese on top of each serving and place the tin on a large baking sheet. Bake in preheated oven until a wooden pick inserted in the center of the cups comes out clean, for about 30 minutes.

To serve, grasp each end of the corn shucks and gently lift the puddings out. Place on individual serving plates and serve hot.

CHAPTER SIX

Taking the Show on the Road

B y the late 1970s Don Strange had firmly established a reputation as a top caterer in Texas. His parties were well known for cutting-edge food presentations as well as the over-the-top innovations around which he designed every event. It seemed to me that when he was asked to do even the simplest event, he would ask himself, "Now, this event should be very easy, so how can I complicate it?" And each time he would do exactly that by adding his special brand of drama to the event, making an everyday event extraordinary.

I guess it was inevitable that word about the *Wow!* factor of the events planned by Don would spread beyond the Texas border. He had been doing events for some of the state's top corporations and the Lone Star rich and famous for several years. They were all quite generous in recommending the company to those requesting the name of a really good Texas caterer.

In 1980 Don was contacted about doing his first out-of-state event. He was asked to do the finger-food course for the American Express Conference for International Retailers, which was to be held in Leesburg, Virginia. Don was really excited about this opportunity, as the

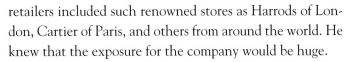

retailers included such renowned stores as Harrods of London, Cartier of Paris, and others from around the world. He knew that the exposure for the company would be huge.

American Express had polled its retailers, asking what type of food they'd like to eat at the conference. The overwhelming majority asked for Texas barbecue. So how would a New York company, in 1980, find out who could throw the best Texas barbecue? Well, they thought they'd just ask one of the most famous Texas families, so they called the owners of the King Ranch, who readily recommended Don Strange.

Now, remember that Don was asked to do only the finger-food course. So off we went to Leesburg to meet with the caterer who was doing the main part of the meal. They treated us as though we were country bumpkins and seemed to assume that Don knew nothing about catering large (or fine) events. Don was told that he would have a thirty-minute time slot in which to serve the finger foods.

When we returned home, he was even more determined to make this event a shining moment after being treated so shabbily. In May Don headed to Leesburg, taking most of the company staff and a caravan of trucks filled with the food and equipment he would need. It was a 2,000-mile trip to serve 100 people. The staff set up the tent and the grills, along with the various stations for each different food. Don prepared his signature barbecued side of beef, which was sliced right off the steer on the grill, arranged on pan de campo, drizzled with barbecue sauce, and handed to the guests. Hand-patted gorditas and quesadillas were also prepared as curious guests, most of whom had never seen Tex-

Longtime employee Irene Correa sets up an avocado bar.

Mex foods, watched. Dozens of huge cheese baskets and hot biscuits were placed at a special station. And, of course, there was an ample supply of margaritas. The guests simply went wild over the variety of unique foods and flavors.

And therein a big problem arose. The finger-food tent was set up in an area well removed from what Don had taken to calling "the real food." After the thirty-minute period was up, the main caterer began to send runners to Don to remind him to get the guests to proceed to the dinner area. Well, the guests simply wouldn't leave Don's party to go eat the other stuff! Finally, Don turned off all of the lights so that the guests had to leave. It was a very successful first venture out of Texas. I'm sure the other caterer wouldn't agree.

That same year, Don received a call from a person representing Pete Rozelle, who was then commissioner of the National Football League. Mr. Rozelle wanted to do a real Texas barbecue for the NFL team owners, coaches, players, and press at his home in White Plains, New York. He had called Clint Murchison, the owner of the Dallas Cowboys back then, to get the name of a great Texas caterer.

Don had done several successful events for the Cowboys, and Mr. Murchison highly recommended him. Mr. Rozelle made a trip to San Antonio to interview Don. I remember the humor in Don's voice when he described the interview. He said that as he described the possible food choices—gorditas, quesadillas, fajitas, the slow-smoked side of beef, margaritas, and more, he realized that Mr. Rozelle had no clue what he was even talking about! But, of course, Don had prepared a little spread for tasting, and the fresh, zesty flavors of the colorful foods sealed the deal. Once again, however, Don was hired for only the first course of the party. Another caterer would be serving a seated dinner of roast beef with traditional accompaniments.

When Don began to call meat purveyors in New York City to source the side of beef, which he would pick up on his way to White Plains, none of them had ever heard of anyone wanting a whole side of beef. Furthermore, not a single one of them could even procure such a thing. He thought perhaps he could get one shipped from Kansas City. Same response—they'd never heard of barbecuing half of a whole steer. He finally decided that the only way the side of beef was going to happen in White Plains was if he took it with him! He purchased the side from his regular meat supplier in San Antonio and froze it. Then he had to get a special crate built for shipping the beef to New York City. When the crate was built to Don's specifications, it looked exactly like a coffin! Nevertheless, it was loaded into the cargo hold of a Braniff Airways flight on which several staff members were also flying. When the plane landed at La Guardia, the staff disembarked and headed to the freight cargo dock to tend the beef and wait for Don and the company caravan. The freight guys said they'd seen hundreds of odd things come across the cargo docks, but the coffin with half a cow in it was definitely the most bizarre piece of cargo they'd ever handled. When Don arrived, he opened the crate so that the cargo handlers could have a look. They were most impressed when he told them the beef would soon be barbecued and consumed by the NFL.

The company's caravan of trucks and staff wound through Manhattan and began the journey to rural White Plains. At the time, Don was still using flamboyantly decorated Mexican street-vendor carts as serving stations. He had loaded the carts onto open trailers, which were pulled by one of the company vans. There were the vans carrying the staff and one pulling the trailer with the carts, followed by the refrigerated trucks and the trucks carrying the equipment, serving pieces, and props. Not far outside of Manhattan, the whole caravan was pulled over by the New York state police. They'd never seen anything quite like Don's catering caravan. They thought this was a band of gypsies going down their highway, and they were certainly going to find out what they were up to! After much explanation, the "gypsies" were on their way to Pete Rozelle's home, which was set in the middle of his private nine-hole golf course.

When the staff finished setting up the tents and the equipment, Don started grilling the side of beef. Soon the aroma of that succulent beef was permeating the air. Don recalled looking up to see Peter Duchin, the famous musician, staring at the side of beef in its rack over the grill. He told Don that he lived across the road and simply couldn't resist the fabulous smells drifting along with the breeze. The side of beef was done, so Don cut off a few slices, wrapped them in a warm piece of pan de campo, added some barbecue sauce, and handed it to Mr. Duchin. He couldn't believe the wonderful taste of the beef and soft texture of the bread. Once the party began, the guests were enjoying themselves so much that they didn't want to go eat the roast beef at the other caterer's area. Even the company's staff had a great time being among their football heroes. One of Don's long-time wait staff recalled that as she was preparing a tray of margaritas to pass through the crowd, she was flanked by Dan Rather and Pat Summerall!

In 1982 Don received a call from a Hollywood publicist on behalf of a "well-known Hollywood celebrity." The publicist also represented Larry Hagman and Linda Gray, stars of the Texas-based TV series *Dallas*. Each year for his birthday, Stacy Winkler, wife of actor and producer Henry Winkler, gave Henry a party built around a theme. When she decided she wanted to do a Texas barbecue, she asked the publicist to call Linda Gray for a recommendation. Ms. Gray had attended a Cattle Baron's Ball that Don had catered in Dallas. She told the publicist that the party had been fabulous—"over the top." So Don and company were off to Hollywood.

The party was held in the Winklers' backyard, where Don set up a bona fide version of a Texas ranch, complete with bales of hay hauled all the way from Texas. The caravan to Los Angeles included a real chuck wagon, his Mexican vendor carts, and an entire antique bar with a mirrored back unit. Of course, Don always liked to take his own food because he knew he could rely on the quality of food from his suppliers. But when he began to research the regulations and health permit requirements for doing events in California, he discovered that he wouldn't be allowed to bring any produce into the state. Since produce plays such a huge role in many of the company's signature dishes, he was worried about finding the necessary variety of produce after he got there. Stacy Winkler assured him that the local farmer's market would have whatever he needed. Don took a few of his crew with him, and they nearly bought out the market, much relieved to know that they would be serving fresh, locally grown produce at the Winkler party. The festivities started at 3 p.m. and lasted until 10 p.m. The guests, of course, were all recognizable celebrities, and they loved Don because neither he nor his staff gaped at them, and no one asked for an autograph. If only they had known that Don never watched television or went to the movies, so he didn't know who they were in the first place!

Although Don invited me to come along on the trip, I didn't go. I truly believed that Hollywood would not be impressed by a little caterer from Texas. And everyone knew that California was known for its trend-setting cuisine, so why would they want the rustic Tex-Mex comfort foods and smoked meats that Don would be serving? I feared that he would be met with a very "ho-hum" attitude and that he would feel crushed.

But the party was a huge success. Don grilled his newly created fajitas and served his stuffed jalapeños; the staff made gorditas and quesadillas in front of the guests. He served his signature chili, fried-to-order shrimp, and much more. Guests were given little red clay tequila tasting cups on colorful strings to be worn around the neck. The Winkers and their guests had never tasted foods with the fresh, vibrant, zesty flavors of Don's offerings. Nor had they seen such attention to detail in the "staging" of a party. Don was asked to do Henry's party again the next year. Stacy Winkler said their friends were calling to get the exact date so that they would be sure to get it on their calendars! In fact, Don did the birthday bash three times, the last time for Henry's fortieth birthday.

"My first impression of Don Strange was one of pure amazement over the magnitude of what he did," says Henry Winkler. "Don Strange had such a huge personality and such grand visions, which translated to pure generosity and a deep desire for people to enjoy themselves. The total experience was an extravaganza—warm, delicious, and fun. It wasn't just the one event, but rather a fabric of imagination. It was the coming together of all the million details that made up the parties this amazing man did. Our friends still talk about those parties, and Don became a legend in Hollywood. To call Don Strange a caterer doesn't do him justice. He didn't *cater* events; he *created* them. I remember him with great fondness and respect."

Shortly after Don got home from the first Winkler party, there was an "incident" involving our son Jason, who was eleven at the time. It seems that he had been doing a lot of bragging at school about his dad going to Hollywood to do a birthday party for "The Fonz," the character played by Henry Winkler on the popular TV series *Happy Days*. One of his friends didn't believe him and challenged Jason to prove it.

Don never, ever threw away anything, so at any given time there would be dozens of little scraps of paper with notes or phone numbers lying on his dresser or stuffed in his wallet. Don had a routine of taking all the dollar bills in his wallet or his pockets and dividing them among the three boys. Jason, in his quest to find proof of the party, asked Don if he had any dollar bills to hand out, thinking he'd get an opportunity to look in his dad's wallet. Right on cue, Don told him that if he did, they'd be in his wallet, which was on his dresser. Jason made a beeline for our bedroom, where he pilfered through Don's wallet, which did contain a few dollar bills and many scraps of paper, one of which had Henry Winkler's home phone number. Jason dutifully brought the bills to Don so they could be divided and carefully stuffed the scrap of paper, his undeniable proof, into his pocket.

Several days later, the phone rang early in the evening and I answered it. It was Stacey Winkler. I guess I must've gotten a very concerned look on my face when she said, "We seem to have a little problem." I noticed that Jason fled up the stairs to his bedroom. Later he said he just knew who was on the other end of the call the minute the phone rang! He'd been waiting for it.

Jason, of course, had taken the phone number to his unbelieving friend, telling him to call and talk to Fonzie. When the Winklers asked the boy where he had gotten their private home phone number, he readily ratted on Jason. Thank goodness, Don was home that evening. I was so upset with Jason that I didn't want to talk to him, so I took on the job of calling his friend's mother to explain the situation and see to it that she took the phone number away from her son.

Don went upstairs to deal with Jason, who had retreated to his closet in tears. Years later Jason told me that he was certain he would get the whipping of his life that night. Instead, Don knocked quietly on the door, saying, "Son, we need to talk." Then he proceeded to tell Jason that what he had done could have caused the Winklers to tell all of their friends that Don Strange had been careless and foolhardy with their private information, causing an unknown amount of potentially lost business, not to mention that he would most likely never be asked to cater an event at the Winklers again. Then word might get back to Texas about what had happened, and it could mean that people would stop using the company because Don was not mindful of his customers' privacy. Jason said that Don went on with this scenario until the company had no business, the employees had all lost their jobs, we had no income and lost everything we had—all because of what he had done. By then, he said, he'd have given anything for that anticipated whipping instead of having to consider the possibly dire consequences of what he'd done.

The second year that Don catered Henry's party, I was anxious to go. I just wanted to watch Don in action in Hollywood! The party almost started out with a disaster. One of the company vans was pulling the trailer that contained Don's Mexican vendor carts. As they were headed down the Hollywood Freeway, the trailer came loose and veered across the freeway. Miraculously it was a level stretch, so the trailer didn't gain any momentum or hit anything. It just coasted to the shoulder and slowed to a stop.

On the morning that Don and the crew began to set up in the Winklers' backyard, I was sitting on a bale of hay having a cup of coffee and a doughnut, which the Winklers had graciously provided for the crew. Henry came out of the house in a bathrobe and sat down next to me. I noticed a price tag dangling from the belt of his robe. He asked why I hadn't come with Don the year before, so I told him of my fears that they wouldn't think Don was very special and that I wouldn't have been able to watch that. He seemed to ponder my comments for a moment, then he paid Don the greatest compliment imaginable when he said, "But, Frances, nobody out here has an imagination that could even come close to Don Strange's." We chatted for a few more minutes, then as he got up to leave, I couldn't stop myself from mentioning the price tag on his belt. I'd just been a mother too long, I guess. I said, "Come here, Henry," and I removed the tag as I asked, "Don't you know it's not cool to leave the price tags on your clothes?" He winked at me and with a devilish grin said, "Well, Frances, I don't have to worry about being cool anymore!"

During the 1980s the company catered dozens of parties all over the country. In the early part of the decade Don did a birthday party for a man in Columbia, South Carolina, who owned several large McDonald's franchises. He had lived in Texas at some point in his life and wanted a real Texas barbecue—with beef, not pork, which is what they call barbecue in the Carolinas. Don packed up the crew and drove to Columbus, where he built his ranch setting and smoked a side of beef for 300 guests. In the mid-1980s he catered a two-day party for 500 people in Miami, Florida. The party was for the Homart Corporation, which was celebrating the opening of yet another spectacular new building.

Don always said that pulling off large events in

faraway places, which often had no kitchens or any type of conventional cooking equipment, was all in the planning. He took everything he thought he might conceivably need, leaving nothing to chance. He and the company's staff would spend a great deal of time planning every piece of equipment and every dish that would be needed as well as the number of staff members. He planned the details right down to taking Texas mesquite wood for cooking the meats. Menus were carefully designed so that the food could be prepared in remote locations. He also knew the importance of having relationships with chefs and suppliers in the places were he catered events, and he spent twenty-five years building those. If last-minute emergencies occurred on the road, those relationships could be tapped for some extra hands on deck, or food, or supplies.

In 1989 the crew traveled to Oklahoma to do an event for the 8,000 members of the National Association of State Legislators at the Williams Center Mall in downtown Tulsa. I can only imagine the challenge of planning such a huge event, considering the supplies and equipment that would have to be transported so far, along with the staff to pull it off! One of the first hurdles Don encountered was one that really baffled him. It seemed that there was a great brouhaha among Tulsa caterers and restaurateurs over the fact that a Texas caterer had been hired for an event in their own backyard. Obviously the grousing and griping reached the officials at the local health department in Tulsa, because they began to come up with all sorts of bizarre requirements that the company would have to adhere to. Don really hated such pettiness. One of their outlandish requirements was that he would have to place "sneeze guards" over every single food station! Now, I'm sure you know what a sneeze guard is if you've ever been to a cafeteria. It's the glass and chrome barrier that covers the food so no one can breathe or sneeze on it. Not too sexy, those sneeze guards! Don was horrified at the thought of having to cover his beautifully designed tables with ugly cages—not to mention the prohibitive cost, which had certainly not been figured into the

company's quote for the various parties. "Have you ever been to a catered event where there were sneeze guards covering the food?" he implored. I had to admit that I'd never heard of such a thing. He made countless sketches trying to devise something that would please the health department officials, something that he could afford and would somehow fit into his design scheme. Presentation, in addition to great food, was one of Don's hallmarks.

Despite some initial mental turmoil, not only did he come up with an affordable solution that the officials had to admit would work, but it was one that appeared to be a featured part of the table design from the beginning— like a display of free-form art suspended above the food. Don bought thin sheets of clear Plexiglas and had them cut to fit each of the food stations. Then he drilled small holes in each corner of the sheets and hung them from the tent's ceiling at an angle, using clear nylon fishing line. By all accounts, the effect was quite dazzling, with the Plexiglas suspended over the tables and carts on the long strands of nylon line, glinting in the candlelight! For certain, no one was heard mentioning "sneeze guards."

Of course, to Don, all of his clients were equally important, and every event—be it for 10 or 10,000—got the same attention to detail and careful planning. Celebrity worship was not a part of his makeup. So although the entire staff was giddy the day in 1990 when the office paged him over the loudspeaker system in the kitchen to say someone from the White House was on the phone, Don treated the call the same as he would from any client calling to inquire about having the company do a party. The caller told Don that the company had been highly recommended by President and Mrs. George H. W. Bush and asked if he would be interested in catering the Annual Congressional Barbecue!

It would be a serious understatement to say that preparations for the two-day event were enormous. First Don and I, along with key staff members who would be handling various facets of the event, went to Washington for

endless interviews. Don also wanted to make notes about the area on the South Lawn where the party would be staged. But it was pouring down rain, so he could only look at the site from the windows. We also visited the White House kitchen, where some of our staff members would be preparing several of the dishes to be on the menu.

When the company caravan arrived at the White House on the appointed date, the staff began the job of setting up the tents and arranging the various food stations, props, and the many grills. The first evening's event would be for the Diplomatic Corps. The second night would be for the congressmen, their families, and guests. After the outside setup was completed, our staff began cooking in the kitchen. I went to the kitchen in the morning to see if they needed anything. As I stepped back out into the hallway, I was stopped by a Secret Service agent, who told me to stand right where I was, as the president was coming! I told him that I was leaving and would be very quick about it, but he was adamant that I wasn't going anywhere. I thought

to myself, "Oh my God, Don is going to kill me for being somewhere I shouldn't have been!" Then I saw President Bush coming down the hallway with Nelson Mandela and his wife, Winnie. As they passed me, the president nodded, said "Good morning," and walked on by. Then I was allowed to move from the spot where I had pasted myself against the wall.

The company's director of sales and marketing, Di-Anna Arias, had a similar experience inside the White House. She had gone to the kitchen to help one of company's waiters carry out huge pottery bowls full of food. They got on the elevator and pushed what they thought to be the right button. But when the elevator door opened with a loud "whoosh," they found themselves facing a dining table. Seated at one end was President Bush and Nelson Mandela at the other. Standing behind each was a personal waiter. They were having lunch. Both men turned toward the door and nodded; then, thankfully, the door whooshed shut.

Don smoked his whole side of beef, along with

Opposite: President and Mrs. Bush;
Congressional Barbecue on the
South Lawn of the White House.
Left: Don Strange of Texas staff with
President and Mrs. Bush.

delicious, tender rib roast. There was a host of salads at their own station, plus myriad side dishes, in addition to the standards—gorditas, quesadillas, avocado halves, and fried stuffed jalapeños, which were specifically requested by the president. Texas peach cobbler was served for dessert. For the Diplomatic Corps dinner, Don had to adapt many of his traditional Texas dishes to adhere to cultural dietary restrictions. The food, in keeping with the Texas ranch theme, was served on blue graniteware.

For the congressional dinner on the second evening, Don added his Grilled White Wings to the menu, grilling them on-site. They were a big hit with most of the guests, but our staff members later told Don that the Kennedys said they were "too hot!"

Don felt that the event had been a great success, but that night as the crew was packing up for the trip back home, he received a very solid vote of confidence. The White House maître d' came down to find Don. He said that the president had asked him to inquire if there had

been any of the delicious meat left, as he'd really like to have some sandwiches made from it. Don gladly gave him two of the smoked prime rib eyes that were not used so that President Bush could enjoy a few more days of Texas flavor! The staff still talks about the time they fed the president and Congress at the White House. President and Mrs. Bush posed for official portraits with the staff members before they left, and each and every staff member received a framed copy of the photograph from the White House.

The company continued to receive requests for doing out-of state-events, and Don eagerly accepted them, considering each one to be a new challenge, a new opportunity to push the limits of his creativity to a new level and the company's reputation into new territory. Today the staff takes such events in stride as an integral part of the business. I'll probably always wonder if Don would have taken on an event out of the country, although I suspect he wouldn't have turned it down and it would've scared the life out of me until it was over!

Don's Chile Con Queso

⭐

2½ pounds pepper-jack cheese, cut into 1-inch cubes

2 cups whole milk

Good-quality corn tortilla chips

The company serves Don's Chile Con Queso at just about every occasion if it doesn't clash with the rest of the menu. People always ask for the recipe, and it's fun to watch their amazement when they find out that it has only two ingredients! Sometimes the simplest things are indeed the best.

Makes about 4 cups

Combine the cheese and milk in the top of a double boiler over gently simmering (not boiling) water. Simmer, stirring often, until cheese has melted and mixture is smooth and thickened, about 15 minutes. Don't rush the process by overheating the water, or the cheese will separate into a stringy, scrambled mess.*

Serve warm in a Crock-Pot set as low as possible or a chafing dish, alongside a basket of corn tortilla chips.

*IF THIS HAPPENS, you might be able to save the queso by quickly pouring the entire contents into the blender. Begin on very low speed, increasing gradually so it will not overflow the top of the blender. Blend until the queso comes together and is smooth and creamy. Return to top of double boiler over low heat. (If it doesn't come back together, then it was overcooked too badly.)

Texas Blue Crab Dip

⭐

---

1 (8-ounce) package cream cheese, softened and cut into 1-inch cubes

½ cup real mayonnaise

1 tablespoon freshly squeezed lemon juice

½ teaspoon Worcestershire sauce

Dash of cayenne pepper

1 teaspoon kosher salt

⅓ cup sliced, skin-on almonds, toasted

2 cups regular lump crabmeat

Toasted French bread rounds

The meat of the Texas blue crab is a great Texas taste. There's just nothing like it, whether it's the basis for a soup, a casserole, or a good dip like this one, which the company began to serve in the 1980s. The deliciously sweet, faintly marine taste of the dip still has clients requesting it over and over.

Makes about 3½ cups

Preheat oven to 350 degrees. Combine cream cheese, mayonnaise, lemon juice, Worcestershire sauce, cayenne, and salt in work bowl of food processor fitted with steel blade. Process until smooth. Turn mixture out into a medium bowl. Gently fold in the almonds and crabmeat, taking care not to break up crabmeat any more than necessary to blend together. Turn mixture out into a 2-quart casserole suitable for serving.

Bake in preheated oven until lightly browned and bubbly, about 25 minutes. Serve hot with toasted French bread rounds.

Mango and Brie Quesadillas

★

With Mexican food being a company specialty, Don loved to create very unique variations on classic dishes. This tasty version of the traditional quesadilla is filled with luscious fresh mango slices and creamy brie cheese, with a zingy taste of green onion.

Makes 24 wedges

Lay the flour tortillas on work surface. Divide cheese wedges into 8 equal portions (about 2 ounces each). Arrange a portion of the cheese wedges on the lower half of each tortilla. Place 4 mango slices on top of the cheese wedges. Top with several slices of avocado. Scatter an equal portion of the green onions (if using) over the mango and avocado slices. Fold the top half of each tortilla over the filling and press down firmly. Place the quesadillas on a parchment paper–lined baking sheet.

Heat a flat-top griddle to medium-high. Place the quesadillas on the griddle, cheese side down, and grill until cheese begins to melt, about 2½ minutes. Carefully turn them over and grill on the other side until filling is warm and quesadillas are sealed together by the melted cheese, another 2½ minutes. Remove from grill and slice each quesadilla into three wedges. Arrange on a platter and serve warm.

8 (6-inch) flour tortillas

1 pound firm brie cheese, rind removed, cut into very thin wedges

2 medium mangos, peeled and cut into 32 thin slices (see below "Peeling and Cutting Mangos")

1 large avocado, peeled, seeded, and cut into thin slices

4 green onions and tops, sliced thin (optional)

HERE'S HOW YOU DO IT

Peeling and Cutting Mangos: Select mangos that aren't too ripe. The flesh should give slightly but still feel firm. One mango will yield about 1 cup of diced mango.

Place mango on a cutting board, resting on one of its flat sides. Using a chef's knife, slice the mango lengthwise, starting about one-third of the way into the mango to avoid the hard seed in the center. Continue cutting all the way through to separate the "cheek" from the fruit. Repeat the cut on the opposite side. Cut the remaining strips of fruit from the seed. Discard the seed.

To dice a mango, carefully cut a crosshatch pattern through the mango pulp in each half, using a sharp paring knife and cutting down to the skin but not through it. Hold a cut half in both hands with your thumbs and palms on top of the ends of the fruit. Gently push upward from below with your fingers, applying pressure to the center of the fruit first.

Continue to ease the remaining flesh upward until the skin is pressed completely inside out and the cubes pop up. Carefully slice off the cubes of pulp by cutting between the fruit and the skin. Discard skin.

To slice the mango, once you have removed the two halves from the seed, make a series of lengthwise cuts through the flesh, as wide as the recipe calls for, cutting down to the skin but not through it. Use the same process to turn the skin inside out and simply slice off the slices by cutting between the skin and your cuts. Discard skin.

Spinach Salad with Raspberry Vinaigrette

1 pound baby spinach leaves

1 cucumber, sliced into thin rounds

2 cups thin-sliced celery

2 ripe avocados, peeled, seeded, and cut into bite-size cubes (see "Peeling and Seeding Avocados" on page 157)

Raspberry Vinaigrette

½ cup sugar

½ teaspoon dry mustard

½ teaspoon salt

⅓ cup raspberry-flavored vinegar

1 slice medium onion, about ½ inch thick and roughly chopped

⅔ cup canola oil

1 teaspoon poppy seeds

2 teaspoons toasted sesame seeds

Salads are an essential element in many Don Strange of Texas events, whether the event is a seated, served dinner, a buffet, or a "station" affair where guests help themselves to whatever dishes they wish. This salad makes a very attractive presentation, either on a glass salad plate or served in a large bowl.

Serves 6 to 8

Make the Raspberry Vinaigrette. Combine all ingredients except poppy and sesame seeds in work bowl of food processor fitted with steel blade. Process until smooth. Turn dressing out into a bowl and whisk in the poppy and sesame seeds. Refrigerate, tightly covered, at least 2 hours before serving.

Place a bed of spinach leaves on each individual serving plate and drizzle a portion of chilled dressing over the top (see below "Dressing Green Salads"). Garnish with cucumber slices, celery, and avocados. (Or you can combine the spinach, cucumber slices, celery, and avocados in a large serving bowl, drizzle the dressing over the top, and toss to moisten all spinach with dressing.)

HERE'S HOW YOU DO IT

Dressing Green Salads: Placing your good homemade salad dressings in squeeze bottles makes it much easier to dress a salad. If the dressing has large particles in it, you may have to trim the squeeze bottle's tip, enlarging the hole to allow large pieces of herb or other ingredients to pass through. Be sure that your dressing, as well as the greens and garnishes, are well chilled. There's nothing worse than a lukewarm salad! If you really want to impress your guests, chill the salad plates and forks.

Always dress the greens before adding any garnishes such as fruit, vegetables (including tomatoes), nuts, or the like. That way, the garnishes are not hidden under a cloak of dressing. To get the best distribution of dressing, squiggle the dressing from the squeeze bottle in a Z pattern across the greens. Then turn the plate 90 degrees and repeat the Z from the opposite direction. Then add your garnishes and serve the salad at once.

Bea's Fried Shrimp with Two Sauces

⭐

Bea Rapelo was a longtime employee who had a special affinity for preparing fried foods. Anything that she fried just tasted better than when someone else did it! Her fried shrimp, especially, was one of the company's most often requested items.

Serves 4 to 6

To make the sauces, combine the respective ingredients in separate bowls and whisk or stir to blend well. Refrigerate, tightly covered, until ready to use.

When ready to fry the shrimp, put the seasoned flour on a plate and set aside. Whisk the egg and milk together in a bowl and set aside. Put the crackers in a large zip-sealing plastic bag and roll them with a rolling pin until ground into fine crumbs. Transfer the cracker crumbs to a separate plate.

Dip a shrimp in the seasoned flour to coat well, shaking off excess. Then dredge the shrimp in the egg wash, coating well. Lastly, coat the shrimp in the cracker crumbs, shaking off excess. Place the shrimp on a baking sheet lined with parchment paper. Repeat with the remaining shrimp, arranging them on the baking sheet in a single layer.

Fry shrimp in small batches, without crowding. Repeat with remaining shrimp, allowing the temperature of the oil to return to 350 degrees before beginning each batch. Drain on a wire rack set over a baking sheet. Serve hot with the two sauces.

All-purpose flour seasoned to taste with seasoned salt and black pepper

1 egg

1 cup milk

1 sleeve of saltine crackers

2 pounds jumbo (16–20 count) shrimp, peeled and deveined, tail sections left intact

Canola oil heated to 350 degrees for deep-frying

Cocktail Sauce

1 cup ketchup

Prepared horseradish to taste

Dash of Tabasco sauce

1 tablespoon Worcestershire sauce

1 tablespoon freshly squeezed lemon juice

Tartar Sauce

1 cup mayonnaise

2 tablespoons drained capers

Juice of half a lemon

1 tablespoon grated onion

¼ cup dill relish

Grill-Smoked Beef Rib Roast

───────────── ★ ─────────────

1 boneless standing rib roast, 6 to 7 pounds (see "Purchasing a Beef Standing Rib Roast" on page 125)

Rub (see recipe below)

Prepared horseradish

Rub

¼ cup granulated garlic

2 tablespoons Lawry's Seasoned Salt

2 tablespoons freshly ground black pepper

⅓ cup sugar

2 teaspoons crushed red pepper flakes

⅓ cup beef base paste (available in upscale specialty markets)

1 tablespoon Kikkoman Teriyaki Marinade & Sauce

2 tablespoons olive oil

Don was always a master at grilling and smoking various cuts of beef. Indeed, the company is known for the many delicious cuts of grilled and smoked beef it has served over the years. Don was particularly fond of a well-marbled rib-eye roast, and when a client was looking for upscale meat presentations, he would often suggest grilling a whole beef rib roast. Cooked to medium-rare and sliced on-site, it was a big hit any time he served it. When Don prepared grilled whole rib-eye for the Congressional Barbecue at the White House in 1990, President Bush requested some of the leftovers! Simply roasting the meat in the oven also produces delicious results.

─────────────

Serves 6 to 8

Build a hardwood charcoal fire in a barbecue pit and allow it to burn down until the coals are glowing red and covered by a layer of white ash, about 20 to 30 minutes.* Meanwhile, combine all the rub ingredients and stir into a smooth paste. Spread the paste evenly over the top fat layer of the roast. Place the meat on grill rack, fat side up, and cook until an instant-read meat thermometer registers 130 to 135 degrees (medium-rare), about 1 hour and 20 minutes, or longer, if desired.

Set the meat aside and cover loosely with foil; allow to rest 15 minutes before slicing. (This will allow the juices of the meat to redistribute throughout the roast, ensuring moist and juicy cuts all the way through.)

Slice the roast into individual portions and serve with prepared horseradish.

*TO USE THE OVEN-ROASTING METHOD, preheat oven to 350 degrees. Place oven rack in middle position. Spread the rub evenly over the top fat layer and sides of the roast. In a heavy open roasting pan, place 1 small onion, quartered; 1 large carrot; 2 celery stalks with leafy tops; and 2 cups rich beef stock. Place a wire rack in the pan and set the roast on the rack, fat side up. Cook in preheated oven 1 hour, then reduce heat to 250 degrees and roast an additional 1 hour and 15 minutes, or until an instant-read meat thermometer registers 130 to 135 degrees (medium-rare). Check the temperature of the meat often, as oven temperatures can vary.

Strain the pan drippings and discard the vegetables. Skim fat from the drippings. Combine drippings with enough beef stock to make 3 cups. Place the drippings in a 2-quart saucepan; add 2 garlic cloves, smashed with the side of a chef's knife, and 2 tablespoons dry red wine. Bring to a boil, then lower heat and simmer 10 minutes. Strain and keep hot. Serve with slices of the roasted meat.

HERE'S HOW YOU DO IT

Purchasing a Beef Standing Rib Roast: Select a standing rib roast of appropriate size—allow about 14 ounces of meat per person. When purchasing the roast, ask for the small end of the rib eye. It is the tenderest portion and may be a bit more expensive, but the taste and tenderness will compensate for the small difference in price. When you have an occasion with a large crowd that calls for a really spectacular creation, buy the whole, lip-on rib eye and grill or roast it, adjusting the quantities in this recipe in relation to the weight of the rib eye.

Venison and Pork Crepes with Hunter's Sauce

───────────────────── ★ ─────────────────────

1 pound venison backstrap, cut into
    julienne strips about 2 inches long

1 pound trimmed pork tenderloin, cut into
    julienne strips about 2 inches long

⅓ cup rice wine or sake

⅔ cup soy sauce

¼ cup sugar

2 tablespoons baking soda

2 teaspoons dark sesame oil

½ cup cornstarch

Crepe Filling

¼ cup olive oil

1¼ cups sliced water chestnuts, drained

1 pound sliced white mushrooms, or sliced
    shiitake mushrooms for a richer flavor

3 garlic cloves, minced

2 cups beef broth

6 green onions and tops, sliced into 1-inch
    slices

18 prepared crepes

Hunter's Sauce (see recipe below)

Minced parsley as garnish

Hunter's Sauce

6 tablespoons unsalted butter

2 shallots, cut into tiny dice

2 tablespoons tomato paste

1 teaspoon Asian chili-garlic sauce

3 tablespoons all-purpose our

2 cups beef broth

¼ cup red currant jelly

⅓ cup dry Madeira

⅓ cup sour cream

Kosher salt and freshly ground black
    pepper to taste

When Don catered the centennial celebration of the famed YO Ranch in 1980, he wanted to create a dish that would be representative of the Texas frontier. Venison, an abundant game meat in early Texas, provided meat for many Texas settlers, so he felt it was a natural choice for a dinner commemorating a Texas frontier ranch. It's an elegant dish that the company has served many times since its debut.

───────────────────

Serves 4 to 6

Place the venison and pork strips in a large zip-sealing plastic bag. Combine rice wine, soy sauce, sugar, baking soda, sesame oil, and cornstarch in a bowl; whisk to blend well and dissolve sugar. Add the marinade to the plastic bag, seal the bag, and turn several times to coat the meat. Place the bag on its side in a baking dish and refrigerate overnight, or for at least 8 hours.

Prepare the Hunter's Sauce. Melt the butter in a heavy-bottomed 12-inch skillet over medium heat. When the butter is foaming, add the shallots and cook, stirring, until they are wilted and transparent but not browned, about 3 to 4 minutes. Stir in the tomato paste and chili-garlic sauce; cook, stirring constantly, until the paste has thickened and darkened, about 5 minutes. Add the flour all at once and stir to incorporate completely. Add the beef broth and bring the sauce to a boil to thicken. Add the red currant jelly and stir to melt. Stir in the Madeira and simmer for 10 minutes. Remove from heat and whisk in the sour cream. Season with salt and pepper. Keep hot.

Prepare the filling. Drain the meat, discarding the marinade. Heat the olive oil in a heavy-bottomed 14-inch skillet over medium-high heat. When the oil is hot, add the meat strips and cook, stirring often to prevent sticking, until well browned and slightly crisp, about 10 minutes. Lower heat to medium and add the water chestnuts, mushrooms, and garlic. Sauté until mushroom liquid has evaporated, about 7 to 8 minutes. Add the beef broth and cook, stirring occasionally, until broth is reduced almost to a glaze, about 15 minutes. Stir in the green onions and remove from heat. Place a portion of the meat mixture in the center of each crepe and fold the sides over to cover the filling. Place desired number of crepes on each serving plate, seam sides down. Spoon a portion of the Hunter's Sauce over each serving and garnish with minced parsley.

Grilled Axis Venison Backstrap with Blackberry-Sage Sauce

⭐

Grilled venison is such a quintessentially Texas dish, and it certainly fits right into the setting of the Don Strange Ranch. Axis venison backstrap, or loin, is available from the Broken Arrow Ranch in Ingram, Texas. It's an all-natural, humanely harvested Texas venison. Of course, if you have a hunter in the family, then you can use the bounty of the hunt. This is a wonderful dish for a special occasion.

Serves 4 to 6

To prepare the venison, trim the loins of any silverskin. Coat with olive oil on all sides and season all over with salt and black pepper. Set aside.

Heat a gas grill to medium heat, or build a hardwood charcoal fire in a barbecue pit and allow it to burn down until the coals are glowing red and covered by a layer of white ash, about 20 to 30 minutes. (Pecan wood is a great choice when grilling venison.) Place the grill rack about 6 inches above the coals. Grill the venison, turning often for even browning, until an instant-read thermometer inserted in the thickest part of the meat registers 130 to 135 degrees (medium-rare). Remove from heat, cover loosely with foil, and allow to rest 10 minutes before slicing.

While the venison is grilling, make the Blackberry-Sage Sauce. Combine the wine and blackberries in a heavy-bottomed saucepan over medium-high heat. Cook, stirring often, until wine is reduced by half and blackberries are very soft, about 15 minutes. Set aside.

While the berries are cooking, melt 2 tablespoons of the butter in a heavy-bottomed skillet over medium heat. When foam subsides, sauté the shallots, sage, and ground cumin until shallots are wilted and transparent, about 7 minutes. Add the demi-glace, lemon juice, and the reserved berry mixture. Simmer, stirring often, until the sauce is thickened, about 5 minutes. Season with salt and black pepper. Cut the remaining 3 tablespoons of butter into small cubes and add to the sauce, whisking rapidly to blend. Do not allow the sauce to boil, or the butter will separate. Remove from heat at once; set aside and keep warm.

Slice the venison loins into ½-inch-thick portions and place the slices, slightly overlapping, on individual plates. Spoon a portion of the Blackberry-Sage Sauce across the meat. Serve hot.

3 axis venison loins, about 8 ounces each

Olive oil

Kosher salt and freshly ground black pepper to taste

Blackberry-Sage Sauce

1½ cups full-bodied dry red wine

2 pints fresh blackberries, rinsed and well drained

5 tablespoons unsalted butter

2 shallots, minced

2 tablespoons minced fresh sage

¼ teaspoon ground cumin

2 cups prepared brown veal demi-glace (see note on page 104)

Juice of half a lemon

Kosher salt or sea salt to taste

Freshly ground black pepper

Traditional Peach Cobbler

Crust

2 cups all-purpose flour

⅔ cup solid shortening

1 teaspoon kosher salt

3 to 5 tablespoons ice water

Peach Filling

2½ pounds fresh peaches, peeled, seeded, and sliced (5 cups)

1 cup sugar

1 teaspoon ground cinnamon

2 tablespoons all-purpose flour

⅓ cup melted butter

1 teaspoon almond extract

Vanilla ice cream (optional)

Peach cobbler has to be one of the best desserts ever created. It's good anytime, but especially when delicious Hill Country peaches are in season. This traditional cobbler has been one of the company's most-requested desserts for many, many years. You can make it an over-the-top experience by adding a scoop of vanilla ice cream to each serving.

Serves 10 to 12

To make the crust, mix the flour, shortening, and salt together with a pastry blender or two knives until it is the consistency of coarse meal. Add the ice water a little at a time and mix together by hand to form a smooth dough. Do not overwork the dough to the point that it becomes springy and elastic. Set aside while making the filling.

Preheat oven to 400 degrees. Grease the bottom and sides of a 9-by-13-inch baking dish; set aide.

Make the filling by placing the peaches in a large bowl. In a separate bowl, stir together the sugar, cinnamon, flour, butter, and almond extract, blending well. Stir into the peaches.

Divide the dough in half. Roll out one-half of the dough on a lightly floured work surface to a ¼-inch-thick rectangle. Cover the bottom and sides of the prepared baking dish with the dough and prick all over with the tines of a fork. Bake in preheated oven until set and light golden brown, about 10 to15 minutes. Remove from oven and turn the filling into the baked bottom crust. Roll out the remaining half of the dough to a thickness of ¼ inch. Cover the top of the cobbler with a solid sheet of the dough, cutting several slits in the top to allow steam to escape; or cut the dough into strips and make a lattice topping.

Bake in preheated oven until crust is golden brown and filling is bubbling, about 1 hour. Serve warm or at room temperature. Add a scoop of vanilla ice cream to each serving, if desired.

CHAPTER SEVEN

Going Where No Caterer Has Ever Gone

Don with staff member Juan Casarnis.

Don Strange of Texas, the company, and Don Strange, the man behind the company, always operated according to the credo associated with the U.S. Postal Service: "Neither snow nor rain nor heat nor gloom of night stays these couriers from the swift completion of their appointed rounds." Don Strange, the man, added: "nor geographical locations or barriers." If there was a job, he'd be there, wherever "there" might turn out to be.

The company's first request to cater an event in a remote, hard-to-access location came in 1976. Bill Blakemore II, a Midland businessman, had used the company to cater several events in Midland and was extremely pleased with the outcome. Mr. Blakemore owned the historic Iron Mountain Ranch outside of Marathon, Texas. The ranch was originally established in 1881 by Captain Albion Sheppard, who first came to the region as a surveyor for the Southern Pacific Railroad when it laid lines through the area. Captain Sheppard later donated the land on which the town of Marathon is located.

The ranch is located northwest of Marathon in northern Brewster County. It's a rugged region, suitable

mainly to cattle grazing. With its 6,000-foot summit, Iron Mountain is an intrusive rock from the Tertiary period and may be up to 66 million years old. The mountain, which spans a half mile at its widest point, stands completely within the ranch. Mr. Blakemore and his first wife, Marian, who was a member of one of the founding families of the King Ranch, began construction of a grand, hacienda-style home at the dark-colored peak of the mountain. The site offers a panoramic view of Gilliland Canyon below.

Upon the untimely death of his wife as the home was nearing completion, Mr. Blakemore halted construction. Six years later he completed the house as a memorial to her and wished to have a party there for fifty guests, including members of the King Ranch families. Don realized that the greatest challenge would lie in getting the company's big equipment and refrigerated food trucks up the mountain. The one-lane dirt and rock road began at the base of the mountain and went up at a very steep incline. There

were no shoulders on the road, meaning there would be no place to pull over and no room for error. To further complicate the event, the company had already scheduled a large event for the opening of a new bank building in Laredo the night before, and Mr. Blakemore planned his party as a late luncheon event at 2 p.m.

Of course, Don booked the event, and *then* he devised a plan for pulling off both parties. He had the staff load trucks with equipment and food for the two separate events, and both caravans headed to their respective destinations, Don going with the group to Laredo. He chartered a private aircraft in Laredo to be waiting for him and his grill cooks at midnight. The rest of the Laredo crew would pack up and head back to San Antonio. They flew to the private airstrip at Iron Mountain Ranch where Mr. Blakemore had a car waiting for them to make the five-mile trip to the ranch headquarters. There they met the other crew from San Antonio, which had arrived in the afternoon, and began setting up for the party. Don said he got two hours of sleep on the plane and felt as good as new.

Mr. Blakemore had told Don that he wanted "something different" from a regular Texas barbecue, and

he wanted the setting to be elegant. Don suggested a "Texas luau" with roast suckling pig slow-smoked on-site. Mr. Blakemore loved the idea. The event was held in the hacienda's courtyard, with its impressive view that spanned miles. The staff had just finished setting and decorating all of the tables when a helicopter carrying a group of the guests flew over the courtyard. All of the napkins, much of the silverware and glassware, and the table decorations were blown in every direction! But Don always allowed a generous amount of time (and extra tableware) for mishaps, and the tables were quickly reset.

Don slow-smoked a suckling pig for each table! After the finger foods and drinks had been served at various stations around the courtyard, the roasted pigs were carried to the tables in a grand procession for the guests to see, then whisked away to be sliced and served. Don said the meal was a spectacular sight. The host and his guests were quite dazzled. After the party, the crew packed up for the trip back to San Antonio. They waited until all of the guests had made it down the mountain, then the caravan began to inch its way down the narrow road. Don rode in one of the large trucks. He told me that he could barely see the edge

of the road from the driver's side and that the 6,000-foot drop-off was eerily dramatic.

The company catered many more events at Iron Mountain Ranch for Bill Blakemore and his second wife, Emily, including a three-day event that involved not only three meals a day but a separate location at another ranch located a few miles down on Highway 90. And the activities at this ranch were sandwiched in the middle of those at Iron Mountain, which meant that the crew had to make several trips up and down the mountain with food and equipment. The event was a combination business meeting and hunting excursion. But Don and his crew made it happen, catching snippets of sleep at the Gage Hotel in Marathon.

In July of 1979 the company went offshore. Literally. Charles Butt, the CEO of Texas's largest grocery chain, H-E-B, had always thought very highly of Don. When he decided he wanted to have a party for 400 people on his private island, near Port Aransas, he hired Don. The island is accessible only by boat. The whole idea of catering a party on an island owned by Charles Butt fascinated Don, and he eagerly accepted the challenge. It was a given that the

Moo, who taught Don a great deal about cooking seafood.

menu would focus on seafood, and he wanted to offer as many varieties of fresh Texas Gulf fish and shellfish as possible. When he learned the island's rich history, he felt a sense of Texas pride from having the opportunity to cater an event there.

The island included one of five remaining lighthouses on the 400-mile-long coastline of Texas. It was constructed by the U.S. government in 1856 on the twenty-five-acre Harbor Island to mark access to Aransas Pass, which leads to the port of Corpus Christi. During the Civil War, control of the lighthouse passed repeatedly between Confederate and Union forces. On Christmas Day of 1862, Confederate General John B. Magruder ordered the destruction of the tower to prevent its use as a point of navigation for federal vessels. Two kegs of powder were exploded inside the lighthouse tower, damaging the upper twenty feet and destroying most of the circular staircase. After the war, the lighthouse was repaired, and it remained in service until 1952, by which time Aransas Pass had slowly inched a mile south of it and a new light was established at Port Aransas.

The lighthouse, which has survived many hurricanes, was sold to a private owner in 1955. In 1971 Charles Butt purchased the property and spent the next few years restoring the lighthouse. He employs keepers to maintain the lighthouse and activate the light each night. There are two cottages on the island in addition to the lighthouse keeper's home.

When Don began strategizing a plan for Charles's party, he realized that he would have to hire a barge to get the equipment and food to the island. He would cook most of the fish and shellfish on-site using his grills, propane-burner cookers, and his Texas Grill Pardners. Don knew that Charles was as excited about the upcoming event as he was. The last time they met to finalize the menu, Charles showed Don one of the T-shirts he had designed as gifts for the guests to commemorate the party.

Staff members who worked the island party still talk about the mouthwatering array of food that Don planned. At the time, one of the company's cooks was a little woman from Thailand whom everyone called "Moo." She happened to be a master at cooking seafood. Don had crab traps put in the water to catch fresh crabs. Then he set up a station near the water's edge where Moo would take the crabs straight from the traps and boil them during the party, along with onions, corn on the cob, and potatoes. As each batch was finished, she'd drain the pot and spread the crabs and vegetables out on a newspaper-lined kiosk. The staff provided wooden mallets for cracking the crab shells. Can't get much fresher than that!

There was a station where the staff sautéed fresh scallops and oysters, which were topped with Ernie sauce. One kiosk featured chicken and shrimp teriyaki roll-ups, grilled as guests watched. There were seafood crepes filled with a delicious mixture of shrimp, crab, and scallops and topped with a sauce of heady white wine and Gruyère cheese. Several huge clam shells filled with mounds of boiled shrimp on ice, served with red cocktail sauce, claimed their own station. At another station steak Diane was prepared to order, and at yet another, snapper meunière. There were watermelon baskets piled high with fresh fruit and an entire table filled with desserts. The stations were decorated with hundreds of palm fronds and great piles of oyster shells. The party was nothing short of spectacular. But, for the first time ever, Don had to hear about the success of the party mostly secondhand. It was a windy day, and the barge was tossed on the swells of the waves all the way from Port Aransas to the island. Don became so wretchedly seasick that he could barely maneuver. After helping his assistant, Dan Schmidt, oversee the setup of the party in the sweltering July heat, he had to be put to bed in one of the air-conditioned cottages. He would come out for a few minutes at a time to check on the progress of the cooking, but in the end he had to trust Dan to tend to the details. Don spent most of the party in the cottage with one foot on the floor, trying to keep the bed from swaying in those waves.

In 2000 the company headed back to the mountains, this time to Sawtooth Mountain, located northwest of Fort Davis. Part of the Davis Mountains, its summit is at a lofty 7,686 feet. In 1941 a group of engineers with the highway department discovered Kit Carson's name carved on a huge boulder in the vicinity with the date December 25, 1839.

Miranda Leonard, who owns the Sawtooth Mountain Ranch, hired the company to cater a three-day event for fifty people. The event was to consist of three separate parties. The first would be held on Friday evening in Fort Davis, where Don would serve a course of heavy hors d'oeuvres at the lovely Veranda Inn. The first course would be followed by a dinner prepared by the staff of Hotel Limpia, where Ms. Leonard stayed when she was in Fort Davis, and served in the hotel's dining room.

For the hors d'oeuvres, Don served his ever-popular grilled baby lamb chops with mango chutney as well as gorditas topped with refried beans, cheese, guacamole, and pico de gallo. There were goat cheese empanadas filled with a creamy mixture of goat cheese and herbs and studded with sun-dried tomatoes as well as vegetable crudités served with dill dip—plus an open bar with several types of beer and special wines provided by Ms. Leonard.

On Saturday morning the crew headed to the ranch to set up for a large dinner that night. The ranch was in the middle of absolutely nowhere. There were no structures, no water, no electricity—nothing but the mountain. So everything needed for the event had to be hauled up to a site near the summit of the mountain, including dozens of huge water containers for drinking and for a dishwashing/sanitation station. Don envisioned a "barbecue on the range" motif for the event. The crew set up tents and a chuck wagon with a canvas tarp extending from its side, where they served some of the foods. Hay bales covered with grain and flour sacks were placed around a large stone fire pit.

The hors d'oeuvres for the Saturday-night party consisted of a steamship round of beef, which was cooked at the site in a barrel roaster, carved, and then served with Jalapeño Béarnaise Sauce, Henry Bain sauce, and petite dinner rolls, along with shrimp Acapulco. There were stations where 16-ounce porterhouse steaks were grilled to order and branded with the ranch's brand for the main course! There were many side dishes and a salad of mixed greens with blue cheese and a light vinaigrette dressing. For dessert the guests were treated to chocolate-raspberry mousse crepes and peach cobbler. Again, there was an open bar. And all this with no electricity. The hostess as well as her guests were delighted with the party in its isolated location. One staff member remarked that it looked as though you could reach up and touch the thousands of stars in the clear night sky.

The final meal, held in the same location on the ranch, was a Sunday brunch. The crew arrived early to set up for it, and everything was ready to go as the guests arrived from Fort Davis. The omelet station was set up to prepare each guest's omelet to order from an array of fillings. It was a gorgeous day with an amazingly brilliant cerulean blue sky. The staff described it as being one of those "grand to be alive" sort of days. Then, from a distance at first, could be heard a concentrated buzzing that became more pronounced with each passing minute. Suddenly, from out of nowhere, a huge swarm of honeybees descended on the party. Within minutes, every plate, bowl, platter, and pitcher—anything containing food—was covered with the bees. The crew was desperately trying to shoo away the bees and get the food covered, but the bees kept on coming. Luckily, only a few people were stung, and not badly. It quickly became evident that no one would be able to eat the food, so the hostess, with great apologies, called off the brunch, and the guests made a hasty exit. That left the staff to tear down the site, get the chuck wagon loaded onto its trailer, pack up the trucks with equipment, tables, chairs, tableware, trash—and hopefully, not the bees!

In the company's history there have been many more events in challenging locations as well as in the worst possible weather. Our son Jason recalls the worst one in his memory—a March 1987 party at the Railroad Museum in Galveston. The event was on Mardi Gras and was given for the Krewe of Maximilian. The weather was freezing cold. Don had Jason, sixteen at the time, cooking Grilled White Wings on a balcony where he had set up a nice station so that folks could wander out and watch the revelers below while enjoying the freshly grilled appetizers. But it was so cold that no one would come out on the balcony. Then it began to snow, so Jason would grill a batch and bring them inside, where they were eagerly devoured, then go out and grill another batch. The party lasted until 4 a.m. When the staff got everything packed up and headed to the Galveston Causeway to cross over to the mainland, they discovered that the causeway was a solid sheet of ice.

A caterer's work is rarely easy, even when the circumstances are ideal and the location easily accessible. But creating stellar events under bizarre conditions or in all-but-unreachable locations would seem damn near impossible to most people. But never to Don Strange.

Nash-Goehring Wedding
at the Gallagher Ranch

Helotes, Texas

Prickly Pear Margaritas and Small Coronitas Beer

Small Hill Country Lamb Chops with Mango Chutney

Grilled White Wings

Mesquite-Grilled Beef Tenderloin with
Jalapeño Béarnaise Sauce and Parker House Rolls

Nopalito Salad in Cilantro-Lime Vinaigrette

Baby Spinach and Romaine Leaves with Rio Grande Valley
Grapefruit, Queso Fresco, Cranberries, and Pecans

Gorditas

Venison Crepes

Fish Tacos with Roasted Chipotle Salsa and Lime

Arroz Con Pollo with Pan de Campo

Avocado Halves Stuffed with Shrimp Ceviche

Bean and Cheese Tacos

Kahlua Freezes

Miranda Leonard Brunch
at Sawtooth Mountain Ranch

Fort Davis, Texas

September 24, 2000

★

Grilled White Wings

Omelets Made to Order

Don Strange Cheese Grits

Hot Biscuits

Assorted Bagels with Salmon and Cream Cheese

Assorted Breakfast Breads & Muffins with Preserves and Butter

Fresh Seasonal Fruit

Coffee and Fruit Juices

Charles Butt Party at Lighthouse Island

Aransas Bay, Texas

July 7, 1979

★

Boiled Blue Crabs Freshly Plucked from the Bay

Chilled Boiled Gulf Shrimp with Red Cocktail Sauce

Sautéed Oysters with Ernie Sauce

Chicken and Shrimp Teriyaki Roll-ups

Watermelon Basket Filled with Fresh Seasonal Melon & Pineapple Dusted with Coconut Flakes

Sautéed Fresh Scallops

Red Snapper Meunière

Seafood Crepes

Steak Diane

Beef Tenderloin Shish Kebabs

Fudgy Brownies

Goat Cheese Empanadas

★

9 ounces soft Texas goat cheese*

9 ounces cream cheese, softened

⅓ cup minced, drained sun-dried tomatoes packed in oil

3 green onions and tops, minced

1 tablespoon minced fresh flat-leaf parsley

1 tablespoon minced fresh basil

3 garlic cloves, minced

1 teaspoon dried Mexican oregano

Kosher salt to taste

90 frozen 12-inch-wide phyllo pastry sheets, thawed

Olive oil

1 cup (4 ounces) grated Parmesan cheese

While these crisp and tasty little triangles are not empanadas in the true sense, as they are made with Greek phyllo dough instead of the usual pastry, Don loved to create freewheeling versions of classic foods. Whatever you may choose to call them, they are delicious finger foods, so be sure to make plenty.

Makes 60 pieces

Preheat oven to 350 degrees. Line a baking sheet with parchment paper and set aside. Combine the goat cheese, cream cheese, sun-dried tomatoes, green onions, parsley, basil, garlic, and oregano in a medium bowl and stir to blend well. Season with salt and set aside.

Place one phyllo sheet on work surface. Keep the remaining sheets covered with plastic wrap and a slightly damp tea towel. Brush the entire sheet with a very light glaze of olive oil. Scatter a portion of the Parmesan cheese over the sheet, being sure that you go all the way to the edges of the pastry. Top with a second sheet of pastry, and repeat the oil and cheese topping. Add a third sheet and glaze with oil and scatter cheese over the sheet. Using the palms of your hands, flatten the pastry stack to stick it together.

Using a sharp knife and definitive cuts, slice the stacked pastry into two 4-inch-wide strips down the length of the sheet. Working with one stacked strip at a time, place a tablespoon of the cheese filling in the center of the bottom of the strip. Fold the left corner of the pastry over the filling to meet the opposite edge of the strip, forming a triangle. Now fold the triangle up from the bottom-right point. Continue to fold in the same manner (this is the same technique used in folding a flag). Brush the small flap remaining at the top with olive oil and fold it onto the empanada, pressing it down. Brush both sides of the empanada lightly with oil; place, folded side down, on prepared baking sheet. Repeat with remaining strip of pastry, then repeat the entire process with the remaining sheets of phyllo dough.

Bake empanadas in preheated oven until golden brown on both sides, about 20 minutes. Serve hot.

*IF YOU OR YOUR GUESTS don't like goat cheese, it may be due to the very assertive flavor of some goat cheeses. Try tasting many of the different artisan goat cheeses being crafted in Texas. Some of them actually have very delicate tastes.

Boiled Blue Crabs

★

Boiling crabs is a great "action" thing. The company has a tradition of serving foods that can be cooked in front of party guests, and boiling up a big pot of spicy court bouillon and throwing in potatoes, onions, corn on the cob, and then live blue crabs is one of the best. The aroma draws people to its source, and when the big pot is drained and the contents spread out on newspapers, you don't ever have to tell folks to "dig in."

Makes 20 party servings

Combine all seasonings in a 40-quart stockpot with a straining basket and place the pot on a butane burner. Add water to fill the pot slightly more than halfway. Bring to a boil and allow the liquid to cook for 30 minutes. This forms a nice, spicy court bouillon in which to cook the vegetables and crabs. Add water as needed to maintain the water level.

Add the corn and potatoes and cook for 10 minutes; then add the onions and cook an additional 5 minutes. Check the crabs to be sure that all are very much alive. Discard any that are dead. Using long tongs, put the crabs in the pot, pushing them down into the water. Cover the pot and cook until the crabs are dark terra-cotta color, about 20 minutes. Carefully and slowly lift the straining basket from the water, taking care that the hot water doesn't spew from the holes in the strainer and cause burns. Spread the veggies and crabs out on newspaper and stand back! Provide several rolls of paper towels.

6 (3-ounce) packages of Zatarin's Shrimp & Crab Boil

2 cups Lawry's Seasoned Salt

12 bay leaves

10 lemons, cut into quarters

½ cup cayenne pepper

2 tablespoons black peppercorns

12 large ears of fresh corn, cut into 2-inch pieces

10 pounds baby red new potatoes

20 large onions, peeled, tops and roots removed

48 live blue crabs

HERE'S HOW YOU DO IT
Making Seafood Stock: If you're not into making your own fish stock from fish heads and bones, there are some easy alternatives that will produce a very usable stock. The Knorr brand shrimp bouillon cubes make a good stock, or you can use bottled clam juice. Or you can prepare a seafood stock using More Than Gourmet's Glace de Fruits de Mer Gold, which can be found with the bouillon cubes and packaged stocks in specialty markets. It's the most expensive of the substitutes, but it is well worth the price. Just follow the directions on the box.

There's also another alternative. Save the shrimp shells each time you peel shrimp for shrimp dishes; freeze those shells (and heads, too, if you buy head-on shrimp) until you have accumulated a gallon bag of shells. You can then make a nice stock. Simply heat a thin glaze of canola oil and sauté some chopped onion, carrot, and celery until the vegetables begin to caramelize, then add a couple of tablespoons of tomato paste, stir, and cook until the tomato paste begins to caramelize. Add the shrimp shells and stir to brown slightly; add about 10 cups of water and bring to a boil. Lower heat and cook for about 1 hour. Drain into a large fine strainer set over a large bowl, pressing down on the shells and vegetables to extract every possible drop of flavorful broth; discard the shells and vegetables. Voilà! You have a homemade stock at very little cost!

Shrimp Acapulco

★

We serve this dish as a chunky salsa-style dip with corn tortilla chips. It would also make a great luncheon salad, served on crisp mixed greens. Either way, it's really tasty!

Makes about 2 quarts

To prepare the dressing, combine the red wine vinegar and mustard in work bowl of food processor fitted with steel blade. Process until smooth and well blended. With machine running, add the combined olive oil and canola oil in a slow, steady stream through the feed tube. Season with salt and pepper. Continue to process an additional 15 seconds to form a strong emulsion.

      Combine the shrimp, bell peppers, onions, cilantro, jalapeños, and avocados in a large bowl, tossing to mix. Add the dressing and stir to coat all ingredients. Refrigerate, covered, until well chilled. Serve in an attractive bowl with a basket of corn tortilla chips alongside.

2½ pounds boiled, peeled, and deveined cocktail (70–90 count) shrimp

1 cup diced red bell pepper

1 cup diced yellow bell pepper

1 cup diced red onion

1 cup thinly sliced green onions and tops

1 cup minced cilantro

¼ cup chopped pickled jalapeños

6 avocados, peeled, seeded, and cut into ½-inch dice (see "Peeling and Seeding Avocados" on page 157)

Good-quality corn tortilla chips

Dressing

¼ cup red wine vinegar

½ cup Dijon-style mustard

⅓ cup extra-virgin olive oil

½ cup canola oil

Kosher salt and freshly ground black pepper to taste

Sautéed Scallops

★

2½ pounds large (U/10) scallops

⅓ cup olive oil

10 medium garlic cloves, peeled and smashed

Kosher salt and freshly ground black pepper to taste

Juice of 1 lemon, preferably Meyer variety

⅔ cup dry white wine, such as chardonnay

Scallops are one of the most delicious and delicate of all shellfish. But there's an art to preparing them without overcooking them. Don taught the staff well, and they would cook the scallops in front of the guests. Party guests clamored for this simple yet elegant and delicious dish. When buying scallops, be sure that they're fresh. They should be moist and have a faintly marine aroma. If they smell *fishy* or of ammonia, then they just aren't fresh. The dish is most impressive when prepared with the giant U/10 scallops, meaning there are only ten of them per pound, but you can also use regular sea scallops. Tiny bay scallops are not recommended.

Serves 4 to 6

Pat the scallops very dry using absorbent paper towels (they won't sear if they have surface moisture). Set aside.

Heat the olive oil in a heavy-bottomed 14-inch skillet over medium-high heat. When the surface of the oil is shimmering, add the garlic. Cook, stirring, until garlic is browned, about 1 minute. Add the scallops and season with salt and pepper. Sear scallops until browned, about 2 minutes per side, turning once. Pour the lemon juice over the scallops and gently stir just until scallops turn white all over. Do not overcook, or they will be tough and rubbery. Remove pan from heat at once and spoon the scallops onto individual serving plates using a slotted spoon.

Return the pan to high heat and add the wine. Using a metal spatula, scrape up browned bits from bottom of pan. Cook quickly to reduce liquid by half. Drizzle the pan sauce over the scallops and serve hot.

Seafood Crepes

★

Don loved to serve crepes filled with elegant, tasty meats and seafood in rich sauces. This was one of his favorites, and it was one of the dishes served at Charles Butt's party on his private island off the coast of Port Aransas. Prepared crepes of excellent quality are available to consumers today at most upscale supermarkets, making this a quick and easy dish to serve.

Serves 6

Heat the olive oil in a heavy-bottomed 12-inch skillet over medium-high heat. When the oil is shimmering and very hot, add the scallops and shrimp; season with salt and pepper and Seafood Magic. Sear, tossing constantly, just until seafood is lightly browned, about 5 minutes. Remove from heat and pour seafood into a wire strainer set over a bowl. Discard the cooking oil, reserving the browned bits on the bottom of the skillet.

   Return the skillet to medium heat and add the butter. When butter has melted and foam has subsided, add the mushrooms, celery, shallots, and remaining seasonings. Sauté, stirring often, until vegetables are wilted and mushroom liquid has evaporated, leaving only the butter in the bottom of the pan, about 10 minutes. Add the flour all at once and stir until no unblended traces of flour remain. Cook, stirring, 2 to 3 minutes. Combine the lemon juice, seafood stock, and white wine; add to the pan and stir rapidly to blend, scraping up any browned bits from the bottom of the pan. Bring the mixture to a full boil to thicken; reduce heat and simmer for 5 minutes. Return the shrimp and scallops to the skillet and stir in the whipping cream. Gently stir in the crabmeat. Cook, stirring often, until the seafood and cream are heated, about 3 minutes. Take care not to break up the lumps of crabmeat. Stir in the cheese and cook, stirring, just long enough to melt the cheese. Remove pan from heat.

   To serve, use a slotted spoon to fill the center of crepes with the seafood mixture. Fold sides of the crepes over the seafood mixture and place 2 crepes on each serving plate, seam side down. Spoon a portion of the sauce remaining in the pan over each serving and garnish with a scattering of the green onion tops. Serve hot.

4 tablespoons olive oil

1 pound small bay scallops

1 pound small (70–90 count) shrimp, peeled and deveined

Kosher salt and freshly ground black pepper to taste

2 tablespoons Chef Paul Prudhomme's Seafood Magic or other Cajun seasoning

6 tablespoons unsalted butter

8 ounces sliced mushrooms

1 large celery stalk, cut into small dice

3 French shallots, minced

¼ teaspoon cayenne pepper

1 teaspoon minced fresh thyme

2 teaspoons minced fresh flat-leaf parsley

1 large fresh bay leaf, minced

½ teaspoon kosher salt

3 tablespoons all-purpose flour

2 tablespoons freshly squeezed lemon juice

2 cups seafood stock or bottled clam juice (see "Making Seafood Stock" on page 140)

1 cup dry white wine, such as chardonnay

¾ cup whipping cream

8 ounces lump crabmeat

1 cup (4 ounces) shredded Gruyère cheese

12 prepared crepes, warmed just before filling

Very thinly sliced green onion tops as garnish

Stuffed Red Snapper

★

1 whole red snapper, about 16 pounds, gutted, cleaned and scaled, with head, tail, and fins intact (see "Buying Fresh Fish (and Making Sure They're Fresh)" on page 146)

Kosher salt and freshly ground black pepper to taste

¾ pound (3 sticks) unsalted butter, divided

2 red bell peppers, chopped

1 yellow bell pepper, chopped

1 green bell pepper, chopped

6 green onions and tops, thinly sliced

4 (4-ounce) jars marinated artichoke hearts, drained and roughly chopped

½ cup minced parsley

1 pound baby spinach leaves, roughly chopped

2 pounds regular lump crabmeat

1 pound feta cheese, crumbled

Short bamboo skewers

Juice of 1 lemon

Chef Paul Prudhomme's Seafood Magic

Lemon slices and fresh dill sprigs as garnish

Don first prepared this very impressive dish for friends visiting us at our house in Rockport. He went to one of the fish markets in Fulton and bought the biggest whole red snapper available. It weighed a little over 16 pounds! He wanted to stuff the fish whole, so the fishmonger, suggested a "pocketbook fillet," which involves removing the entire bone structure of the fish through the stomach side. A good fish market will do it for you. It's a really spectacular dish when presented on a huge platter.

Serves about 15

Spray a large fish-grilling rack with nonstick cooking spray; set aside. To fillet the fish for stuffing, use kitchen shears or scissors to cut the rib bones away from the flesh at the stomach opening. Using a sharp boning or fish filleting knife, cut the flesh away from the ribs and backbone of the fish, taking care not to puncture the skin by keeping the boning knife angled toward the bones, not the flesh. Using the shears, cut the backbone loose at the head. Pull out the backbone and ribs from the head end. Rinse the boned cavity of the fish, then pat dry using absorbent paper towels. Season the cavity with salt and pepper. Place the fish on a large baking sheet and refrigerate while making the stuffing.

To make the stuffing, melt 2 sticks of the butter in a heavy-bottomed 14-inch skillet. When the foam subsides, add the bell peppers, green onions, artichoke hearts, and parsley. Sauté, stirring often, until the peppers are limp, about 7 minutes. Add the spinach and quickly sauté just until the spinach begins to wilt, about 2 minutes. Remove from heat and turn the mixture out into a large bowl. Set aside and allow to cool.

Gently fold the crabmeat and feta cheese into the cooled mixture, taking care not to break up the lumps of crabmeat. Season to taste with salt and pepper.

Remove the fish from the refrigerator, leaving it on the large baking sheet. Stuff with the stuffing mixture, packing it tightly into the cavity. Using the bamboo skewers, seal the slit by crisscrossing the skewers through both sides of the open edge. (If you used a fish smaller than 16 pounds and have some leftover stuffing, bake it separately in a baking dish for about 15 minutes at 350 degrees, or until heated through and golden brown on top.) Melt the remaining stick of butter with the lemon juice. Brush both sides of the fish with the butter and season liberally with the Seafood Magic. Transfer the fish to the prepared grilling rack.

Heat a gas grill to medium heat, or build a hardwood charcoal fire in a barbecue pit and allow it to burn down until the coals are glowing red and covered by a layer of white ash, about 20 to 30 minutes. Position grill rack 8 to 10 inches above the coals. Place the fish on the grill and grill for 20 minutes. Turn the fish rack over and grill the other side for an additional 20 minutes, or until the flesh is opaque throughout and the stuffing reaches an internal temperature of 150 degrees (using an instant-read meat thermometer inserted into the thickest part of the fish from the open side).

Place fish on a large platter or wooden plank. Garnish the platter or plank with lemon slices and fresh dill sprigs. Slice the fish into individual portions and serve hot.

HERE'S HOW YOU DO IT
Buying Fresh Fish (and Making Sure They're Fresh):
When you can, it's always best to select from whole fresh fish at the seafood market or seafood counter at your favorite market. The fish at the counter should be stored on ice on a perforated surface so that the melting ice will drain off. There are many telltale signs that will mark a fish that is definitely past its prime. Look for fish with clear, not clouded eyes. The eyes should never be shrunken, but rather full and bulging. The gills should be bright red, never brown, which indicates a sign of age. Ask the person at the counter to let you feel and smell the fish. The skin should be firm to the touch, much like your own skin, and never mushy. It should be slightly moist, but never with a slimy or sticky feel. Lastly, the fish should not smell *fishy*, only with a faint marine smell.

Now that you've selected a pristinely fresh fish, you can ask the fishmonger to prepare it as you wish—filleted, cut into steaks if it is a large fish, or pocket-filleted if you wish to stuff it. If you have the fish filleted, ask the fishmonger to remove the skin. When you cook skinned fish fillets, always start with the skinned side down so the fish won't curl up.

If you must select from already filleted fish, then you must rely on the flesh being firm and never slimy. The aroma is a good indicator of freshness. If it smells fishy, it will taste fishy!

Grilled Baby Lamb Chops with Mango Chutney

These little grilled baby lamb chops are a must at most Don Strange of Texas parties. They're piled on platters, and company waiters walk through the crowd as guests are arriving, passing out the tasty little morsels. The meat is cut away from the top slender portion of the bone (called "French Cut"), so they're held by the bone, allowing guests to munch away without getting their fingers messy.

Makes 16 chops

Make the Mango Chutney. Combine the sugar and vinegar in a heavy-bottomed 4-quart saucepan over medium-high heat. Bring to a boil, stirring to dissolve the sugar. Add the onion, garlic, ginger, serrano chile, and salt. Return to a boil, then lower heat to a simmer and cook 15 minutes, stirring often. Add the mangos, lime juice, and raisins. Cook an additional 10 minutes, stirring often, or until the mixture reaches the consistency of marmalade. Allow the chutney to cool, then refrigerate, covered, for at least 24 hours. Serve at room temperature.

To grill the lamb chops, heat a gas grill to medium heat, or build a hardwood charcoal fire in a barbecue pit and allow it to burn down until the coals are glowing red and covered by a layer of white ash, about 20 to 30 minutes. Slice the lamb racks between each bone to make 16 chops. Glaze both sides with olive oil and season both sides with salt and pepper.

Place the chops on the grill and cook until an instant-read thermometer registers about 128 degrees (medium-rare), the recommended level of doneness, about 10 to 14 minutes, turning once.

Serve the chops hot with the Mango Chutney.

2 (8-bone) New Zealand baby lamb racks, about 1½ pounds each, "Frenched"

Olive oil

Kosher salt and freshly ground black pepper to taste

Mango Chutney

1 cup firmly packed brown sugar

1 cup apple cider vinegar

1 large onion, chopped

2 medium garlic cloves, minced

1 tablespoon minced fresh ginger

1 serrano chile, seeds and veins removed, minced

1 tablespoon kosher salt

2 large ripe mangos, peeled, seeded, and cut into 1-inch cubes (see "Peeling and Cutting Mangos" on page 121)

¼ cup freshly squeezed lime juice

½ cup golden raisins

Chocolate-Raspberry Mousse Crepes

★

8 ounces bittersweet chocolate, chopped

3 tablespoons water

3 large egg yolks

¼ cup powdered sugar

2 ounces (½ cup) hazelnuts, ground and toasted

3 tablespoons raspberry liqueur

1½ cups whipping cream, beaten to stiff peaks

Sweetened Whipped Cream (see recipe below)

2 pints fresh raspberries (6 per crepe), plus additional for garnish

Chocolate curls

Powdered sugar

Mint sprigs

Chocolate Crepes

2 eggs

¼ cup powdered sugar

½ cup all-purpose flour

2 tablespoons butter, melted

2 teaspoons vanilla extract

2 tablespoons cocoa

1 cup milk

Unsalted butter for cooking the crepes

Sweetened Whipped Cream

2 cups well-chilled whipping cream

2 tablespoons well-chilled sour cream

3 tablespoons powdered sugar

1 tablespoon vanilla extract

The days of the oil boom brought a new level of sophistication to the Texas palate. Clients wanted elegant, fancy dishes, and anything rolled into a crepe was de rigueur. This delicious chocolate dessert crepe became a party favorite. Interestingly enough, crepes are making a comeback, showing up on upscale restaurant menus around the country. You can make the component parts ahead and assemble the dish at the last minute.

Serves 6

Melt the bittersweet chocolate in top of double boiler over simmering water, stirring until smooth. Remove from heat and set aside to cool briefly.

Meanwhile, combine water, yolks, and powdered sugar in a large metal bowl. Set bowl over simmering water in base of double boiler and whisk vigorously until the mixture is frothy and a candy thermometer registers 160 degrees, about 6 minutes. Remove bowl from top of double boiler. Using electric mixer, beat egg mixture until thick and cool, about 3 minutes. Fold cooled chocolate into the mixture; then add hazelnuts and raspberry liqueur. Fold the whipping cream into the chocolate mixture in 3 additions. Refrigerate, tightly covered, until ready to use.

To make the Sweetened Whipped Cream, combine all ingredients in bowl of electric mixer and beat until soft, floppy peaks form. Seal tightly with plastic wrap and refrigerate until ready to use. (If the cream loses its body before serving, simply whisk it vigorously and it will stiffen again.)

Make the Chocolate Crepes. Combine the eggs and sugar in electric mixer and beat until mixture is thickened and light lemon yellow in color, about 4 minutes. Add the flour and beat to blend well. Add melted butter, vanilla, cocoa, and milk and beat until a smooth batter forms, about 4 minutes.

To make each crepe, melt about a teaspoon of butter in a 6-inch crepe pan over medium heat. Swirl the butter to coat the bottom of the pan. Add 2 tablespoons (⅛ cup) of the crepe batter all at once and swirl quickly to cover the bottom of the pan. Cook just until the crepe is set, about 1 minute, then turn and quickly cook the other side, about 20 seconds. Repeat with remaining batter to make a total of 12 crepes, wiping the pan clean with a paper towel between each crepe. (See "Making Crepes" on page 74.)

To serve the crepes, place a portion of the chilled mousse in the center of each crepe. Press about 6 raspberries into the mousse and fold the sides of the crepes over the filling. Place 2 crepes, seam side down, on each serving plate. Spoon a portion of the Sweetened Whipped Cream over the center of each serving. Scatter a few chocolate curls on top of the cream. Place the powdered sugar in a small wire strainer and dust it over each serving, letting some of the powdered sugar fall on the empty portion of the plate. Garnish plate with a mint sprig and a few fresh raspberries; serve.

CHAPTER EIGHT

We Need a Ranch

After the crash of the oil industry in the early 1980s, Don, the eternal optimist, remained just that, an optimist. Instead of lamenting the business that had been lost, he was on a mission to find ways to replace it. He had faith that weddings would become a lifeline for the company because people will continue to fall in love and get married, despite what's happening with the economy. But he also wanted to be in a position to do private events for convention groups meeting in San Antonio. He'd always talked about having a ranch where he could stage large events where the guests would be totally immersed in Texas culture while dining on iconic Texas cuisine. At a time when other businesses were scaling back, Don viewed the oil bust as a challenge, saying, "Times like these are a way to expand into other areas that we may not have considered before."

He always loved to look at real estate property, although I hated it! He had catered so many events at ranches all over the state and around the country—private events for the ranch owners as well as Cattle Baron's Balls, held on ranches that the ranch owners would make available for these occasions. But the ranches were never

equipped for large-scale catering, so the company had to transport large quantities of tables and chairs and other equipment to the site. It was always a monumental task to pull off these ranch-based parties.

Don envisioned having a place that was within thirty minutes of San Antonio, one that looked like a real working ranch where he could hold events. He would make it a place where people could get away for a day and feel as though they were visiting an authentic Texas ranch. Only *his* ranch would be specifically equipped for catering.

For his birthday in January of 1982, Don told me the only present he wanted was for me to go with him to look at a couple of pieces of property that a real estate agent had located for him. Well, what could I say? It was his birthday wish. When that Sunday dawned, it was the nastiest-looking day you could imagine. We trudged through the rain and gloom to three or four pieces of property, none of which excited either one of us. I kept reminding myself, "It's his birthday . . ." Then we turned onto a bumpy road, sadly in need of work, that led to the last property that the realtor wanted to show us, an eighty-nine-acre ranch. The place was badly run down, but we could both immediately see the potential, and the location was ideal—just off I-10 near the community of Welfare and yet just far enough from the interstate that it was quiet and had a feeling of being remote. We loved that fact that the property had a rock

house, built in 1869, that had seen a lot of Texas history. The steps leading to the house had fallen away long before, so we could only stand on our tiptoes and look through the windows. There were no roads and not much else, but we just knew this was the right place. Don got so excited over the find that we both forgot the terrible weather.

We bought the property in February of 1982 and named it the Welfare Ranch because Don, being the unassuming person he was, didn't feel right about naming it after himself! However, the name caused a great deal of, well, "confusion." It seems that a lot of the people who drove by, seeing the sign "Welfare Ranch," just happened to be *on* welfare, so they would drive on in, assuming it to be another of their benefits! A San Antonio newspaper offered to run a "Name the Ranch of Don Strange" contest, which Don thought would be a splendid idea. When the most popular name submitted was simply "The Don Strange Ranch," he couldn't argue with the consensus of local folks. So the ranch officially became the Don Strange Ranch.

I was consumed with anxiety at the time about how we would ever pay for the place. We took out a mortgage for the purchase price. But the oil bust had just taken away over half of our business, and here was Don insisting that we were going to pay for the improvements "out of the

days the guys would work outside, whittling down the huge beams that they would use to build the barn.

When the house was completed, Don turned his full attention to building the barn. It is a unique structure in that every beam joint is dovetailed and pegged. Not a single nail or screw was used in its construction. Each section of the beams was raised into place by hoisting it up by ropes attached to pickup trucks. It looks for all the world as though it's been there as long as the house. Next came the installation of all the plumbing and electricity required for large parties as well as reinforcement of the cattle guards to accommodate large buses. Then Don was in business. He bought an ornate antique counter and mirrored-back bar from the old Staffel's Feed Store in San Antonio and installed it in the barn to serve as the bar. Additional covered pavilions were added to the sides and front of the barn to provide a total of 10,125 square feet. During the construction, Don began to collect artifacts like antique wagons, wagon wheels, a real chuck wagon, and other ranching paraphernalia to make the ranch as true to its 1860s origin as possible.

Don built a bona fide rodeo arena where groups can

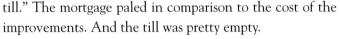

till." The mortgage paled in comparison to the cost of the improvements. And the till was pretty empty.

But somehow he did it. First he restored the house. He'd wanted to build a barn first so that he could begin to schedule events, but it was a winter of continuous heavy rains, so he started on the house. He hired skilled local craftsmen who loved to work with wood to do the job. There were no plans. Don would simply draw out a plan on a scrap of paper, room by room, of what he wanted the space to look like, and they would construct it. On sunny

opt to have a full-fledged rodeo, with real cowboys, at their events. Hosts can include a hayride in old wooden wagons filled with hay and drawn by an antique Farmall tractor. There's a herd of longhorn cattle that are very fond of being petted.

The ranch has been the scene of so many weddings, corporate functions, fund-raising events, and even landmark events. The now internationally famous Dixie Chicks played two of their earliest gigs at the Don Strange Ranch. One of these marked the first time they'd ever used an amplifier!

One of the more memorable events at the ranch was held on February 20, 1988. It was a fund-raiser for George H. W. Bush on his San Antonio campaign stop during his bid for the presidency. Both George and Barbara Bush attended the one-day event, for which the setup took an entire week. First the Secret Service moved onto the ranch early in the week to install extra phone lines and who-knows-what other gizmos. Then they brought helicopters and took aerial photos of the ranch and surrounding area from every imaginable angle. When the food was loaded onto the company's refrigerated trucks at the San

Antonio commissary early on the morning of the party, USDA inspectors supervised the operation and sealed the trucks for the drive to the ranch. The inspectors traveled with the convoy to the ranch, unsealed the trucks, and then supervised the placement of all the food. Later in the morning, bomb-sniffing dogs were brought in to sniff out the ranch. However, this procedure almost went amuck because there was so much meat being grilled on open pits that it was hard for the handlers to keep the dogs' attention on their bomb-sniffing duties! Don served his celebrated fried stuffed jalapeños, and George Bush loved them so much that he asked for a few to take on the road. As Don was carrying the delicious snacks to the candidate's car, Mr. Bush thanked him and told him that if all went well, he'd invite the company to do an event at the White House. True to his word, two years later the president asked Don to cater the Annual Congressional Barbecue. Remembering the stuffed jalapeños, he asked Don to serve them at the barbecue.

As our sons took on active roles in the operation of the business, Don began to rely heavily on them, as well as his experienced staff, to be the eyes and ears of the company.

He knew they were the ones out there interfacing with the clients every day. He believed that they knew best how to keep the business in the vanguard.

So when Jason, who was then twenty-four years old, came to us in 1996 with the idea of building a ropes and challenge course on the Don Strange Ranch, Don listened. Jason had participated in ropes courses throughout high school and college and saw them as a popular trend that was sure to grow. The courses are designed as corporate team-building venues to demonstrate life's lessons in a nurturing environment that fosters problem-solving skills. Jason asked to meet with us, and we were both impressed that he had explored the cost of building and maintaining the course, had gotten reports from other courses, and compiled facts and figures on growth in the industry—everything we needed to know to consider his proposal.

At first we scrutinized Jason's idea closely because the ranch was already generating a strong return for the company. But, true to form, Jason persevered, and we agreed to build the course as yet another ranch facility. Jason located a firm that he thought would do the best job in constructing the course. We contracted with Alpine Towers, Inc, a renowned ropes-course consulting firm, to design the twenty-five-acre course, located near Kendall Creek.

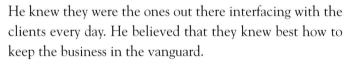

The course includes a fifty-foot-high climbing structure, two giant swings, two high-ropes partner climbs, a low-ropes course, a fifty-foot-high climbing pole, and a ninety-foot-long rope bridge that spans Zink Creek. Together, the structures allow people to explore climbing as a metaphor for accomplishing goals and achieving personal growth. The Don Strange Adventure Challenge Course is the only handicapped-accessible course in Texas and regularly hosts physically challenged client groups. Programs have been custom-designed for many large corporations, including McDonald's and Marriott International.

In 1997, after the Adventure Challenge Course had proven to be a popular attraction, Don added the Kendall Creek facility to the ranch, thinking that it might be beneficial to have a place nearby where groups participating in the challenge course could schedule meals and meetings. Due to the immense popularity of the ranch and the fact that it was heavily booked, he had already been talking about the need for another facility to expand the ranch's event capacity. Now two events can be scheduled

simultaneously at the Don Strange Ranch, doubling the income potential of the original investment.

The facility at Kendall Creek, known now as Kendall Creek Ranch, was designed as a lodge-style venue and has a completely different feel from that of the original party barn. The 8,000-square-foot pavilion, which seats up to 400 for a seated dinner and up to 1,000 for a picnic-style event, is nestled among oak, mesquite, and pecan trees. It has a large indoor-outdoor fireplace, a rock patio, and a kitchen. The giant doors surrounding the pavilion can be closed to provide an intimate ambiance or protection from the vagaries of weather.

In 2008 the Food Network filmed a segment of its series *The Secret Life of . . . Caterers* at the Don Strange Ranch. The host, George Duran, wanted to film a real-life party. Don scanned the event schedule book and determined that a large fund-raiser for the Rotary Club's scholarship fund would be an ideal event. Don was tremendous in the episode, portraying himself as he always was—the ultimate host. The video can be viewed on the Don Strange of Texas website (www.donstrange.com).

Once again, Don's uncanny optimism paid off when he bought the ranch and transformed it into a special place. He liked to say that the Don Strange Ranch is "where a new friend, a good rain, and a new baby calf are always welcome."

Today the Don Strange Ranch accounts for about 40 percent of the company's revenue.

Maggie's Guacamole

★

3 large ripe avocados, peeled and seeded, seeds reserved* (see "Peeling and Seeding Avocados" on page 157)

1 white onion, chopped fine

1 ripe tomato, seeded and chopped

1 medium garlic clove, minced

3 serrano chiles, seeds and veins removed, minced

1 tablespoon minced cilantro leaves and tender top stems

Freshly squeezed Key lime juice to taste

Kosher salt to taste

You can bet there's one dish that will be present at 99 percent of Don Strange of Texas parties—guacamole. It's used as one of the toppings on Don's famous gorditas, which have been a favorite at parties since the early days of the company. You can vary the heat level in this recipe by using fewer or more serrano chiles. Don always preferred the serrano chile in guacamole because of its clean, biting heat and pleasantly high acidity. Green and red serranos can be used interchangeably, but the red will be somewhat sweeter. They also add nice color when used as a garnish.

Makes about 4 cups

Mash the avocados in a medium bowl. Add the onion, tomato, garlic, chiles, and cilantro. Stir to blend well. Season with lime juice and salt. If the guacamole tastes a bit flat and boring, try adding a bit more salt. (Salt is a natural flavor enhancer and often is just what is needed to crank up the volume on taste!) Refrigerate, covered, until ready to serve.

*BEFORE REFRIGERATING THE GUACAMOLE, push the avocado seeds into the surface of the dip, then cover with plastic wrap. The seeds will retard the darkening of the guacamole for about 3 hours.

Don Strange Ranch Coleslaw

★

1 (20-ounce) can Dole pineapple chunks, well drained

1 (16-ounce) bag prepared coleslaw mix with carrots

1¼ cups real mayonnaise, whisked with 2 tablespoons sugar

Not overly fond of traditional coleslaw recipes, which he found to be bland and somewhat boring, Don created this delightfully unique slaw made with chunks of pineapple. It goes with just about everything and makes a great addition to an al fresco dinner.

Serves 6 to 8

Combine all ingredients in a medium bowl, stirring to coat pineapple and slaw with the mayonnaise. Chill, covered, for at least 1 hour before serving.

HERE'S HOW YOU DO IT

Peeling and Seeding Avocados: There's a simple, easy way to peel thick-skinned avocados and remove the large seed, which is firmly embedded in the flesh. First be sure to purchase ripe avocados. Always buy the dark, bumpy-skinned Haas avocados, as their flavor and texture are superior. The best way to tell if an avocado is ripe is by feel. Hold the avocado in your hand and give it a gentle squeeze. An unripe one will be very hard, like a stone. The flesh of a perfect avocado will yield somewhat under the pressure of your gentle squeeze. It should actually be about the same consistency as the flesh of your palm. Avoid those that feel loose in their skin, as they are overripe.

To peel the avocado, grip it gently on one side with your hand. With a large, sharp knife, cut the avocado as if you were cutting it in half, *lengthwise*, going all the way around the fruit and slicing through to the seed. Rotate the halves and open them to expose the seed. Tap the seed with the blade of your knife, using enough force to wedge the knife into the seed. Take care not to miss the seed and cut your hand! Now simply twist the knife to remove the seed. Place the blunt edge of the knife in your hand and use your thumb and forefinger to push the seed off the blade of the knife.

Now you can scoop out the pulp from both halves using a spoon. Discard the tough skins. If you wish to dice the avocado, do so before removing the pulp from the skin. Using a small dinner knife, make gentle crosshatch cuts in the pulp, being sure that you don't cut through the skin. Then use a spoon to scoop out the diced flesh, scooping against the skin.

To make avocado slices for a sandwich or salad, use a sharp paring knife to cut slices all the way through the skin of each half. Simply use your fingers to peel away the slices from their skin.

Mixed Green Salad with Nopalitos

★

Salads are an added treat to a meal. The company typically sets up a salad station where party guests can custom-make their salads. This salad, with its delicious blue cheese dressing, has always been a party favorite.

Serves 4 to 6

Prepare the Blue Cheese Dressing first. Combine mayonnaise, sour cream, 2 tablespoons of the blue cheese, vinegar, garlic, Worcestershire sauce, and Tabasco sauce in work bowl of food processor fitted with steel blade. Process until smooth. Turn out into a bowl.

    Crumble the remaining 4 ounces of blue cheese into the dressing and stir to blend well. Cover tightly and refrigerate for at least 4 hours to allow the flavors to meld together before using.

    To serve, combine the salad greens in a large bowl, tossing to mix well. Place a portion of the greens on each serving plate. Drizzle a portion of the dressing over the greens (see "Dressing Green Salads" on page 122); garnish with tomatoes, cucumber slices, onion slivers, pecans, and nopalitos as desired.

8 cups mixed salad greens such as romaine, Bibb, radicchio, frisée, and arugula

Tomato wedges or cherry tomatoes

Thinly sliced cucumbers

Slivered red onions

Whole toasted pecans

Thornless small nopalitos

Blue Cheese Dressing

1 cup real mayonnaise

1 cup sour cream

4 ounces plus 2 tablespoons blue cheese, preferably a blue goat cheese

2 teaspoons apple cider vinegar

1 garlic clove, minced

½ teaspoon Worcestershire sauce

Dash of Tabasco sauce

Chilled Pasta Salad

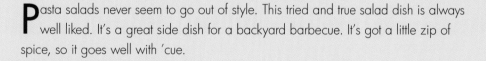

Pasta salads never seem to go out of style. This tried and true salad dish is always well liked. It's a great side dish for a backyard barbecue. It's got a little zip of spice, so it goes well with 'cue.

Serves 6 to 8

Place the drained pasta in a large bowl and toss with the tomatoes and chiles, olives, green onions, and celery; set aside. In a separate bowl whisk together the mayonnaise and cumin; add salt and pepper. Fold the mayonnaise mixture into the pasta mixture, blending well. Refrigerate, covered, and serve chilled.

1 (16-ounce) box penne rigate pasta, cooked al dente and drained

1 (10-ounce) can Ro-tel tomatoes with diced green chiles, well drained

⅔ cup sliced green pimento-stuffed olives

6 green onions and tops, sliced thin

½ cup chopped celery

⅔ cup mayonnaise

1 teaspoon ground cumin

Kosher salt and black pepper to taste

Tacos al Carbón with Avocado Pico de Gallo

★

3 pounds boneless beef rib-eye roast,
    trimmed of fat

Olive oil

Kosher salt and freshly ground black
    pepper to taste

14 flour tortillas, warmed

Avocado Pico de Gallo (see recipe below)

Sour cream (optional)

Avocado Pico de Gallo

1 pint grape tomatoes, quartered

1 medium avocado, peeled, seeded,
    and cut into small dice (see "Peeling
    and Seeding Avocados" on page 157)

⅔ cup chopped cilantro

6 green onions and tops, sliced thin

6 pequín chiles, minced, including seeds

Juice of 1 lime

Kosher salt to taste

The Spanish term *al carbón* refers to something grilled. The concept of tacos *al carbón* is an old one in Tex-Mex cuisine and involves grilling various cuts of beef that are then cut into small strips. The beef strips are piled onto warm flour tortillas and topped with various toppings. Generally the dish is made from strips of beef brisket or skirt steak, but Don wanted a cut that would be tender and highly flavorful, so he chose rib eye for his version of tacos al carbon. The company serves them at parties with freshly made flour tortillas and a pico de gallo made with avocados.

Serves 6 to 8

Make the Avocado Pico de Gallo. Combine all ingredients in a bowl and toss to blend well. Refrigerate in a tightly covered container until ready to serve. If making it ahead of time, don't add the salt until ready to serve.

Heat a gas grill to medium heat, or build a hardwood charcoal fire in a barbecue pit and allow it to burn down until the coals are glowing red and covered by a layer of white ash, about 20 to 30 minutes. Cut the meat into ½-inch-thick steaks. Glaze both sides of each cut with olive oil and season with salt and pepper.

Grill the meat until it is medium done, about 136 degrees, turning once, about 4 minutes per side. Remove from heat and slice into thin strips, trimming off any fat. Pile a portion of the meat in the center of each warm tortilla and top with a portion of the Avocado Pico de Gallo and sour cream. Fold the tortillas in half and stand them on a serving platter. Serve at once.

Carne Guisada

⭐

Carne guisada is a classic Tex-Mex dish. It's a comfort food that can be prepared using leftover scraps of meat or less expensive cuts. Don first discovered the dish when he was back in the company's commissary kitchen one day. The staff had prepared a staff lunch using some leftover brisket and scraps of other meats. Don tasted the concoction and loved it, proclaiming that it would no longer be simply a kitchen staff lunch! He began to serve the dish at parties, where it was spooned onto warm Pan de Campo and handed to the guests. It was an instant hit and is still served often at Don Strange of Texas parties. As an entrée, it can be served over cooked white rice instead of Pan de Campo.

Serves 8 to 10

Heat ½ cup of the canola oil in a heavy-bottomed Dutch oven over medium-high heat. When the surface of the oil is shimmering with heat, add the beef cubes and cook, stirring often, until they are browned and seared on all sides, about 8 minutes. Lower heat to medium and add the onion, bell pepper, tomato, bay leaves, chili powder, cumin, granulated garlic, and pepper. Cook, stirring often, until vegetables are wilted, about 10 minutes. Stir in the beef stock; scrape bottom of pan to remove browned bits of meat and vegetable glaze. Season with salt. Cover and reduce heat to a simmer. Cook, stirring occasionally, until the meat is very, very tender, about 1 hour.

While the stew is cooking, heat the remaining ⅔ cup of canola oil in a separate heavy-bottomed 10-inch skillet, preferably cast-iron, over medium heat. When the oil is hot, stir in the flour all at once. Cook, whisking constantly, until a hazelnut-colored roux forms, about 15 minutes. Remove from heat and continue to whisk for about 4 minutes. Turn the roux out into a metal bowl (take care not to let the hot roux come in contact with your skin). Continue to whisk the roux occasionally as it cools. (If it separates, reheat it and whisk; it will come back together.) Set aside.

When the beef cubes are very tender, bring the stew to a full, rolling boil. Add the roux by spoonfuls until all has been added. Continue to cook until the stew has thickened to form a thick, rich gravy.

Serve hot, piled in the center of warm Pan de Campo and folded over like a taco.

½ cup plus ⅔ cup canola oil

3 pounds beef chuck roast, trimmed of fat and tendons, cut into 1-inch cubes

1 large yellow onion, cut into 1-inch dice

1 large green bell pepper, cut into 1-inch dice

1 large ripe tomato, peeled and chopped

2 fresh bay leaves, minced

1 tablespoon chili powder

1 tablespoon ground cumin

2 tablespoons granulated garlic

1 tablespoon freshly ground black pepper

1 quart beef stock

Kosher salt to taste

⅔ cup all-purpose flour

Pan de Campo (see page 169)

Shrimp and Crab Corn Cakes with Two Sauces

★

These delicious cakes were one of Don's last major creations. Regular crab cakes were being served everywhere, so he wanted a dish that would take the concept of the crab cake one level higher—one with his personal signature. The dish has been hungrily embraced by customers and is served with a choice of two sauces, Lime Mayonnaise or Tanqueray Mayonnaise.

Makes 16 small (3½-inch) cakes

Lime Mayonnaise

1 cup H-E-B Mayonesa (lime mayonnaise)

2 tablespoons freshly squeezed lime juice

1 teaspoon minced chipotle chile in adobo sauce

¼ teaspoon salt

1 tablespoon minced cilantro

Tanqueray Mayonnaise

1½ cups real mayonnaise

¼ cup sour cream

½ teaspoon salt

½ teaspoon cayenne pepper

⅓ cup Tanqueray gin

1 tablespoon minced parsley

1 cup all-purpose flour

1 cup masa harina

1½ cups unseasoned bread crumbs

2 teaspoons baking powder

1 tablespoon sugar

1½ teaspoons kosher salt

½ teaspoon freshly ground black pepper

1 cup milk

1 tablespoon canola oil

2 eggs

1¼ cups frozen whole-kernel corn, thawed and well drained

1 cup tiny diced roasted red bell pepper

1 cup tiny diced green bell pepper

2 jalapeño chiles, seeds and veins removed, minced

1 tablespoon minced fresh cilantro

3 tablespoons minced shallots

1 pound lump crabmeat

1 pound tiny (70–90 count) peeled and deveined shrimp, chopped

1 (6-ounce) bag panko (Japanese-style) bread crumbs

Canola oil for sautéing

Lime Mayonnaise (at left)

Tanqueray Mayonnaise (at left)

Make the Lime Mayonnaise by combining all ingredients in work bowl of food processor fitted with steel blade. Process until smooth. To make the Tanqueray Mayonnaise, combine all ingredients in a medium bowl and whisk to blend well. Refrigerate the mayonnaises until ready to use.

Line a large baking sheet with parchment paper. Place a wire cooling rack on a second baking sheet. Set both aside.

In a large bowl, toss together the flour, masa harina, bread crumbs, baking powder, sugar, salt, and pepper; set aside. In a separate bowl whisk together the milk, canola oil, and eggs, blending well. Fold the milk mixture into the dry mixture, mixing thoroughly. Stir in the corn, bell peppers, jalapeños, cilantro, and shallots, blending well. Gently stir in the crabmeat and shrimp, taking care not to break up the lumps of crabmeat.

Place the panko bread crumbs in a shallow bowl or baking dish. Tightly pat ½ cup of the seafood mixture into cakes about 3½ inches in diameter. Dredge each cake in the panko crumbs, patting the crumbs firmly onto the cakes. Place the cakes on the prepared parchment-lined baking sheet.

Heat a thin glaze of canola oil in a heavy 12-inch skillet over medium heat. Place as many cakes as will fit in a single layer, not touching, in the hot oil. Sauté for 5 minutes on each side, turning once, or until golden brown. Remove cakes to the wire rack on the second baking sheet; keep warm in a low oven while sautéing the remaining cakes. Serve hot with the two mayonnaises.

Fried Fresh Corn

4 large ears of corn, shucked

4 tablespoons (½ stick) butter

Lawry's Seasoning Salt

Freshly ground black pepper

Almost nothing tastes better than fresh corn scraped right off the cob at its juicy best and cooked in butter. The company has served it at events for years, and no one ever tires of it.

Serves 4 to 6

Using a sharp knife, cut the corn kernels off the cobs into a bowl. Then scrape the cobs a second time to get the corn "milk." Stir to blend the corn and its juice together. Melt the butter in a heavy-bottomed skillet over medium heat. When butter is sizzling, add the corn. Season to taste with seasoned salt and pepper. Cook, stirring often, until corn is lightly browned, about 10 minutes. Serve hot.

Corn Relish

2 cups frozen whole-kernel corn, thawed and well drained

⅓ cup diced roasted red bell pepper

2 tablespoons well drained canned diced green chiles

2 tablespoons vinaigrette-style Italian salad dressing

2 tablespoons finely chopped green onions

¼ teaspoon granulated garlic

Kosher salt and freshly ground black pepper to taste

This relish is one of our most dependable side dishes. It's great with barbecue and burgers or any picnic or al fresco setting. It's also a great "make-ahead" dish, as the flavor actually improves after a day in the refrigerator.

Makes about 2½ cups

Combine all ingredients except salt and pepper in a medium bowl and stir to blend well. Season with salt and pepper. Cover and refrigerate until ready to serve.

Don Strange Cheese Grits

2 cups whole milk

2 cups half-and-half

¼ pound (1 stick) unsalted butter, cut into small dice

1 cup quick-cooking grits

Kosher salt to taste

¼ cup whipping cream

1 cup (4 ounces) shredded Monterey Jack cheese*

1 cup (4 ounces) grated Parmesan cheese*

This grits dish, one of the company's most versatile, is served with steaks and fish dishes as well as for brunch. Grits are always a real Texas treat to party guests.

Serves 6

Combine the milk, half-and-half, and butter in a heavy-bottomed 3-quart saucepan over medium heat. Bring to a boil, then stir in the grits. Cook, stirring, until grits begin to thicken, about 5 minutes. Add salt and whipping cream. Cook, stirring, just until the cream is heated and the grits are still soft and creamy. Remove from heat and add the cheeses, stirring until all the cheese is melted. Serve hot.

*TO VARY THIS RECIPE, substitute 2 cups shredded Cheddar cheese (for Cheddar Grits) *or* 2 cups Gorgonzola cheese (Blue Cheese Grits) for the Monterey Jack and Parmesan cheeses.

Pan de Campo

★

Pan de Campo is a rustic camp bread that was prepared by chuck-wagon cooks in Dutch ovens over open fires. Don adapted the bread for cooking on a flat grill, or *comal*, set on a barbecue pit over glowing coals. When done, the breads are topped with slices cut from a spit-smoked side of beef and doused with barbecue sauce. Guests fold the bread over the beef and chow down! The company also serves Pan de Campo at indoor events, where they are cooked on the *comal* over small propane burners in front of the guests and topped with Carne Guisada. Pan de Campo with sliced beef was a highlight of the feature on the Don Strange Ranch that appeared on a segment of the Food Network's *The Secret Life of…Caterers,* taped in 2008. Pan de Campo is also delicious slathered with butter and some good preserves or blackstrap molasses for a real cowboy breakfast.

1½ tablespoons instant-rise yeast

1 cup warm water (105–115 degrees)

2 tablespoons sugar, divided

5¼ cups all-purpose flour plus additional as needed

1 tablespoon kosher salt

¾ teaspoon baking soda

¾ teaspoon baking powder

1½ cups buttermilk

⅔ cup canola oil

Makes 36 breads

Stir the yeast into the warm water in a 2-cup Pyrex measuring cup. Gently whisk in 1 tablespoon of the sugar. Set aside until the yeast has dissolved and the mixture is foamy.

Combine the flour, salt, baking soda, baking powder, and the remaining tablespoon of sugar in work bowl of food processor fitted with steel blade. Pulse 3 or 4 times to blend dry ingredients well. Add the yeast mixture, buttermilk, and canola oil. Process until the dough forms a ball. If the dough is sticky, add additional flour, 1 tablespoon at a time, as needed to form a soft, smooth dough. Process to blend after each addition. Turn dough out onto work surface and knead four or five times. Place the dough in a large, lightly oiled bowl and turn to coat all surfaces. Cover the bowl tightly with plastic wrap and set aside in a warm, draft-free spot to rise until doubled in bulk, about 1 hour.

Punch the dough down until no air remains. Divide the dough into 36 portions; shape each portion into a ball about the size of a golf ball. Using a rolling pin, roll each ball into a 6-inch disk. Refrigerate while heating the grill.

Heat a flat griddle on the stovetop or on a char-grill. When the grill is medium-hot, place as many of the dough rounds as will fit on the grill in a single layer, not touching. Cook the breads until lightly browned on both sides or small bubbles appear on the top surface of the dough, about 1½ minutes per side, turning once with a metal spatula. Serve hot.

Longtime company employee, Dan Schmidt.

Café Mystique

1⅓ cups crushed ice

1⅓ cups cold espresso, or strong black coffee

1⅓ cups Kahlúa liqueur

½ cup Carnation powdered malt mix

Sweetened whipped cream, beaten to stiff peaks (optional)

Café Mystique is a chilled coffee drink that goes back to the early days of the company, and it's still a party favorite today. It's delicious and refreshing, with a low alcohol content, so it's perfect for outdoor events. James Beard loved the drink so much that he asked Don for the recipe. Don called this drink "Café Mystique" for a reason. There were all sorts of variations, depending on what the crew had brought with them or what the client had in the liquor cabinet. A simple variation can be made with just vanilla ice cream, black coffee, and coffee-flavored liqueur.

Makes four 8-ounce drinks

Combine the crushed ice, espresso, Kahlúa, and malt mix in blender. Process until smooth and well blended. Serve over ice in tall glasses. Top each drink with a generous dollop of the whipped cream.

CHAPTER NINE

The Waring General Store

By 1986 I was beginning to feel somewhat confident that we were going to survive financially after the oil bust and the purchase of the ranch. But I should've known that after four years of no major wild hairs, Don would be restless and looking for the next major challenge. However, when he came home and told me that he had bought the general store in Waring, Texas, as well as the piece of property across the street from it, I really lost it! Don kept telling me that the store was such a bargain he felt he couldn't let the opportunity pass. "I bought the whole place for $15,000, honey. The place has history. It was the Waring Post Office, and it was built in the 1920s. And the lot across the street I got for $1,000. It'll be great for staff parking," he reasoned. But we didn't have $16,000. We had sons in college!

Jason recalls his dad's admission that purchasing the store had caused a major sore spot in our marriage. So the Waring General Store sort of languished on the back burner for a while, although once again Don miraculously conjured up a way to pay for it! He eased into cleaning up the place to make it suitable as another venue for events. The main room had a dirt floor, and the entire space was

piled with junk. Most recently it had been a Case farm implements store. A room at the front of the building had served as the Waring Post Office. The other space in the front was the Waring General Store and Gas Station. It definitely cried out for a creative hand.

Driving into Waring, located on the banks of the Guadalupe River forty minutes north of San Antonio off I-10, is like traveling back to another era. It's a sleepy little town, like nearby Welfare, with a few simple clapboard buildings and the Waring General Store. The town was founded in 1887 as Waringford, then shortened to Waring in 1901. At one point in its history Waring boasted two general stores, a corn and grist mill, a gin, a stone quarry, a lumberyard, a hotel, and other establishments.

Don left the front of the building pretty much the way it was—with the two eight-foot-tall red Texaco Fire Chief gas pumps, their cylindrical glass gas tanks framing the entry, alongside two ancient Mobilgas pumps with the old winged Pegasus logo.

An interesting bit of history regarding the store has

to do with the weathered "Waring" that's painted on the tin roof in huge letters. Don was told that during World War I, Waring was on the final approach path for military planes flying into the old Kelly Field in San Antonio, later renamed Kelly Air Force Base, which became the oldest continuously operating flying base in the history of the U.S. Air Force. Initially the base was devoted to flight training and served as a reception and testing center for recruits. Pilot trainees would use the store's roof as a navigational guidepost—when they saw "Waring" on that rooftop, they knew they were on the right path to home base.

Don intended for the store to be another venue for parties, albeit smaller ones. He put in a tile floor in the large room and added a small stage for entertainment, turning it into a rustic dining and dance hall. The decor is pure "country nostalgia," including many old advertising signs

made of metal and vitreous enamel that Don scouted up from around the country as well as a cozy antique wood-burning stove. He added a large rock courtyard off the dining room and turned the spacious back property into a picnic-style eating spot.

But most of our marketing focus was directed toward the ranch, so the store was never a great revenue source as a party venue. Then Jason, remembering his dad's advice about the best way to make money was to use what you had rather than buying something new, came up with an idea for the space. In his travels as a young man, he had been to an old rural general store somewhere that featured a "steak night" once a week. They offered a simple menu—a grilled steak, a couple of side dishes, a salad, and dessert—for a set price. He liked the idea and saw firsthand that it could generate not only good revenue but traffic. So he proposed trying the idea at the Waring General Store.

Anxious to see the place produce a steady income and to finally soothe my feathers, Don agreed. On Wednesday, March 19, 1998, the first Steak Nite was held at the Waring General Store. It was a smashing success, drawing local folks as well as those from nearby Boerne, Comfort, and more distant towns. Eventually tour buses from

San Antonio would come, bringing entire busloads of people from the city to enjoy a nice dinner in the country. Wednesdays began to breathe new life into Waring. The Rust family, from whom Don bought the store, has been most appreciative of the attention that the Waring General Store has brought to the town. During any one event at the store, the town's population might quadruple!

Jason kept the menu simple and the price reasonable. Staff members from the commissary kitchen grill gorditas and quesadillas at a display cooking station, serving them hot off the grill, along with Don's famous chile con queso dip before dinner. There's a huge bowl of green salad, with a choice of dressings, as well as mashed potatoes to go with the New York strip steaks, which are grilled to order in the courtyard. Grilled chicken breast is also available. There are always three or four desserts, made in the commissary kitchen from my mother's delicious recipes, which have been favorites at company events for years.

Don added a second stage where bands provide entertainment at the edge of the picnic area in the back. Often our son Brian and his sons, Austin and Jake, perform as Brian Strange and the Strange Brothers. There's a large grassy area where kids can romp and play or throw footballs around. Steak Nite has become a great way for families to get out for an evening, enjoy a steak dinner with entertainment, and turn the kids loose to play. Folks get groups of

their friends together and travel to Waring for a night out. Walking in on Steak Nite in full swing, you get the impression that you've been invited to a family reunion! There's plenty of good iced tea and coffee. Sodas, bottled water, and wine and beer are also available for purchase.

As Jason had imagined, the traffic that Steak Nite brought to the Waring General Store also brought increased public awareness of the store as a venue for private functions. The inside dining hall can accommodate roughly 200 guests. The outside dining area seats approximately 400. The facility is available for private parties and receptions every day of the week—except, of course, Wednesday.

In the fourteen years since Steak Nite originated,

over 120,000 Texas steaks have been served. And since its opening night, Steak Nite has been cancelled only four times—the store was either flooded or frozen!

In the spring of 2010, Brian, Jason, and I fulfilled the dream that Don and I had talked about for so long—the possibility of having some sort of retail store where people could buy the products that are available through our online store, Don Strange Market Place, Inc. We both felt that the two "sites" would be of mutual benefit. We opened the Don Strange Market Place in the front of the Waring General Store, taking in the spaces that formerly housed the Waring Post Office and the original general store. Now folks passing through the old town or coming for Steak Nite can purchase the condiments and sauces that have become the company's most requested signature flavors over the years, as well as packages of Grilled White Wings, Christmas Bacon, Double-Barrel Brownies, Texas Two-Bite Pecan Tarts, Kendall Creek Honey Bars, and the Texas Grill Pardner. Once again, Don was right. I feel certain that somewhere in the cubbyholes of his mind he knew that his $15,000 investment would be the one that would take the company into exciting new territory as a retail marketplace.

Grilled Steaks with Steak Nite Marinade

★

4 New York strip or rib-eye steaks, 10 to
    12 ounces each

Kosher salt and freshly ground black
    pepper to taste

Steak Nite Marinade

3 cups Worcestershire sauce

¼ cup Yucatan Sunshine Habañero Hot
    Sauce (available at H-E-B)

Juice of 4 limes

1 cup extra-virgin olive oil

½ cup golden rum

6 bacon slices, cooked crisp and crumbled

Don purchased the Waring General Store mainly for use as another venue for parties. However, once Jason's idea for Steak Nite was implemented, the delicious steak dinners brought crowds of families with kids, groups of friends, and even busloads of folks from San Antonio. Be sure to make the marinade at least 4 hours in advance to allow the flavors time to meld together.

Serves 4

Make the Steak Nite Steak Marinade. Combine all ingredients in a medium bowl and whisk until well blended.

    Build a hardwood charcoal fire in a barbecue pit and allow it to burn down until the coals are glowing red and covered by a layer of white ash, about 20 to 30 minutes. Place the steaks in a large baking dish and pour enough of the marinade over them to barely cover. (Any unused marinade can be refrigerated for up to a week.) Marinate steaks for 10 minutes, turning once. Remove from the marinade and discard marinade. Season steaks with salt and pepper and grill to desired degree of doneness.

Steaks on the grill at the Waring General Store seared with the official brand of the Don Strange Ranch, reflecting the letters *d* and *f* for Don and Frances.

Mother's Basic Custard

★

2 cups milk

3 eggs

½ cup sugar

4 tablespoons all-purpose flour

1 teaspoon vanilla extract

Mother uses this custard in many of her marvelous desserts. It's a good one, and you can vary it with any flavor you wish by adding nuts, berries, coconut—the possibilities for flavored custard are limited only by your own creativity!

Makes about 2½ cups

Heat the milk in a heavy-bottomed 2-quart saucepan over medium heat until hot. In bowl of electric stand mixer, beat the eggs, sugar, and flour until light and fluffy, about 5 minutes. Stirring, gradually add the egg mixture to the hot milk and continue to stir until the custard is thickened. Remove from heat immediately. Allow to cool; add vanilla extract.

Banana Pudding

★

1 recipe Mother's Basic Custard

1 box vanilla wafers

4 to 6 bananas, peeled and sliced

Banana pudding has got to be one of the most universally popular desserts on the planet. My mother made this pudding when I was a child, and it's a crowd favorite at Steak Nite.

Serves 8 to 10

Prepare Mother's Basic Custard according to recipe. Layer vanilla wafers in the bottom of a 9-by-13-inch baking dish; reserve a few wafers for the topping. Cover the wafers with sliced bananas and pour the custard over the bananas. Crush the reserved wafers and scatter over the top of the pudding. Refrigerate until ready to serve.

Chocolate Ice Box Pie

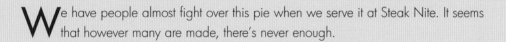

We have people almost fight over this pie when we serve it at Steak Nite. It seems that however many are made, there's never enough.

Makes one 9-inch pie

Prepare Mother's Basic Custard according to recipe instructions. When the custard has thickened, stir in the chocolate chips. Continue to stir until the chocolate has melted and mixture is smooth. Turn the chocolate filling out into the prepared pie shell and refrigerate until well chilled.

When ready to serve, combine the cream, sugar, and vanilla and beat until stiff and fluffy. Spread over the top of the pie and slice into wedges to serve.

1 single pie shell, baked (see Pie Pastry recipe on page 185)

1 recipe Mother's Basic Custard (see page 180)

6 ounces semisweet chocolate chips

1 cup heavy cream

⅓ cup powdered sugar

1 teaspoon vanilla extract

Coconut Cream Pie

Lovers of coconut cream pie swear that Mother's version is the best they've ever had. We know for sure that there's never a scrap of it left when it's served at Steak Nite!

Makes one 9-inch pie

Prepare Mother's Basic Custard according to recipe. When the custard is thickened, stir in the coconut, blending well. Turn custard mixture out into pie crust and refrigerate until firm.

When ready to serve, combine the cream, powdered sugar, and vanilla and beat until stiff peaks form. Spread over the top of the pie and slice into wedges to serve.

1 single pie shell, baked and cooled (see Pie Pastry recipe on page 185)

1 recipe Mother's Basic Custard (see page 180)

1½ cups sweetened flaked coconut

1 cup heavy cream

⅓ cup powdered sugar

1 teaspoon vanilla extract

Boston Cream Pie

★

1 recipe Mother's Basic Cake using yellow cake mix (see page 186)

1 recipe Mother's Basic Custard (see page 180)

1 recipe Chocolate Fudge Icing (see page 187)

This delicious version of the classic Boston Cream Pie has been a favorite at Steak Nite since its inception. It's also a favorite with our family. In fact, it's Matt's favorite dessert. He requested this cake for his groom's cake, and Mother made twenty-three of them for the wedding reception!

Makes one 9-inch dessert

Prepare the yellow cake and bake according to package instructions in two 9-inch cake pans. Cool on wire racks.

Prepare Mother's Basic Custard according to recipe and chill until firm. Prepare the Chocolate Fudge Icing according to recipe and cool slightly.

To assemble, place one of the cake layers on a serving plate. Top with the custard. Place the second layer over the custard. Spread the top of the second layer with the icing, allowing it to drizzle down the side of the cake slightly. Refrigerate until ready to slice into wedges and serve.

Lemon Meringue Pie

★

1 single pie shell, baked (see Pie Pastry recipe on page 185)

2½ cups water

½ cup cornstarch

1½ cups sugar

4 egg yolks, beaten

1 teaspoon minced lemon zest

3 tablespoons butter

½ cup freshly squeezed lemon juice

Meringue

4 to 6 egg whites (4 for average height; 6 for a real towering meringue)

½ to ¾ teaspoon cream of tartar*

½ cup sugar

½ teaspoon vanilla extract

A pie topped with a towering toasted meringue is just too inviting to resist. Mother has always been a master of the meringue. She says that the secret of a good meringue is to avoid overbeating it and to spread it all the way onto the pie crust (which holds it in place).

Makes one 9-inch pie

Make the meringue (see "Making a Successful Meringue" on page 184). Combine the egg whites and cream of tartar in bowl of electric mixer and beat at high speed just until foamy. Gradually add sugar, 1 tablespoon at a time, beating until stiff peaks form and sugar dissolves, about 2 to 4 minutes. Add vanilla, beating well. Set aside.

Preheat oven to 375 degrees. Prepare the pie filling. Heat water, cornstarch, and sugar in a heavy-bottomed 4-quart saucepan over medium heat. Bring to a full boil to thicken. Lower heat to medium-low and whisk in the egg yolks. Cook just to thicken, then add the lemon zest, butter, and lemon juice, whisking to blend well. Cook until the mixture becomes thick again. Remove from heat and fold in 1 heaping tablespoon of the prepared meringue gently but thoroughly. Turn the mixture out into prepared pie shell and spread the remaining meringue over the top, spreading it to the outside edge of the pastry.

Bake 10 to 15 minutes in preheated oven to brown the meringue. Allow the filling to cool before slicing.

*CREAM OF TARTAR increases the stability of egg whites.

HERE'S HOW YOU DO IT

Making a Successful Meringue: Meringues, for many home cooks, are a real "iffy" proposition. But once you're armed with a few facts, then making successful meringues is simple.

Meringues are classified as either soft or hard. Soft meringues are glossy, smooth, and tender. They're used as pie toppings and cake frosting, and are folded into puddings and other desserts. They can also be folded into cake batters to lighten them.

Hard meringues are generally sweeter and are baked to form crisp dry meringue shells or cookies.

Here are some "insider tips for making a perfect soft meringue.

Avoid making meringue on a humid day, as the sugar will absorb moisture and the meringue will be unstable.

For meringue with the greatest volume, let the egg whites stand at room temperature for a full 30 minutes before beating.

Use the size of bowl called for in the recipe. Copper, stainless steel, or glass bowls work best for beating egg whites.

Be sure the electric mixer beaters and bowl are squeaky clean, with no traces of fat. Even the tiniest bit of oil or grease can keep the whites from beating to their full volume.

Begin to add the sugar gradually as soon as the whites are frothy.

After adding all the sugar, continue beating until stiff peaks form and the sugar is completely dissolved. Rub a little of the meringue between your fingers; it should feel completely smooth with no traces of sugar granules.

Do not overbeat the whites. If overbeaten, they will appear "rocky" and will eventually break down. Overbeaten whites must be discarded, and you will have to start over with fresh egg whites.

Spread the meringue quickly onto the hot filling. When soft meringue on a pie weeps, it's usually because the meringue was not spread on the pie while the filling was hot and therefore did not get thoroughly cooked on the bottom.

Anchor the meringue by spreading it to the edge of the pastry to seal completely and keep it from shrinking.

Bake the pie immediately after adding the meringue. After baking, allow the pie to cool away from drafts.

Always let a meringue pie cool completely before slicing. If sliced while even the least bit warm, the filling will most likely be runny. For this reason, it's best to make a meringue pie several hours in advance. Using a hot, wet knife to slice the pie will also make it easier to get a neat slice.

Pie Pastry

★

My mother developed this tried-and-true pastry recipe long before I remember. It is the pastry used for most of the pies baked in the commissary kitchen. The secret to making great pie pastry lies in not overworking the dough.

2 cups all-purpose flour

1 teaspoon kosher salt

1 teaspoon sugar

1 cup solid shortening

4 to 6 tablespoons ice-cold water

Makes two 9-inch pie shells or one double-crust pie

Place the flour, salt, and sugar in a large bowl; toss to blend well. Add the shortening. Using a pastry blender or two knives, cut the shortening into the flour until the mixture resembles coarse meal. Incorporate the water until the dough comes together into a loose mass. Turn out onto lightly floured work surface; using your hands, bring the dough together to form a smooth, cohesive pastry. Divide the dough in half and form each piece into a round disk. Wrap each disk in plastic wrap and refrigerate until ready to use.

To roll out the dough, flour the work surface lightly. (Too much flour makes a heavy, tough pastry.) Roll the dough out into a large circle about 1/16 to 1/8 inch thick. Roll the dough loosely around the rolling pin, then unroll it into a 9-inch pie pan. Lift the edges of the pastry and let it fall into the bottom and against the sides of the pan. Don't stretch the dough or it will shrink when you bake it. Gently pat into bottom and sides of pan. Cut off excess pastry, leaving a 1-inch overhang at the rim.

If making a single-crust pie, turn the overhanging pastry under and press lightly to seal. Flute edge as desired, or press with the tines of a fork. If making a pie with an unbaked filling, bake pie shell according to instructions below. If making a single-crust pie with a baked filling, bake as directed in the recipe.

If making a double-crust pie, add filling to bottom pastry, roll out top pastry, and unroll it over the filling. Cut off excess pastry, leaving about a 1-inch overhang. Fold both the top and bottom pastries under at the rim. Flute edge as desired, or press with the tines of a fork. Bake as directed in the recipe.

To bake the pie shell before filling, preheat oven to 375 degrees. Prick the bottom of the pastry all over with a fork, then line the bottom and sides with a double thickness of foil. Turn the foil over the edge of the pastry also. Weight the foil with uncooked rice or beans; bake for about 20 minutes in preheated oven. Remove foil and weights and bake an additional 10 minutes, or until pastry is golden brown. Cool before filling.

Di-Anna Arias, Don Strange of Texas Director of Sales and Marketing.

Buttermilk Pie

★

1 single pie shell, unbaked (see Pie Pastry recipe on page 185)

1 cup sugar

Dash of kosher salt

3 tablespoons all-purpose flour

3 eggs, lightly beaten

2 cups buttermilk

¼ pound (1 stick) butter, melted

2 teaspoons vanilla extract

1 teaspoon minced lemon zest

You don't have to like buttermilk to love a good buttermilk pie. It's a comfort-food dessert that's a universal favorite.

Makes one 9-inch pie

Preheat oven to 425 degrees. Toss together the sugar, salt, and flour, blending well. In bowl of electric mixer, combine the sugar mixture with the eggs and beat until blended and fluffy, about 5 minutes. Add the buttermilk, butter, vanilla, and lemon zest. Beat thoroughly.

Turn the mixture out into prepared pie shell. Bake for 5 minutes in preheated oven, then reduce oven temperature to 325 degrees and bake an additional 45 to 50 minutes, or until filling is firm when pie is jiggled slightly. Allow to cool. Refrigerate until chilled before slicing.

Mother's Basic Cake

★

1 box Duncan Hines cake, any flavor

1 small box instant vanilla pudding, or substitute any flavor to match cake mix

⅔ cup sour cream

3 eggs

1 cup water

¼ cup canola oil

When my mother, Mary Singleton, worked for the company, she created a number of recipes that the kitchen still uses today, including her delicious cakes. She developed this basic cake batter for many of the cakes that are served at Steak Nite.

Combine all ingredients in bowl of electric mixer and beat for 2 minutes. Proceed as directed in separate cake recipe (see the recipes for Boston Cream Pie, Italian Cream Cake, and Triple Chocolate Cake). Or spread batter in greased and floured cake pan(s) and bake according to directions on package, or until a wooden pick inserted in center of cake comes out clean.

Italian Cream Cake

Italian Cream Cake is another Steak Nite favorite, and for good reason. It's rich and delicious, with lots of great texture from the coconut and pecans.

Makes one 9-inch cake

Prepare batter of Mother's Basic Cake as directed in recipe. Add the coconut and pecans; beat just to blend. Turn mixture out into two 9-inch cake pans and bake according to package instructions. Cool on wire racks.

    To make the icing, combine the cream cheese and butter in bowl of electric stand mixer and beat until very light and fluffy, about 10 minutes. Add the vanilla extract, then gradually add the powdered sugar, scraping down sides of bowl after each addition; beat until icing is fluffy and well blended. Frost the cooled cake with the icing. Press additional coconut and pecans into the icing on the top and sides of the cake. Slice into wedges to serve.

1 recipe Mother's Basic Cake using French Vanilla cake mix and vanilla pudding (see page 186)

1 cup shredded coconut plus additional for decoration

1 cup finely chopped pecans plus additional for decoration

Cream Cheese Icing

1 (8-ounce) package cream cheese, softened

½ pound (2 sticks) unsalted butter, softened

1 teaspoon vanilla extract

1 pound powdered sugar

Triple Chocolate Cake

This cake is really devilishly chocolate—a favorite with chocoholics. Be sure to include the step of flouring the chocolate chips. It keeps them from sinking to the bottom of the batter and ensures that they melt evenly throughout the cake.

Makes one 9-inch cake

Grease and flour two 9-inch cake pans and set aside. Prepare batter of Mother's Basic Cake as directed in recipe. Toss chocolate chips with flour, then transfer to a wire strainer and shake off excess flour. Add the chocolate chips to the cake batter and beat just to blend. Turn batter out into prepared cake pans and bake according to package instructions. Cool completely on wire racks.

    To make the icing, combine butter, milk, and sugar in a heavy-bottomed 2-quart saucepan over medium-high heat. Bring to a boil, stirring often, and cook for 1 minute, stirring constantly. Remove from heat and whisk in the chocolate chips. Continue to whisk until chips are melted and icing is smooth. Allow to cool for 10 to 15 minutes before frosting cooled cake. Slice cake into wedges to serve.

1 recipe Mother's Basic Cake using Devil's Food cake mix and chocolate pudding (see page 186)

1 cup semisweet chocolate chips

¼ cup all-purpose flour

Chocolate Fudge Icing

4 tablespoons (½ stick) unsalted butter

¼ cup milk

1 cup sugar

1 cup semisweet chocolate chips

Carrot Cake

Many of our family members think that Mother's desserts are a great part of the success of Steak Nite. People jockey for position at the dessert station, and regulars even check out the desserts first to determine how much room they need to leave for their favorite desserts! This cake is a perennial favorite.

Makes one 9-inch cake

Preheat oven to 350 degrees. Grease and flour a 9-by-13-inch baking pan and set aside. Combine sugar, oil, eggs, and vanilla in bowl of electric mixer. Beat until well blended, about 5 minutes. In a separate bowl sift together all dry ingredients. Add to the egg mixture and beat just to blend. Do not overbeat. By hand, stir in the carrots, pineapple, and pecans and mix just until blended. Turn mixture out into prepared baking pan and bake for 35 minutes, or until a wooden pick inserted in center of cake comes out clean.

    Cool on wire rack and frost with Cream Cheese Icing. Cut into squares to serve.

2 cups sugar

1½ cups canola oil

4 eggs

1 teaspoon vanilla extract

2⅓ cups all-purpose flour

2 teaspoons ground cinnamon

½ teaspoon kosher salt

1 teaspoon baking soda

3 cups freshly grated carrots

1 (8¼-ounce) can crushed pineapple, undrained

1 cup chopped pecans

Cream Cheese Icing (see Italian Cream Cake recipe on page 187)

Fresh Apple Cake

This recipe is a fall favorite at Steak Nite when apples are fresh and ripe. Granny Smith apples have a full, rich flavor and firm texture, which makes them an ideal apple for cooking.

Serves 10 to 12

Preheat oven to 325 degrees. Butter and flour a 9-by-13-inch baking pan; set aside. In the bowl of an electric stand mixer combine the canola oil and sugar. Beat until fluffy and light lemon yellow in color, about 5 minutes. Add the eggs and beat to blend well. Combine the baking soda and flour and add to the batter. Beat just until ingredients are well incorporated. Add the pecans, vanilla, and apples; beat just to mix.

    Pour the batter into the prepared pan and bake in preheated oven for 45 minutes, or until a wooden pick inserted in the center of the cake comes out clean. Cool on wire rack.

    While the cake is cooling, make the glaze. Combine all ingredients in a heavy-bottomed 2-quart saucepan and bring to a boil, stirring. Cook just long enough to melt the sugar. Pour the hot glaze evenly over the cake. Allow glaze to cool before cutting. Cut into squares to serve.

1½ cups canola oil

2 cups sugar

3 eggs

1 teaspoon baking soda

3 cups all-purpose flour

1 cup chopped pecans

2 teaspoons vanilla extract

1¼ pounds medium Granny Smith apples, peeled, cored, and chopped (3 cups)

Glaze

¼ pound (1 stick) butter

1 cup firmly packed light brown sugar

¼ cup evaporated milk

Peanut Butter Blossoms

★

1¾ cups all-purpose flour

1 teaspoon baking soda

½ teaspoon kosher salt

½ cup sugar plus additional for coating

½ cup firmly packed light brown sugar

¼ pound (1 stick) butter

½ cup smooth peanut butter

1 egg, beaten

2 tablespoons vanilla extract

48 Hershey's Milk Chocolate Kisses

I think Mother was making these delightful cookies before the Reese's Peanut Butter Cup was a commercial success! They're my favorite cookies and are often served at parties for the perfect sweet nibble.

Makes 48 cookies

Preheat oven to 375 degrees. Combine all ingredients except the chocolate candies in bowl of electric mixer. Beat on low speed until a smooth dough forms. Form the dough into 48 balls using about 1 teaspoon of dough for each. Roll each ball in sugar to coat and place on ungreased cookie sheet about 1½ inches apart. Bake for 10 to 12 minutes. Remove from oven and press one of the Hershey's Kisses into the center of each cookie until the cookie begins to crack. Using a metal spatula, transfer the cookies to a wire rack and cool completely before serving.

Mother's Brownies

★

1 cup plus 1½ tablespoons unsweetened cocoa

¾ teaspoon baking soda

1 cup canola oil

⅔ cup boiling water

2½ cups sugar

4 eggs, beaten

1½ cups plus 2 tablespoons all-purpose flour

2 teaspoons vanilla extract

½ teaspoon kosher salt

If you like your brownies soft and cakelike, but ultimately chocolate-y, then you'll love this recipe, which Mother developed in the commissary kitchen years ago. It's become the "official" Don Strange of Texas brownie. They're served at party-planning conferences and other meetings, at parties, and often at Steak Nite, when guests have one or two before their steaks, heeding the advice "Life is short—eat dessert first!" To make them even more decadent, top them with Chocolate Fudge Icing (see page 187).

Makes 24 brownies

Preheat oven to 350 degrees. Grease and flour a 9-by-13-inch baking pan, tapping out all excess flour; set aside. Toss together the cocoa and baking soda in a large bowl, blending well. Whisk in ¼ cup of the canola oil. Add the boiling water and whisk until well blended and thick. Stir in the sugar, eggs, and remaining canola oil. Stir until smooth. Add the flour, vanilla, and salt, stirring to mix well.

Turn the batter out into prepared baking pan and bake until a wooden pick inserted in center comes out clean, 25 to 30 minutes. Cool on wire rack before slicing into 2-inch squares.

CHAPTER TEN

A Downtown Presence at the Buckhorn Saloon

For a number of years Don had known that the company needed a permanent site in downtown San Antonio for on-premise events. He felt that this location should be very close to the downtown hotels, the River Walk, the Alamodome, and other downtown convention venues so that he would be in a better position to draw business from conventions and corporate meetings. And he envisioned it as a fairly upscale setting where he could also cater weddings and wedding receptions when clients preferred an option to the rustic setting at the Don Strange Ranch. However, even Don, the eternal dreamer, knew that available downtown San Antonio real estate was a finite, precious commodity and that its price reflected its scarcity.

In 1999 one more dream came true for Don. The Buckhorn Saloon, originally established in 1881, was reopened on Houston Street and the owners approached Don about being the exclusive caterer for private events at the saloon. After negotiating an agreement that worked for both parties, Don began to decorate the 6,500-square-foot area upstairs, turning it into just the space he'd been dreaming about for a long time.

Left to right: Alexandra, Matt, Kelly, Frances, Molly, and Jason.

The Buckhorn Saloon itself has a very colorful history. When Albert Friedrich opened a saloon in 1881 on Dolorosa Street, it quickly became a popular watering hole in its downtown location. Friedrich soon learned that some of the dusty cowboys who came in fresh from the trail didn't have much money. So he proclaimed that he would trade deer antlers for a shot of whiskey or a beer. As his collection of horns began to grow, his father, Wenzel, began to make furniture from some of the horns. Friedrich extended the offer to include rattlesnake rattles, from which his wife, Emilie, fashioned signs and artwork. Over the years the collection grew to include thousands of mounts from over 520 species of animals from around the world, including a large gorilla that Albert named "The Guard" and positioned in the front window.

During 1898, Teddy Roosevelt frequented the Buckhorn, now located at Soledad and West Houston streets, and recruited members of his famous Roughriders at the bar. The saloon was also visited by Will Rogers and O. Henry. During World War I, many military recruits training in San Antonio patronized the Buckhorn, taking its story with them all over the world.

The Buckhorn Saloon closed with the advent of Prohibition, but reopened as a curio shop and café at another location on West Houston Street. After the move the Buckhorn also offered vaudeville entertainers. During World War II San Antonio again became the training center for many soldiers who visited the Buckhorn and further spread its reputation around the globe.

In 1956 the Lone Star Brewing Company acquired the famous Buckhorn Collection and opened the Lone Star Buckhorn Hall of Horns at its San Antonio brewery. In 1973 the Hall of Feathers and Hall of Fins were added. The collection includes many record-breaking mounts that are documented in the Boone and Crockett record books, such as a 78-point whitetail deer that Friedrich bought in 1890 for $100. Other highlights of the collection are a record 1,056-pound black marlin and the skull and horns of a 10,000-year-old giant deer, now extinct and known as "the Irish elk." There's a chandelier made from 4,000 horns

as well as a chair made for Teddy Roosevelt by Wenzel Friedrich out of sixty-two pairs of buffalo horns.

When Lone Star was sold to Stroh's Beer in 1998, the old brewery was closed and its brewing operations moved to Longview, Texas. To keep the Buckhorn Collection in San Antonio, Mary Friedrich Rogers, granddaughter of Buckhorn founder Albert Friedrich, and her husband, Wallace Rogers, acquired the collection and reopened the Buckhorn Saloon in its present location on Houston Street, just a few blocks from its original location.

To Don, it was more than a dream come true. Having grown up in San Antonio, he regarded the Buckhorn as one of the city's icons and confessed to having some personal memories of visits to the legendary bar.

Now he was faced with the challenge of naming his new venue. As the many exhibits were being placed at the new Buckhorn, he had been particularly enthralled with one of them, located adjacent to the catering space. The exhibit features the famous Texas sharpshooting couple Adolph "Ad" Toepperwein and his wife, Elizabeth. Ad Toepperwein, born in Boerne, Texas, in 1869 and the son of a gunsmith, became a trick shooter on the vaudeville circuit and then an exhibition shooter for the Winchester Repeating Arms Company. Elizabeth, born in New Haven,

Connecticut, in 1882, married Ad in 1903 and soon received her first shooting lesson from him. Within three weeks she was able to shoot one-inch pieces of chalk from between his fingers, earning her the nickname "Plinky" (because she liked to "plink 'em"). The pair went on to break records for marksmanship around the world. They became legends in the early 1900s and visited the Buckhorn regularly, recounting tales from their travels for all who would listen. The Buckhorn Collection contains a bust outline of an Indian chief that Ad created on a piece of sheet metal with precise consecutive shots from a .22 rifle. Plinky was known to shoot even better than famed Annie Oakley, who once told her, "Mrs. Topp, you're the greatest shot I've ever seen." The first woman to score a perfect 100 shooting at clay pigeons, Plinky died in 1945; Ad lived to the ripe old age of ninety-three, spending his later years teaching gun safety and shooting skills to youngsters.

Don was so fascinated with the Toepperweins' story that he decided to name his newest catering venture after them, and the Toepperwein Room was born. The new Buckhorn Saloon and the Toepperwein Room opened to the public in the fall of 1999.

The saloon is located on the main floor of the building. It's a space that very accurately captures the feeling of a late-1800s frontier saloon with its large antique bar, vintage furnishings, and flooring of tiny hexagonal tiles. Many of the animal mounts are displayed in the saloon. Initially Don had agreed to operate a café for the public within the saloon, but after a short time he remembered from years earlier the frustration his parents had felt when they tried to operate the old Broiler restaurant. Like them, Don knew nothing about operating a restaurant. The logistics were just too difficult to handle, so he gave up the café concession.

When Don entered into the Buckhorn agreement, it was the first time in his life that he had taken on a venture in which he didn't "own the dirt," so he had to learn to make some compromises and mental adjustments to fully understand the concept of operating a business within a business. Don and the management became quite comfortable with each other's agendas, and the association has been a successful venture for both parties.

The restoration of the Toepperwein Room was a lofty undertaking. The building had been vacant for several years, and the space was desperately in need of a loving hand. Don commissioned the late Ken Graves, a noted San Antonio architect, for the project. Don wanted the restoration to be mindful and respectful of the building's rich history, so the original beams and columns were left in place, and the architect worked within the space to accommodate the 1,500-square-foot kitchen, a stage, dance floor, and various seating arrangements.

Don and his employees worked diligently with the team of experts, poring over historical documents pertaining to the building, color samples, linen patterns, and seating options, planning the space in a manner that would preserve its integrity. The walls were painted in subdued shades of brown, khaki, beige, and terra-cotta. The dramatic fifteen-foot ceilings and twelve-foot-high plantation-style windows are striking design elements, giving the space a very grand feel while offering a view of historic Houston Street below.

In keeping with Don's desire to create a complete "environment" for his events, the room was planned to be

at once entertaining, comfortable, and charming. The original hardwood floors were stained dark brown, leather chair rails were added, and four large wrought-iron light fixtures found in the Hill Country were mounted on each side of the large weight-bearing columns. Hand-knotted Persian rugs in rich autumn hues were laid over the entire floor to add dimension and flair as well as to insulate the room against echoing noise.

The design team found antique wooden chairs and tables reminiscent of the turn-of-the-century period. Don amassed a collection of linens from which clients can select to create the look they're trying to achieve for their events. He collected an array of colorfully painted Mexican terra-cotta pottery plates, platters, and bowls, which he arranged on custom-made wooden shelves, placed just inside the doors to provide a perfect accent. The room has the feel of the era when the Buckhorn was born, blended seamlessly with an upscale Hill Country flair. In deference to clients who might not want to view animal heads while hosting a party or meeting, the Toepperwein Room contains no mounts, and a private entrance, separate from the saloon, is offered off of Houston Street. But for those who want

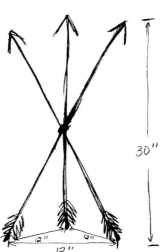

the museum experience as part of their event, the banquet facility's doors can be opened and food and beverage stations set up among the collection.

The 4,000-square-foot Toepperwein Room can accommodate seated dinners for 500 people. A client with a very large guest list can opt to have the event spread over the entire facility, including the main downstairs saloon, which is normally closed during private events. The entire space can accommodate 2,000 people. Whenever clients chose to have their parties on both floors of the Buckhorn, Don, in his quest to provide the ultimate experience, offered the option of bringing Jenny, our late donkey from the ranch, to the event. She was brought to the Buckhorn by her longtime handler, Miguel Hernandez, manager of the Don Strange Ranch, who dressed in his authentic cowboy attire and led her in through the main doors of the saloon.

It appeared as though a cowboy were ambling in to have a beer with his donkey in tow! Then he would slowly lead Jenny through the crowds of guests, who soon discovered that her saddlebags were filled with cold miniature Coronas! Over the years Jenny became a favorite at Buckhorn parties, and we hope there's another Jenny in our future.

In addition to seated dinners, the Toepperwein Room is a popular place for brunches. Don Strange of Texas pulls out all the stops to create elegant and entertaining mid-morning events. I've included a great brunch menu in this chapter that you can use for special occasions like a New Year's Day brunch, a bridal shower brunch, anniversary brunch, or another special occasion in your life.

The association with the Buckhorn Saloon has proven to be another example of Don's genius for entrepreneurial foresight. The company has catered hundreds of successful parties there, and the award-winning Toepperwein Room is highly sought after as a venue for a wide range of events.

Ad and Plinky, I'm sure, have raised a glass or two to Don.

Don Strange of Texas Brunch

Cheese Blintzes with Blueberries

Sautéed Salmon with Asparagus and
Hollandaise Sauce

Christmas Bacon

Brunch Crawfish and Grits

Chipotle Torte

Chocolate Mousse Crepes

Cheese Blintzes

After our first trip to San Francisco, when Don discovered crepes and all the dishes that could be prepared with them, he added Cheese Blintzes to his brunch menu. They were a big-time hit and are still popular today.

Serves 6

Combine the cheese, egg, sugar, salt, and cinnamon in a small bowl and whisk to blend well. Place the crepes browned side up and spoon a portion of the cheese mixture down the center of each. Roll the crepes up and set aside. Heat the butter in a heavy-bottomed 12-inch sauté pan. When the foam subsides, fry the blintzes until browned on all sides.

To serve, place 2 blintzes on each serving plate, seam side down. Top with a dollop of sour cream and scatter some of the berries over the crepes. Drizzle a bit of the honey over each serving and serve warm, garnished with a mint sprig.

2 cups (8 ounces) farmer cheese

1 egg, beaten

2 tablespoons sugar

Pinch of kosher salt

½ teaspoon ground cinnamon

12 prepared crepes

2 tablespoons unsalted butter

Sour cream

Fresh blueberries or sliced fresh strawberries

Honey

Mint sprigs as garnish

Baked Brie

This dish is often served at the appetizer station. Guests love it, with its mingling of flavors interspersed in layers with the creaminess of the brie cheese.

Serves 14 to 18 as finger food

Preheat oven to 350 degrees. Line the bottom of an 8-inch springform cake pan with parchment paper. Spray parchment and sides of pan with nonstick cooking spray; set aside.

Remove all the rind from the cheese. Using a thin-bladed slicing knife, cut the cheese wheel in half horizontally. Place the bottom half, cut side up, in the parchment-lined pan. In a medium bowl, combine the sour cream, salt, green onions, and garlic, whisking to blend well. Spread half of the mixture on top of the cheese. Top with half of the sun-dried tomatoes and all of the parsley and basil. Place the remaining half of the cheese on top of the tomatoes, cut side down. Top with the remaining sun-dried tomatoes, sour cream, and the sliced almonds.

Bake in preheated oven until almonds are browned and the brie is very soft, about 15 minutes. Remove pan from oven and place on wire rack. Allow to cool until lukewarm, then remove sides of pan and slide brie onto a serving platter. Serve with a basket of toasted French bread rounds.

1 (8-inch) wheel of brie cheese

1 cup sour cream

1 teaspoon kosher salt

5 green onions and tops, sliced thin

3 garlic cloves, minced

2 cups sun-dried tomatoes, chopped

⅓ cup minced fresh parsley

⅓ cup minced fresh basil

1 cup skin-on sliced almonds

Toasted French bread rounds

Chipotle Torte

★

6 (8-ounce) packages cream cheese, softened

8 ounces mascarpone cheese, softened

1 cup chopped soft, but not oil-cured, sun-dried tomatoes

⅓ cup minced chipotle chiles in adobo sauce

8 ounces prepared basil pesto

½ cup minced cilantro

French Bread Crostini (see recipe below)

French Bread Crostini

2 cups extra-virgin olive oil

⅓ cup minced garlic cloves

2 teaspoons kosher salt or sea salt

2 French bread baguettes, sliced into ¼-inch-thick rounds

Don Strange of Texas often serves this colorful torte at the finger-food station. It's an attractive, delicious dish with an exciting blend of flavors and a nice little hint of spice. It can be made up to two days ahead of time, if kept covered and refrigerated. Serve with a basket of the crostini.

Serves up to 20 as finger food

Line a deep, straight-sided, 8-inch-diameter bowl (such as a soufflé dish) with plastic wrap, allowing wrap to hang over the top edge by about 6 inches; set aside. Combine the cream cheese and mascarpone cheese in work bowl of food processor fitted with steel blade. Process until smooth and well blended. Turn out into a mixing bowl and set aside. In a separate bowl, combine the tomatoes and chipotle chiles, blending well; set aside.

Divide the cheese mixture into 3 equal portions. Spread a third of the cheese evenly in the bottom of the prepared bowl, extending the cheese layer all the way to the sides of the bowl. Spread half of the pesto over the cheese, all the way to the edge, then scatter half of the tomato mixture evenly over the pesto. Spread another third of the cheese mixture over the tomato mixture. Repeat with the remaining pesto and tomato mixture; top with remaining third of the cheese mixture, spreading the top evenly. Fold the overhanging plastic wrap over the top of the cheese, pressing down gently to compact the torte. Refrigerate at least overnight and for up to 48 hours.

Make the French Bread Crostini. Preheat oven to 375 degrees. Combine the olive oil, garlic, and salt in a small saucepan over medium heat. Bring to a boil, then lower heat and simmer for 5 minutes. Remove from heat and let sit until oil is cool, about 30 minutes. Strain through a fine strainer, pressing down on the garlic pulp to extract flavor. Discard garlic pulp.

Using a pastry brush, coat one side of each bread slice with the garlic oil and place on baking sheets. Toast until very lightly toasted, about 6 to 7 minutes. The toasts should not brown! Cool on wire racks. (If making in advance, store in tightly sealed zip-sealing bags and serve within two days.)

To serve the torte, unfold the plastic wrap from the top of the torte. Place a serving platter, serving side down, on top of the bowl and invert the bowl. Carefully remove the bowl from the torte, then the plastic wrap. Scatter the cilantro on top of the torte, allowing some to fall around the plate. Serve with a basket of French Bread Crostini.

Smoked Salmon Tartare

★

Smoked salmon is a universally favorite party food. We've had rave reviews time and time again when we serve this "tartare" made with smoked salmon. Of course, it's really cooked, but the presentation is the same as for beef tartare, which is made from raw beef and not a universally favorite party food!

Serves about 20

Combine salmon, ½ cup of the shallots, ½ cup of the chives, 3 tablespoons of the capers, mustard, and pepper in a large bowl and stir with a large fork to blend well. Form the mixture into an oval and place in the center of a large platter. Overlap the cucumber slices around the salmon. Place the chopped eggs, cream cheese, remaining capers and shallots, and lemon wedges in lettuce leaves around the edge of the platter, with appropriate serving utensils. Scatter chopped chives over the salmon. Serve the French bread rounds in a basket alongside the platter.

1½ pounds smoked salmon, finely chopped

½ cup plus ⅓ cup minced shallots

½ cup chopped fresh chives plus additional for garnish

½ cup drained capers plus 3 tablespoons, chopped

3 tablespoons Dijon-style mustard

½ teaspoon freshly ground black pepper

2 cucumbers, sliced thin

5 hard-boiled eggs, chopped fine

1 (8-ounce) package cream cheese, whipped in food processor

4 lemons, cut into small wedges

5 large green leaf lettuce leaves

Toasted French bread rounds

Sautéed Salmon with Asparagus and Hollandaise Sauce

★

12 fresh asparagus spears

Kosher salt and freshly ground black pepper to taste

¼ cup olive oil

1½ pounds wild-caught salmon fillet, cut into 4 pieces (see "Buying Fresh Fish [and Making Sure They're Fresh]" on page 146)

Prepared hollandaise sauce (see "Making Foolproof Hollandaise Sauce in the Food Processor" on page 201)

Lemon wheel (see "Making Lemon Wheels" on page 240)

Paprika for garnish

This dish is often served at our brunches because it makes a very nice presentation and is fairly light, befitting the brunch hour. Be sure to use only wild-caught salmon— it's much better-tasting and a better choice for the environment, too.

Serves 4

Line up the tops of the asparagus spears evenly on a cutting board and trim off the tough, woody ends, about 2½ inches, and discard ends. Using a sharp, swivel-bladed vegetable peeler, peel a very thin layer from each spear, beginning about 1 inch below the tips; take care not to peel so deeply that the spears break. Place in a microwave-safe dish and add water to cover. Cover and microwave on high for 3 minutes, then drain and plunge the asparagus into a bowl of ice water to stop the cooking process and refresh the color. When cool, pat dry and return to the microwave-safe dish. Season with salt; cover and set aside.

Heat the olive oil in a heavy-bottomed 12-inch skillet over medium-high heat. Add the salmon pieces and season with salt and pepper. Sear for about 2 minutes, then turn and cook an additional 3 to 4 minutes. Take care not to overcook. (The salmon pieces should be slightly underdone in the center, as they will continue to cook; the flesh should not be flaking apart.) Return the asparagus to the microwave and cook on high for 3 minutes.

Using a slotted spatula, place a piece of salmon in the center of each serving plate. Angle 3 asparagus spears on top and drizzle with a liberal portion of the hollandaise sauce. Garnish with a twisted lemon wheel and dust with paprika. Serve at once.

HERE'S HOW YOU DO IT
Making Foolproof Hollandaise Sauce in the Food Processor: Many home cooks avoid making this classic, delicious sauce because the risk of failure is so great—and also because it takes a lot of time and elbow grease to do all of that whisking. But the invention of the food processor has made the sauce quick, easy, and virtually foolproof. No whisking is required to make a perfect hollandaise every time!

Food Processor Hollandaise Sauce

Makes 1½ cups

3 egg yolks

1 tablespoon fresh lemon juice

2 teaspoons Dijon-style mustard

¾ teaspoon kosher salt

¼ teaspoon cayenne pepper

¾ pound (3 sticks) unsalted butter, melted and hot

Place the egg yolks, lemon juice, mustard, salt, and cayenne pepper in work bowl of food processor fitted with steel blade. Process for about 3 minutes, or until the yolk mixture is thickened and very light lemon yellow in color. With the machine running, add the hot butter in a slow, steady stream through the feed tube until all has been added. Process an additional 15 to 20 seconds to form a strong emulsion. Turn the sauce out into a stainless steel bowl and keep warm over a pan of hot (not simmering) water. Hollandaise should be thought of a sauce that is served warm, not hot. The heat of the food on which it is served will warm the sauce. It cannot be reheated or the eggs will scramble.

Brunch Crawfish and Grits

★

Shrimp and grits, as every Southerner knows, is an iconic Southern dish. Don always liked the dish but wanted to make it a bit more Texan, so he added crawfish. The result was a flavor-packed dish that became a guest favorite at parties and brunches. It's easy to prepare and makes a delicious addition to the brunch table. The secret to the dish is to not overcook the grits. They should be soft and creamy.

Serves 6

Toss the peeled crawfish tails with the seasoning blend, coating well; set aside. Sauté the bacon in a heavy-bottomed 12-inch skillet over medium heat until it is almost crisp and has rendered most of its fat. Remove bacon pieces with a slotted spoon; reserve. Add the seasoned crawfish to the hot fat and toss quickly; sear until slightly brown. Remove with a slotted spoon and set aside. Add the onion, celery, bell pepper, garlic, thyme, oregano, cayenne pepper, and black pepper to the pan. Sauté, stirring often, until vegetables are wilted and transparent, about 10 minutes. Add the flour and stir to blend well. Cook, stirring, about 3 to 4 minutes, then add the stock and lemon juice. While stirring, bring the mixture to a boil to thicken. Reduce heat, stir in the whipping cream, blending well, and simmer mixture about 15 minutes. Stir in the reserved crawfish and bacon; cook just to heat the crawfish, about 5 minutes.

While crawfish mixture is cooking, make the grits. Combine the milk, half-and-half, and butter in a heavy-bottomed 3-quart saucepan over medium heat. Bring to a boil, then stir in the grits. Continue to stir until grits begin to thicken, about 5 minutes. Add salt and stir in the whipping cream. Cook just to warm the cream. Remove from heat while grits are still soft and creamy.

To serve, place a portion of the grits on each serving plate and top with a portion of the crawfish mixture. Scatter a bit of the minced parsley and sliced green onions over the top of each serving.

1½ pounds peeled crawfish tails

2 tablespoons Chef Paul Prudhomme's Seafood Magic seasoning

8 bacon slices, cut into ½-inch dice

1 large onion, chopped

2 celery stalks, chopped

1 green bell pepper, chopped

2 garlic cloves, minced

1 teaspoon minced fresh thyme

½ teaspoon dried Mexican oregano

½ teaspoon cayenne pepper

½ teaspoon freshly ground black pepper

2 tablespoons all-purpose flour

2 cups shrimp stock, or substitute chicken stock

¼ cup freshly squeezed lemon juice

½ cup whipping cream

Minced flat-leaf parsley and thin-sliced green onions as garnish

Grits

2 cups whole milk

2 cups half-and-half

¼ pound (1 stick) unsalted butter, cut into small dice

1 cup quick-cooking grits

Kosher salt to taste

¼ cup whipping cream

Chicken-Fried Quail with Jalapeño Cream Gravy

★

18 semi-boneless quail

4 cups all-purpose flour, seasoned liberally with kosher salt and freshly ground black pepper

3 eggs, beaten well with 5 cups evaporated milk

6 cups panko (Japanese-style) bread crumbs, seasoned with 1 tablespoon each kosher salt, ground black pepper, cayenne pepper, and granulated garlic

1 inch of canola oil in a 12-inch skillet, heated to 350 degrees

Jalapeño Cream Gravy

½ cup bacon and or sausage drippings

2 jalapeños, seeds and veins removed, minced

½ cup all-purpose flour

½ teaspoon freshly ground black pepper plus additional for garnish

4 cups whole milk, or more as needed

½ of a Knorr chicken bouillon cube

Don was never one to simply copy trendy dishes; rather, he expanded them to new levels of great taste. Instead of serving the ubiquitous chicken-fried steak, he created Chicken-Fried Quail, combining the delicious taste of the succulent, juicy little birds with a crisp fried panko breading. And no ordinary cream gravy for this dish, either! Don added his own innovative spin to it by stirring in fresh jalapeños, turning the humble white gravy into a flavor-packed sauce with a nice little zing.

Serves 8 to 10

Preheat oven to 300 degrees. Pat quail dry using absorbent paper towels. Dredge quail in the seasoned flour, coating well and shaking off excess. Dip quail in the egg wash, coating well. Dredge quail in the seasoned panko bread crumbs, patting the crumbs into the egg wash and coating well. Shake off excess. Arrange quail, not touching, on a large baking sheet lined with parchment paper. Fry the quail in batches, about 6 at a time and without crowding, in the preheated oil. Cook about 6 to 7 minutes per side, turning once. Arrange quail in a single layer on a cooling rack set over a baking sheet. Keep hot in preheated oven while frying the remaining quail.

To make the gravy, heat the drippings in a deep-sided, heavy-bottomed 12-inch skillet over medium heat. When the fat is hot, add the jalapeños and cook, stirring, for about 2 minutes. Add the flour and black pepper. Cook, stirring constantly, for 2 minutes. Whisk in the milk and the ½ bouillon cube, blending well with the flour. Bring to a boil to thicken, whisking often to dissolve the bouillon cube.

Pile the quail on a large serving platter and pour the gravy into a bowl. Serve hot.

4 skin-on, boneless duck breasts, about 8 ounces each

Marinade (see recipe below)

⅓ cup teriyaki glaze

¾ teaspoon minced fresh ginger

3 green onions and tops, chopped

1 medium carrot, chopped

1 tablespoon minced cilantro

Green tops from 6 leeks (see "Using Leeks" on page 76)

18 frozen phyllo pastry sheets, thawed

Melted butter

Marinade

2 tablespoons canola oil

2 teaspoons sesame oil

3 whole dried arbol chiles or dried Thai chiles

6 (¼-inch-thick) slices fresh ginger, smashed

6 garlic cloves, peeled and smashed

2 tablespoons minced orange zest

1 teaspoon coriander seeds, toasted and ground

1 teaspoon freshly ground black pepper

¾ cup hoisin sauce

½ cup soy sauce

2 tablespoons honey

2 tablespoons firmly packed dark brown sugar

Don loved to work with duck, but it was not always a popular meat with party hosts. He created this tasty finger food using duck breasts, and the crispy little pockets proved to be a popular way to present duck. If you're making these for a home party, they can be frozen and then baked while still frozen. Allow an extra five minutes of cooking time if they are frozen.

Makes about 96 pockets

To make the marinade, heat the canola and sesame oil in a heavy 10-inch skillet over medium heat. When the oil is hot, add the chiles, ginger, and garlic. Cook, tossing often, until ginger and garlic are well browned, about 6 minutes. Add all remaining ingredients and stir to blend well. Lower heat and simmer for 25 minutes. Allow marinade to cool in the pan, then strain through a fine strainer. Set aside.

Place the duck breasts in a nonreactive baking dish and cover with the marinade. Refrigerate for 8 hours or overnight. When ready to assemble the pockets, heat a gas grill to medium heat, or build a hardwood charcoal fire in a barbecue pit and allow it to burn down until the coals are glowing red and covered by a layer of white ash, about 20 to 30 minutes.

Remove the breasts from the marinade; discard marinade. Grill the breasts for about 8 minutes per side, or until medium, 145 degrees. Remove from grill and set aside to rest for 10 minutes.

Remove the skin and cut the grilled breasts into 1-inch cubes. Combine the duck meat, teriyaki glaze, ginger, green onions, and carrot in work bowl of food processor fitted with steel blade. Process, using the pulse feature, until the mixture is broken up into a mixture that resembles hamburger meat. Turn out into a bowl and stir in the minced cilantro. Set aside.

Bring 3 cups of water to a rolling boil in a deep-sided 8-inch skillet. When water comes to a boil, add the leek tops. Blanch for 2 minutes, then drain into a colander and plunge into a bowl of ice water. When well chilled, drain the tops and lay them on a double thickness of paper towels. Cut or tear each piece into small strips and set aside.

Lay a sheet of phyllo pastry on work surface, leaving the rest covered with plastic wrap and a damp tea towel. Brush the pastry sheet with a thin glaze of melted butter. Lay a second sheet on top and brush it also lightly with butter. Repeat with a third sheet. Cut the stacked sheets, lengthwise, into four strips 4 inches wide. Now cut each strip, crosswise, into 4-inch squares.

Preheat oven to 350 degrees. Spray 8 miniature (12-cup, 2-inch-diameter cups) muffin tins with nonstick vegetable spray; set aside.

Place 2 teaspoons of the duck mixture in the center of each square of phyllo dough. Gather corners together over the filling and twist, allowing some of the filling to extend above the twist. Tie with a strip of the blanched leek tops. Place each pocket in a cup of the prepared muffin tins. Repeat with remaining pastry sheets. Bake pockets in preheated oven until pastry is golden brown and crisp, about 25 minutes. Serve hot.

Pork Loin with Tangy Sauce

Roasted, center-cut pork loin makes a very impressive presentation, and the taste is equally impressive. This dish is often served at parties at the Buckhorn Saloon.

Serves 10 to 12

Preheat oven to 350 degrees. Mix chili powder and garlic salt together, blending well. Rub the spice mixture on the pork, covering all surfaces. Place the pork in a large open roasting pan and bake for 2 hours in preheated oven, or until an instant-read thermometer inserted in thickest part of the meat registers 160 degrees.

While the pork is roasting, make the sauce. Combine all ingredients in a heavy-bottomed 2-quart saucepan over medium heat. Bring to a boil, stirring often. About 20 minutes before the roast is done, spoon some of the sauce over the meat.

When meat is done, set aside to rest for 10 minutes before slicing to desired thickness. Reheat remaining sauce and serve with the pork.

½ cup chili powder

½ cup garlic salt

1 boneless, center-cut pork loin roast, 6 to 8 pounds, with a good layer of fat on the top

Tangy Sauce

1 cup ketchup

1 cup apple jelly

2 tablespoons chili powder

1 tablespoon apple cider vinegar

Haystack of Peppers

This side dish not only adds color to a plate but also has an outstanding flavor, with the seared peppers and onions blending together. Serve them in a stack on the plate, a technique best achieved by picking them up with chef's tongs and making a "haystack."

Serves 4 to 6

Heat the olive oil in a heavy-bottomed 14-inch skillet over medium heat. When oil is very hot, add the peppers and onions. Cook, tossing often with tongs, until all the vegetables are slightly browned but still crisp tender, about 10 minutes. Season with salt and serve hot.

3 tablespoons olive oil

2 red bell peppers, seeds and veins removed, cut into julienne strips

2 green bell peppers, seeds and veins removed, cut into julienne strips

2 yellow bell peppers, seeds and veins removed, cut into julienne strips

2 large red onions, peeled and halved from stem to root, then sliced into julienne strips

Kosher salt or sea salt to taste

Blue Cheese Mashed Potatoes

★

One of Don's favorite flavor combinations was beef and blue cheese. Whenever he served a beef dish, he loved to include blue cheese, either in the beef or in a side dish. This is an excellent example of how he would add flavors to simple dishes like mashed potatoes to turn them into stellar side dishes that perfectly complemented the meat entrée. This is a great dish to accompany grilled steaks.

Serves 4 to 6

Place the potatoes in a heavy-bottomed 4-quart saucepan. Add cold water to cover and bring to a rolling boil over medium-high heat. Lower heat to a gentle boil and cook until potatoes are very tender, about 20 minutes. Strain into a colander, shaking out all excess water. Transfer the potatoes to a large mixing bowl and add the crumbled cheese. Mash the potatoes and cheese together, blending well to desired consistency. Add the evaporated milk and pepper, stirring until well blended. If the potatoes are too stiff, add additional evaporated milk, a little at a time, stirring to blend after each addition. Season with salt and serve hot.

Variation: Garlic and Herb Mashed Potatoes

Delete the Stilton cheese and black pepper. Add 8 large roasted garlic cloves (see "Roasting Garlic" below), mashed to a paste, 1 teaspoon minced fresh rosemary, and ½ teaspoon white pepper.

2½ pounds Idaho potatoes, peeled and diced

½ cup crumbled Stilton cheese

½ cup evaporated milk plus additional as needed

½ teaspoon freshly ground black pepper

Kosher salt to taste

Opposite: Pork Loin with Tangy Sauce, Haystack of Peppers, Garlic and Herb Mashed Potatoes (on plate), and Parker House Rolls (in background).

HERE'S HOW YOU DO IT

Roasting Garlic: To roast garlic, preheat oven to 350 degrees. Slice the top ⅜-inch off the whole head of garlic. Place in a small casserole dish and drizzle with olive oil. Season with kosher salt and black pepper. Cover tightly with foil and bake in preheated oven for 30 to 45 minutes, or until garlic is well browned and the individual cloves are very soft and pulpy. Allow garlic to cool completely, then squeeze the pulp from each clove. Mash to a paste to use.

Exotic Mushroom Sauté

★

⅔ cup extra-virgin olive oil

14 garlic cloves, peeled and sliced thin

3 large French shallots, minced

6 ounces shiitake mushrooms, stems removed

6 ounces oyster mushrooms, bottom stems removed and discarded, roughly chopped

6 ounces cremini mushrooms, quartered

6 small portabella mushrooms, cut into ½-inch strips

2 pounds small white button mushrooms, halved

½ teaspoon crushed red pepper flakes

1 teaspoon freshly ground black pepper

½ cup dry white wine, such as chardonnay

1 tablespoon minced fresh basil

1 tablespoon minced flat-leaf parsley

Kosher salt to taste

½ cup finely grated Pecorino Romano cheese

Party guests just love this dish, which proves that sometimes the simplest of foods can also be the most flavorful. The mushrooms are sautéed in olive oil with the herbs and seasonings in giant paella pans as the guests watch in mouthwatering anticipation. You can vary the type of mushrooms you use. Each variety has its own unique woodsy, earthy flavor, even plain white mushrooms. Serve the mushrooms with a variety of sliced whole grain breads. Add several handfuls of baby spinach leaves to the pan during the last minute of cooking to give a splash of color to the dish.

Serves 15 to 20 as finger food

Heat the olive oil in a heavy-bottomed 14-inch skillet over medium heat. When the oil is hot, add the garlic and shallots. Cook, stirring constantly, just until shallots are wilted and transparent and garlic is beginning to brown, about 3 minutes. Add the mushrooms, red pepper, and black pepper; stir to blend. Stirring often, cook until the mushrooms are limp and any excess mushroom liquid has evaporated, about 10 minutes. Stir in the wine and cook, stirring frequently, until it has evaporated. Add the basil and parsley. Stir to blend and cook for a couple of minutes. Season with salt. Stir in the cheese and remove pan from heat. Transfer to a chafing dish over low heat and serve hot with a basket of sliced whole-grain breads.

Parker House Rolls

★

2 tablespoons instant-rise active dry yeast

1¼ cups sugar

2 cups warm water (105–115 degrees) plus additional as needed

¼ cup honey

7 cups bread flour plus additional as needed

1½ teaspoons kosher salt

2 eggs, beaten

⅓ cup canola oil

4 tablespoons (½ stick) melted butter

The commissary kitchen has been cranking out these much-loved rolls for years. They're served at most of our events as well as at Steak Nite at the Waring General Store. Once baked, the rolls freeze well if wrapped in aluminum foil. When you want to reheat them, simply place them in a preheated 350-degree oven, without opening the foil, for fifteen minutes, then open the foil and cook an additional five minutes to crisp the tops of the rolls. They'll look and taste freshly baked.

Makes about 36 rolls

Combine the yeast, sugar, water, and honey in a 4-cup Pyrex measuring cup; whisk to blend well. Set aside until the yeast has dissolved and the mixture is very bubbly, about 3 to 4 minutes.

In bowl of electric stand mixer fitted with dough hook, combine the flour and salt. Pour in the yeast mixture, using a rubber spatula to scrape the measuring cup. With mixer on low speed, begin to beat the mixture. When the flour is slightly moistened, add the remaining ingredients except melted butter. Start again on low speed, beating until all ingredients are well blended. Increase speed, beating for about 1 minute. Stop and check consistency of the dough. It should not be sticky. (If it is too wet, add additional bread flour, about 1 tablespoon at a time. Beat to blend the additional flour after each addition. If dough is too dry, add additional warm water about 1 tablespoon at a time, beating to blend after each addition.) When dough is the proper consistency, increase speed and knead with the dough hook for about 8 minutes, or until dough is very elastic and springs back when pulled.

Grease a large bowl and turn the dough out into the bowl, turning it to coat all sides. Cover with plastic wrap and set aside to rise in a warm, draft-free spot until doubled in size, about 1 hour. Punch the dough down, then cover, and let rise again until doubled.

Turn the dough out onto work surface and punch down again, removing all air. Roll the dough out to a thickness of about ½ inch. Using a 3-inch biscuit cutter, cut the dough into rounds. Stretch each round into an oval and fold in half, joining the two rounded sides. Combine and roll out scraps; cut into additional rolls. Place the folded rolls on large baking sheets, about 2 inches apart. Brush the tops of the rolls with melted butter, cover very loosely with plastic wrap, and set aside to rise until almost doubled, 30 to 45 minutes.

Preheat oven to 350 degrees. Bake rolls in preheated oven for 20 to 25 minutes, or until golden brown and rolls sound hollow when tapped on the bottom. Cool on wire rack or serve hot with lots of butter!

White Hot Chocolate

⭐

The staff created this recipe for several events that were held during the Christmas holidays in 2009. It made a beautiful addition to the silver and white decorations, as it is pristinely white and was served in white mugs, topped with whipped cream and a single mint leaf with one red raspberry. It's the perfect nonalcoholic winter beverage—guaranteed to warm you up!

Makes five 8-ounce servings

Combine all ingredients except nutmeg and garnishes in a heavy-bottomed 2-quart saucepan over medium-low heat. Cook, stirring often, until all ingredients are well blended and chocolate chips are melted. When the mixture is hot but not boiling, stir in the nutmeg, mixing well. Serve hot in mugs topped with a rosette of the whipped cream. Garnish with a single mint leaf and a raspberry.

2 cups whole milk

2 cups evaporated milk

½ cup whipping cream

1 cup white chocolate chips

1 teaspoon white vanilla extract

⅛ teaspoon freshly grated nutmeg

Sweetened whipped cream, beaten to stiff peaks

Large mint leaves (optional)

5 raspberries (optional)

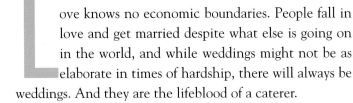

CHAPTER ELEVEN

Storybook Weddings

Love knows no economic boundaries. People fall in love and get married despite what else is going on in the world, and while weddings might not be as elaborate in times of hardship, there will always be weddings. And they are the lifeblood of a caterer.

Throughout the history of Don Strange of Texas there have been economic ups and downs that affected the company's bottom line. In times of economic downturns the first thing that both individuals and businesses dispense with is entertaining. So Don knew well the sinking feeling of parties being cancelled, or regularly held events not being rescheduled and phones sitting silent at the office. But there was always one category of event that didn't depend on the state of the economy—weddings.

Don loved to plan weddings. With the Don Strange Ranch and the Toepperwein Room at the Buckhorn Saloon, he had the freedom to add to weddings whatever features sprang from his imagination. He was in his element when he was planning a wedding with the prospective bride and groom and their families. He was so in tune with every bride's desire for her wedding to be a storybook affair, an occasion to be remembered for years, that they all adored

him by the day of the wedding. Wedding planners loved him, too, for his over-the-top ideas that made every wedding zing with excitement, regardless of how small the budget might be.

The company has done countless weddings over the years. In fact, we recently tried to count them, but it proved to be an impossible task, since in the early years of the company the events were recorded only by client name, with no notation of what type of event it was. Our employees in the office said it would be safe to say, however, that the company has done over 3,200 weddings!

Of course, I heard about most of the weddings through Don's stories and by looking at the countless photographs taken by the staff. One of my favorite of his wedding stories shows how funny people are about their food, especially leftovers. It is very common for people to start worrying about the leftovers before their party even begins. In the early days of the business, Don was catering a wedding reception at a time when all the transportation of food and staff was done in vans. As he was loading one of the vans used for the wedding, he came upon the bride, wedding dress pulled up between her knees, going through the leftovers. When he told me about the incident, I almost died laughing, picturing the bride in the dress of her dreams, going through the leftovers. He never said what the outcome was, but I'm sure he gave her whatever she needed.

There were so many beautiful settings and so many lovely brides. But there is one wedding that I remember firsthand, that of our son Matt in August of 1990. The wedding was held at the Don Strange Ranch. Don was in heaven planning this wedding with Matt and his fiancée, Kelly, and her family. The wedding ceremony was held on the grassy lawn that slopes down from the old house at the

ranch. Don wanted Kelly and her dad to arrive at the ceremony in a horse-drawn carriage, so he went downtown to Alamo Street, where there are carriages for hire. He interviewed several independent drivers and selected one that used a vintage white carriage.

The carriage arrived at the ranch on the day of the wedding and was positioned totally out of sight. Kelly dressed at the ranch house before the guests assembled, then she and her father were taken to the carriage in one of the company vehicles. Don timed how long it took the carriage to make the trip to the grassy lawn and arranged to have someone ring the huge dinner bell at the barn as a signal to the carriage driver to begin his drive to the wedding. Every detail was meant to suggest a wedding on the grounds of a rural church before the turn of the century. Don wanted it to appear that the bride's father was riding from home to the church with his daughter for her wedding.

It was a picture-perfect day. When the guests were all seated, the bridesmaids, flower girl, and ring bearer began the procession from the house, making their way down the hill and up the aisle to their positions. As the guests turned to see the bride, they heard the clip-clop of the horse and

carriage and watched in awe as it turned onto the lawn and the ushers helped Kelly down. She linked arms with her dad, and they walked down the aisle. It was such a dramatic moment. There wasn't a dry eye in the crowd.

The reception was held in the open barn, and there was enough food for an army. Matt didn't want a traditional groom's cake. His favorite dessert was my mother's Boston Cream Pie, so she made twenty-three of them, all of them arranged on magnolia leaves on the groom's table. It's a wedding I'll certainly never forget.

Don told me about a wedding at the Don Strange Ranch where a "movie-script moment" occurred. As he told the story, I could picture the chain of events so vividly that I laughed until my sides hurt. This wedding was staged under the huge oak tree that stands by the barn. The wedding procession made its way from the house and across the

road, proceeding up the aisle between the seated guests. Just as the bride and her father started across the road, the flock of ducks from the ranch's pond fell into formation behind them, as if on cue. They began to waddle along behind the pair toward the aisle. The guests began to giggle at the sight. Then, just as the bride reached the last row of seated guests and began walking down the actual "aisle," the ranch dog decided to get into the act, running up behind the ducks. The dog began to bark, the ducks began to quack, and then Jenny, the ranch donkey, began to bray. By now, the ducks were in a state; suddenly, in perfect formation, they took flight—up and over the bride they went, spreading out in every direction above the wedding party and the oak tree, then flying out of sight. The dog fell silent; the donkey stopped braying. All was quiet as the bride stepped up to take her place beside her groom!

To the very last person, the guests honestly thought that Don had staged the whole thing! And knowing him like I did, I was certain that he never denied it. For months,

young women who called to inquire about having the company do their weddings would ask about including "the duck feature."

One of the weddings that Don catered at the Buckhorn Saloon was in 2003 for one of our staff members, Lorissa Pattison. Lorissa wanted an Asian theme for her wedding, so Don moved all of the vintage, turn-of-the-century furnishings out of the Toepperwein Room and refurnished it with square, Asian-inspired tables and black Chiavari chairs with black cushions. He had a baby grand piano hauled up to the second floor. A lavish seafood buffet featuring tiger crab claws, shrimp, and lobster was served on black and white platters set on red velvet table linens. Square black plates and black linen napkins were used. Scallop shells were scattered around the seafood table for use as small plates. A fifteen-foot "tree" of bare branches intertwined with coral-painted branches rose dramatically from the center of the table, its branches arching out across the ceiling above. The tree was hung with balls of orchids and surrounded by votive candles of varying heights. Black demitasse coffee cups were placed at a separate coffee station adjacent to the wedding cake. Fabrics were draped on standing panels around the room, creating intimate niches. It was a very elegant, dramatic presentation.

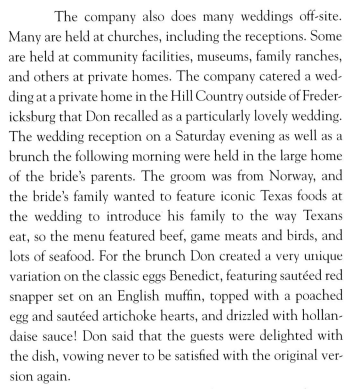

The company also does many weddings off-site. Many are held at churches, including the receptions. Some are held at community facilities, museums, family ranches, and others at private homes. The company catered a wedding at a private home in the Hill Country outside of Fredericksburg that Don recalled as a particularly lovely wedding. The wedding reception on a Saturday evening as well as a brunch the following morning were held in the large home of the bride's parents. The groom was from Norway, and the bride's family wanted to feature iconic Texas foods at the wedding to introduce his family to the way Texans eat, so the menu featured beef, game meats and birds, and lots of seafood. For the brunch Don created a very unique variation on the classic eggs Benedict, featuring sautéed red snapper set on an English muffin, topped with a poached egg and sautéed artichoke hearts, and drizzled with hollandaise sauce! Don said that the guests were delighted with the dish, vowing never to be satisfied with the original version again.

Don was delighted to see the emergence of a new trend: the involvement of the fathers of the brides, along with the mothers, in the planning of their daughters' weddings. He recalled a wedding for the daughter of a family from England in which the father did most of the planning.

The man wanted many English traditions included in the reception, such as the custom of having a chimney sweep hug the bride and put a smudge of soot on her cheek. It was a symbol of good luck for the marriage. This father also specified that the bride and groom should leave the church in an authentic English cab. I never knew where or how Don managed to source some of the things requested by clients, but he never failed to fulfill even the strangest requests. Over the years he amassed a variety of contacts that he could call on to find just about anything. At any rate, the soot-smudged bride and her beloved were swept away in an English cab to begin their lives together with a dose of good luck.

I'd have to say that the most lavish wedding that Don ever catered was the wedding of Faryl Cohen and Drew Greller in 2006. It was one wedding that I was certain would never come off smoothly! Don and the bride's mother, San Antonio events planner Lainey Berkus, spent an entire year planning it. There were more minute details to that wedding than my memory could hold in a lifetime. I

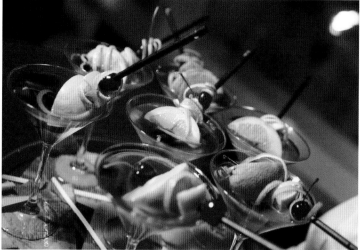

filled with bright and colorful rum martinis—frozen pineapple, strawberry, and blueberry creations were presented with floating orchids, a black chopstick, and large pieces of pineapple, lime curls, and cherries. An open bar was also available for guests with specific drink requests. As guests explored the various niche stations of the reception, they discovered dozens of tasty treats, with eye-catching entertainment at almost every station.

There was an omelet station where square omelets Benedict were prepared to order—fluffy beaten eggs were sautéed in square skillets and filled with smoked salmon, then folded into square pockets, topped with sour cream and caviar, placed on an English muffin, then drizzled with hollandaise sauce and served on square plates. At each end of the omelet station, costumed jugglers were juggling fresh eggs! Trays of eggs were set between the cooking stations, with each egg lettered, monogram style, with the initials of the bride and groom.

In the foyer Don had arranged his Outlandish Crudités Table, featuring marinated artichokes and roasted red, yellow, and green peppers, asparagus, French haricots verts, eggplant, and carrots—all piled about a foot high. Also at the crudités station were Don's signature avocado halves with various condiments, including caviar, soft ripened

couldn't imagine anybody, not even Don, seeing all of those details through to fruition without glitches. There was also a wedding planner involved, in addition to Don and Lainey. What the two of them couldn't plot and plan, the wedding planner did! The 350 invited guests would travel from as far away as Australia to attend the ceremony and reception. I heard the ever-evolving plans for the wedding night and day for a solid year.

The wedding was a traditional Jewish ceremony, held at Temple Beth-El in San Antonio. With the groom's stepping on a glass and breaking it, the wedding ceremony ended and the guests left the temple for a one-of-a-kind, fairy-tale reception.

Waitstaff lined the hallway leading to the multiple reception areas, holding trays of oversized martini glasses

cheeses, a Kosher cracker assortment, and cheese straws stacked high in cylindrical glass containers.

In the richly appointed Stahl Gallery at the temple, Don set up a sushi station, where the waitstaff wore colorful traditional Japanese costumes. Guests could sample pot stickers, California rolls, and tuna and salmon sashimi. There was a large ice carving in the center of the table and clear acrylic trays of sushi were set on large blocks of ice.

A special station featured traditional Israeli fare, such as falafel, hummus, and a Jerusalem sandwich of avocado and tahini in pita breads. A mushroom bar offered an assortment of mushrooms—shiitake, oyster, cremini, portabella, and button—all brushed with olive oil, spices, and garlic, then grilled in giant paella pans in front of the guests and served with whole grain breads and crackers.

The outdoor courtyard was lit with elegant torches and featured a station where chefs were hand-tossing pizza dough high in the air. Pizzas were grilled and piled with toppings of the guest's choice, including Parmesan and mozzarella cheeses, artichoke hearts, smoked salmon, anchovies, olives, and roasted red peppers.

In yet another area, motionless "mannequins" were dressed in exquisite French couture bridesmaid dresses and stationed on pedestals. The display drew the curious to examine the elegant gowns. Imagine the stir created when the models moved into new poses! As part of this same display, a "stagehand" parted the gathering crowd, instructing them to make way as he hoisted one of the motionless models over his shoulder and moved her to an empty pedestal on the opposite end of the reception area, where she assumed yet another pose. Nearby, a large ice sculpture of a mermaid watched over the mimes, wearing a headdress of flowers, grasses, beads, and feathers in sea colors of blues, greens, and purples.

Even the ladies' room was given a personal touch, as Don surrounded the sink with a special flower display.

The finger food and entertainment continued for an hour before Don's second act began. Glass replicas of candy kisses were made for the event and signed by San Antonio glass artist Gini Garcia. They were used to guide guests to their respective tables. The tables were adorned with hundreds of the silver kisses in a multitude of sizes,

along with silver-framed photos of many brides and grooms from the Cohen, Berkus, and Greller families set on platinum silk overlays.

The ballroom doors opened, and guests made their way to their seats at the white linen–covered tables as a live band played. The first course of the wedding feast was served—a Cylinder Salad Tower made with layers of white and green asparagus, vine-ripened red and yellow tomatoes, mozzarella cheese, and cucumbers dressed with aged balsamic vinegar. Each salad was presented with a salmon cake on the side, topped with lime mayonnaise and flamed with lavender rum.

Then the lights dimmed, and the band took up the strains of Aaron Copland's "Fanfare for the Common Man," featuring the sharp notes of a lone trombone, as the white-gloved waitstaff lined an entire wall of the ballroom, each holding a spectacular flaming ice sculpture lighted by votive candles—a display of fire and ice. The servers wound through the room, placing three of the sculptures on each table, where they cast a mystical glow. They were followed by waiters serving a chilled roasted red pepper soup garnished with sprigs of blooming berries and presented in cone-shaped clear glass vessels nested in underliner bowls filled with ice crystals.

The main course was an individual fillet of perfectly seared red snapper served on a bed of basil pesto tossed with pasta and sun-dried tomatoes.

For the dessert course, Don served a dessert he aptly named Cloud 9, a billowing creation made with raspberry sherbet, cherries jubilee, and vanilla bean ice cream—all topped with white cotton candy and served in a tall pilsner glass.

Keep in mind that there were 350 servings of each dish prepared!

After the dinner and the wedding cakes, which Don said were pure pastry artistry, the traditional hora dance brought all of the hundreds of guests to their feet as the bride and groom were lifted high in chairs on the shoulders of their guests, holding the ends of a handkerchief. As the celebration continued into the night, a white Rolls Royce awaited the couple outside the temple. As they made their exit, the guests held hundreds of sparklers high in the night sky.

Can you even imagine such an evening? It was pure Don Strange. From that moment on, I never doubted that he could pull off anything.

Hill Country Wedding Brunch

Grilled Baby Lamb Chops with Mango Chutney

Corn Tortillas Filled with Barbecued Cabrito and Papaya and
Lime Pico de Gallo

Brioche French Toast with Bananas Foster and Warm Maple Syrup

Black Skillet Breakfast Meats (Fresh Alsatian Sausages, Pork and
Sage Patty Sausage, Peppercorn Apple-Smoked Thick-Sliced Bacon,
and Country Ham)

Broiled Red Snapper and Artichoke Hearts Benedict

Baked Brie with Rustic Crackers

Blue Cheese Grits

Berries and Cream with Sliced Fresh Seasonal Fruits

Miniature Cinnamon Rolls with Peach Glaze

Iced Tea and Watermelon Agua Fresca

Freshly Brewed Coffee and Hot Tea

Fresh-Squeezed Orange and Grapefruit Juices

Hill Country Wedding Dinner

Appetizers

Grilled White Wings

Escargot and Wild Mushroom Strudel

Tiny Squares of Choice Beef Tenderloin Medallions on
Wedges of Olive Bread

Fresh Asian Sushi and Sashimi

Sautéed Scallops Served in Sake Cups
with Ernie Sauce

Caviar Table

First Course

Chilled Avocado Soup Garnished with Crème Fraiche

Second Course

Gulf Coast Red Snapper with Caper Cream Sauce

Main Course

Axis Tenderloin Medallions with
Jalapeño Béarnaise Sauce

Quail-Stuffed Chiles Relleños

Cornshuck Pudding

Parker House Rolls

Salad Course

Fresh Spinach Salad with Hill Country Peaches,
Pecans, Mexican Cheese, and
Peach-Champagne Vinaigrette Dressing

Dessert Course

Wedding Cake

Coffee Service

Fire and Ice Red Pepper Soup

★

4 large red bell peppers, about 2 pounds, blistered, peeled, seeded, and roughly chopped

2 pounds yellow heirloom tomatoes, roughly chopped

3 green onions, trimmed and roughly chopped

1 teaspoon minced thyme plus additional whole sprigs as garnish

1½ teaspoons minced flat-leaf parsley

¼ teaspoon crushed red pepper flakes

1 quart plus 1 cup vegetable broth

2 teaspoons Louisiana Hot Sauce

1 cup whipping cream

½ teaspoon freshly ground black pepper

Kosher salt to taste

This soup is both delicious and impressive. Don created it for the soup course of a seated dinner at a very lavish wedding.

Serves 6 to 8

Place the red peppers, tomatoes, green onions, thyme, parsley, and red pepper flakes in blender. Add about 1 cup of the vegetable broth and puree the vegetables until smooth. Add the remaining vegetable broth and the hot sauce; blend until there are no visible particles. Turn mixture out into a medium bowl and whisk in the cream and black pepper, blending well. Season with salt. (Oversalt slightly when seasoning the soup at room temperature. Chilling the soup will dull the salty taste.) Cover the soup with plastic wrap and refrigerate until well chilled. Serve chilled, garnished with sprigs of thyme.

Avocado Soup

★

1 medium onion, roughly chopped, plus
    2 tablespoons minced onion

6 medium avocados, peeled, seeded,
    and roughly chopped (see "Peeling and
    Seeding Avocados" on page 157)

1 (10¾-ounce) can cream of chicken soup

1 cup sour cream

2 tablespoons chopped chives plus
    additional as garnish

2 tablespoons freshly squeezed lemon juice

3 cups evaporated milk

Kosher salt and freshly ground white
    pepper to taste

When the company first started serving this soup in the early years, it was very cutting-edge. Clients clamored for it, and the kitchen was making it in five-gallon batches. Today avocado soup is pretty mainstream, but this is still a very good version. The soup was originally served in small, house-made pumpernickel breads that were baked as round loaves and hollowed out as bowls.

Serves 6

Place the chopped onion in work bowl of food processor fitted with steel blade. Process until totally pureed. Turn the onion out into a fine strainer placed over a bowl. Press down on the pulp to extract ¼ cup of onion juice; reserve juice. Discard the pulp.

Combine the minced onion, avocados, chicken soup, sour cream, 2 tablespoons of the chives, and lemon juice in a blender. Process until smooth, adding the evaporated milk a little at a time. When the soup is smooth and well blended, turn out into a bowl and season with salt and white pepper. (Oversalt slightly when seasoning the soup at room temperature. Chilling the soup will dull the salty taste.)

Refrigerate until well chilled before serving. Garnish each serving with a scattering of chopped chives.

HERE'S HOW YOU DO IT

Pureeing Liquids in the Blender: When pureeing liquids, especially hot ones, in the blender, never fill the container more than one-third full, and make sure that the lid to the container is securely in place. Start blending on low speed, increasing the speed slowly only when you're sure that the liquid won't overflow the top of the container. Otherwise, the hot liquid could blow the lid off the blender, causing nasty burns and, least of all, a horrendous mess!

Wild Mushroom Bisque

★

This delicious soup was served in white cups as the first course at a chilly winter wedding in the Toepperwein Room. It was really a hit, and a perfect example of how Don would often create a recipe for an event that was not a part of the company's regular repertoire. He had the uncanny ability to sense when an occasion called for a specific dish, and he never missed the mark!

Serves 6

Melt the stick of butter in a heavy-bottomed 4-quart saucepan over medium heat. When the sizzling subsides, add the wild and button mushrooms. Cook, stirring often, until the mushrooms are limp and their liquid has evaporated, about 10 minutes. (The butter should be the only liquid left in the pan.) Add the shallots, leek, sage, and pepper. Cook, stirring occasionally, until the shallots and leek are wilted and transparent, about 5 minutes.

Stir in the flour, blending well. Cook, stirring constantly, for 2 to 3 minutes. Add the chicken and beef stocks, stir well, and bring to a full boil to thicken the soup. Cook over low heat for 20 minutes.

Puree the soup in a blender until smooth; puree in batches (see "Pureeing Liquids in the Blender" on page 226). Return to clean soup pot. Add cream and port wine. Cook to heat through. Keep hot while preparing garnishes.

To make the garnishes, melt the butter in a heavy-bottomed, 10-inch skillet over medium heat. When the sizzling subsides, add the chanterelles and season with salt and pepper. Cook, stirring often, until the chanterelles are lightly browned and smell very nutty, about 7 minutes. Use a slotted spoon to remove the chanterelles to a double layer of absorbent paper towels. Set aside to keep warm. Leave the butter in the pan.

Rinse the sage leaves and lay flat on a double layer of paper towels; cover with more towels and press gently to flatten and dry the leaves. Reheat the butter in the skillet until hot. Add the sage leaves in a single layer and cook until they turn dark and crisp, about 4 minutes. Remove gently with chef's tongs and drain on more paper towels (be careful when moving them, as they are very crisp and can break easily). Sprinkle with salt. Use at once or store between layers of paper towels in an airtight container at room temperature.

To serve, divide the soup among 6 shallow soup plates or small bowls. Place 1 tablespoon of the sour cream in the center of each serving. Place a portion of the chanterelles on and around the sour cream, and stick a fried sage leaf in the center of the sour cream with the stem end up. Serve hot.

- ¼ pound (1 stick) unsalted butter
- 24 ounces mixed wild mushrooms (shiitake, cremini, and oyster), roughly chopped
- 8 ounces white button mushrooms, roughly chopped
- 2 large shallots, roughly chopped
- 1 leek, white portion only, cleaned and roughly chopped (see "Using Leeks" on page 76)
- 2 teaspoons minced fresh sage
- ½ teaspoon freshly ground black pepper
- 6 tablespoons all-purpose flour
- 1⅔ cups warm chicken stock
- 1⅔ cups warm beef stock
- ⅔ cup heavy cream
- ⅓ cup port wine
- Kosher salt to taste

Garnishes

- 4 tablespoons (½ stick) butter
- 6 ounces chanterelle mushrooms, sliced thin
- Kosher salt and freshly ground black pepper to taste
- 6 large fresh sage leaves with stems
- 6 tablespoons sour cream

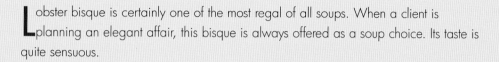

Don Strange of Texas Lobster Bisque

Lobster bisque is certainly one of the most regal of all soups. When a client is planning an elegant affair, this bisque is always offered as a soup choice. Its taste is quite sensuous.

Serves 8

Heat the canola oil in a heavy-bottomed 12-inch skillet over medium heat. When the oil is hot, sauté the onion, celery, green onions, parsley, and garlic, stirring often, until onion is wilted and transparent, about 7 minutes. Set aside.

In a heavy-bottomed 6-quart soup pot over medium heat, melt the butter. When the foam subsides, stir in the flour, blending well. Cook, stirring constantly, until a golden brown roux forms, about 10 minutes. Add the seafood stock, bay leaf, thyme, salt, pepper, and paprika. Bring to a boil to thicken.

Add the reserved vegetables to the pot and simmer, covered, for 30 minutes. Puree the soup in a blender until smooth (see "Pureeing Liquids in the Blender" on page 226); puree in batches, filling the container no more than one-third full with each batch. Return pureed soup to a clean pot and stir in the whipping cream and lobster meat. Cook, stirring often, to heat the cream and lobster. Add the Tabasco and stir to blend well. Serve hot.

¼ cup canola oil

1 large onion, finely chopped (1½ cups)

2 medium stalks celery, finely chopped (1 cup)

½ cup finely chopped green onions and tops

3 tablespoons minced flat-leaf parsley

2 tablespoons minced garlic

¼ pound plus 4 tablespoons (1½ sticks) unsalted butter

¾ cup all-purpose flour

1 quart warm seafood stock (see "Making Seafood Stock" on page 140)

1 fresh bay leaf

1 teaspoon minced thyme

1 teaspoon kosher salt or to taste

⅛ teaspoon freshly ground white pepper

¼ teaspoon paprika

1 quart whipping cream

1 pound cooked lobster meat, cut into ½-inch pieces

1 teaspoon Tabasco sauce

Left to right: Don Strange of Texas Lobster Bisque, Avocado Soup, and Wild Mushroom Bisque.

Spinach Salad with Hill Country Peaches, Pecans, Mexican Cheese, and Peach–Champagne Vinaigrette Dressing

★

12 ounces baby spinach leaves, washed, dried, and chilled

2 large Hill Country peaches, peeled, seeded, and sliced

¼ of a small red onion, very thinly sliced

Toasted pecan pieces

4 ounces queso fresco or Cotija cheese, crumbled

Peach–Champagne Vinaigrette Dressing

2 French shallots, minced

⅓ cup champagne vinegar

1 tablespoon Dijon-style mustard

2 tablespoons honey

¼ cup peach nectar

1 teaspoon kosher salt

2 teaspoons minced cilantro

⅓ cup canola oil

⅓ cup extra-virgin olive oil

In the early summer when Hill Country peaches are ripe, the company serves this salad. Everyone loves it. The dressing is at its best when made several hours before serving so that the flavors have a chance to meld together. It will keep in the refrigerator, tightly covered, for about three days.

Serves 4

To make the dressing, combine all ingredients except olive oil in work bowl of food processor fitted with steel blade. Process until smooth and well blended. With machine running, add the olive oil in a slow, steady stream until all has been added. Process an additional 15 seconds to form a strong emulsion. Refrigerate, tightly covered, until ready to use. Shake well or whisk before using.

To assemble the salad, arrange the spinach leaves on 4 chilled salad plates. Drizzle desired portion of the dressing on each salad (see "Dressing Green Salads" on page 122). Arrange peach slices over the spinach and toss a few onion slices around the fruit. Scatter pecans and crumbled cheese on top. Serve at once.

Eggplant Caviar

★

"It's our Texas version—only a whole lot cheaper," Don always said of this popular party spread. The ingredients are grown all over Texas, another reason he loved to serve the dish. He could get the ingredients fresh from local sources, supporting Texas agriculture and presenting a better quality of food to his clients.

Makes about 1 quart

Preheat oven to 350 degrees. Slice the eggplants in half lengthwise. Brush all sides with about 2 tablespoons of the olive oil and lay them, cut sides down, in a baking dish. Roast in preheated oven until eggplant is very tender and actually collapses, about 45 minutes. Remove from oven and allow to cool in the baking dish.

Peel the tomatoes by dipping them in boiling water for about 20 seconds. Slip the skins off and discard. Cut the tomatoes in half and gently squeeze out the seeds; discard seeds. Chop tomatoes coarsely and set aside.

Scrape out the eggplant pulp, reserving the juices in the baking dish; discard skins. Roughly chop the pulp and combine with the onion, tomatoes, and parsley; set aside.

With the machine running, drop the garlic cloves through the feed tube of the food processor to mince. Stop machine and scrape down the sides of the bowl. Add the eggplant mixture and the reserved juices from the baking dish. Pulse 3 or 4 times to blend the vegetables. With the machine running, add the remaining olive oil in a slow, steady stream through the feed tube. The mixture should have a fine consistency. Turn out into a bowl and season with salt and pepper. Refrigerate until ready to serve.

To serve, place the chilled spread in a decorative serving bowl and set a basket of French bread rounds alongside.

2 large eggplants

⅓ cup extra-virgin olive oil, divided

2 medium tomatoes

1 small onion, peeled and roughly chopped

¼ cup minced fresh parsley, preferably flat-leaf

2 large garlic cloves, peeled

Kosher salt and freshly ground black pepper to taste

Soft French bread rounds for serving

Caprisi Skewers

★

Caprisi salad, which has become extremely popular, originated in the Campania region of Italy. The salad's three main ingredients—tomatoes, mozzarella, and basil—represent the colors of the Italian flag. Don began to get requests for the salad to be served at parties, but of course he wanted to create his own version. Guests loved the presentation of the dish on clear Lucite skewers, transforming the salad into a finger food.

Serves 6 to 8

Thread the tomatoes, cheese balls, and basil leaves onto the skewers, alternating among each ingredient. Place the skewers on a large serving platter; drizzle olive oil over each skewer. Season with salt and pepper. Serve chilled or at room temperature.

48 small red teardrop tomatoes

24 small balls of whole-milk mozzarella cheese

48 small fresh basil leaves

24 clear Lucite or bamboo skewers

Extra-virgin olive oil

Kosher salt and freshly ground black pepper to taste

Macaroni and Cheese Baskets

★

Everybody loves good old American "mac and cheese." Knowing this, Don wanted to create a way to serve the iconic dish that would be both tasty and indicative of his totally-out-of-the-ordinary style. He hit upon the idea of filling miniature pastry "baskets" with a bite of macaroni and cheese and serving them as finger foods at parties. Hosts and their guests loved the concept, and the baskets became a regular feature on the Don Strange of Texas menu.

Makes 50 baskets

Begin by making the Pastry Baskets. (They can be made several hours ahead of time or the day before. If making them a day ahead, cool them completely after baking and store in an airtight container at room temperature.) Combine the flour, salt, and sugar in work bowl of food processor fitted with steel blade. Pulse 3 or 4 times to blend the ingredients. Add the butter cubes and pulse until butter is broken up into pea-size bits. Add the water over the surface of the pastry mixture and process just until the water is blended and the mixture is still crumbly. To check the consistency of the dough, gather a small amount in the palm of your hand and squeeze together. It should form a cohesive dough ball. If the mixture is too dry and crumbly, add another couple of teaspoons of water and process just to blend. Spray 50 miniature (2-inch-diameter) muffin tins with nonstick vegetable spray; set aside.

Turn the dough out onto work surface and gather together, kneading 3 or 4 times to form a dough. Break off portions of the dough and roll into 50 small balls about 1 inch in diameter. Using your palms, flatten the dough balls into rounds about 2½ inches in diameter. Ease the rounds into the prepared muffin tins, tamping dough into the bottom and up the sides. (The dough should come to the top of the tins.) Prick the bottom of the pastries with a fork to prevent puffing while baking. Chill in the freezer for 30 minutes. Preheat oven to 350 degrees.

Remove the muffin tins from the freezer and place on a large baking sheet. Bake in preheated oven until lightly browned and crisp, about 15 minutes. Carefully turn the pastries out onto a wire rack to cool. Leave the oven on and spray an 8-inch-square baking dish with nonstick vegetable spray; set aside.

Prepare the macaroni and cheese filling. Bring a 6-quart pot filled halfway with salted water to a full boil. Add the macaroni and cook at a brisk boil for 10 minutes, or until al dente. Drain into a colander, shake to remove the water, and return to the pot; set aside.

While the macaroni is cooking, melt the butter in a heavy-bottomed 3-quart saucepan over medium heat. When butter has melted, stir in the flour, blending well. Cook, stirring constantly, for 3 to 4 minutes. Add the milk, salt, and cayenne pepper. Whisk until mixture thickens. Add the American cheese and 1 cup of the Cheddar cheese. Stir vigorously until the cheeses are melted and well blended. Pour the cheese mixture over the macaroni and stir to distribute well. Turn the mixture out into the prepared baking dish and scatter the remaining ¼ cup of Cheddar cheese evenly over the top. Bake in preheated oven until the cheese on the top has melted, about 15 minutes.

Working quickly, spoon about 1 tablespoon of the macaroni and cheese into each pastry basket and serve hot.

8 ounces elbow macaroni

2 tablespoons unsalted butter

2 tablespoons all-purpose flour

¾ cup whole milk

1 teaspoon kosher salt

½ teaspoon cayenne pepper, or to taste

1 cup (4 ounces) shredded American cheese

1¼ cups (5 ounces) shredded sharp Cheddar cheese, divided

Pastry Baskets

1½ cups all-purpose flour

1 teaspoon salt

1 teaspoon sugar

12 tablespoons (1½ sticks) unsalted butter, frozen and cut into 1-inch cubes

3 to 4 tablespoons ice-cold water

Opposite: Macaroni and Cheese Baskets with Caprisi Skewers.

Brioche French Toast with Bananas Foster

1 cup whole milk

1 cup whipping cream

4 eggs

1 teaspoon ground cinnamon

½ teaspoon freshly ground nutmeg

Butter

8 (⅝-inch-thick) slices of day-old brioche

Bananas Foster (see recipe below)

Sweetened whipped cream

Cinnamon or nutmeg for garnish

Mint sprigs as garnish

Bananas Foster

⅓ cup firmly packed light-brown sugar

1 teaspoon ground cinnamon

4 tablespoons (½ stick) unsalted butter

½ cup crème de banana or other banana-
flavored liqueur

½ cup dark rum

4 bananas, peeled and cut into ½-inch
slices

The very thought of this dish is enough to make you hungry! Don had a flair for creating elaborate, extravagant brunch dishes. This is one that he served at a lovely wedding brunch outside of Fredericksburg in the Texas Hill Country.

Serves 4 to 6

Make the Bananas Foster. In a small bowl, combine brown sugar and cinnamon with a fork; set aside. Melt butter in a heavy-bottomed 12-inch skillet over medium heat. Add cinnamon-sugar mixture, stirring until sugar dissolves. Add the banana liqueur and ¼ cup of the rum. Cook, stirring, until syrupy and thickened, about 5 minutes. Add the banana slices and lightly coat with the syrup. Add the remaining rum. Quickly swirl the pan, tilting it toward the flame, to ignite the rum. (If you are using an electric stove, light the rum with a long match.) Swirl the pan, basting bananas with the sauce, until flame subsides. Remove pan from heat, set aside, and keep warm.

To make the French toast, combine the milk, cream, eggs, cinnamon, and nutmeg in a medium bowl; whisk until eggs are well beaten and the batter is smooth. Melt some butter on a flat griddle over medium heat.

Dip the brioche slices in the egg batter, coating both sides. Allow excess batter to drip off. Place the battered breads on hot griddle, without touching. (Cook in batches, if necessary, to avoid crowding.) Cook until golden brown, turning once, about 2 minutes per side. Keep hot in a warm oven while cooking the remaining slices.

To serve, stack slices of the French toast on each serving plate. Place banana slices on each serving and drizzle some of the pan sauce over the top. Top with a generous dollop of the whipped cream. Garnish each serving with a sprinkle of cinnamon or nutmeg then add a mint sprig. Serve at once.

Miniature Cinnamon Rolls with Peach Glaze

★

These delicious little rolls—perfect for breakfast or brunch or with afternoon coffee or tea—are served often at Don Strange of Texas brunches. The rolls can be made and baked ahead of time, then frozen, but don't add the glaze. When you're ready to serve the rolls, thaw them and reheat for 20 minutes in a 350-degree oven. Drizzle the glaze on the hot rolls and serve at once.

Makes 24 rolls

Make the Peach Glaze. Combine all ingredients in a bowl and blend well, whisking until there are no lumps of powdered sugar. Refrigerate, covered, while making the rolls.

To make the dough, combine the yeast, sugar, water, and honey in a 2-cup Pyrex measuring cup; whisk to blend well. Set aside until the yeast has dissolved and the mixture is very bubbly, about 3 to 4 minutes.

In work bowl of food processor fitted with steel blade, combine 3½ cups of bread flour and salt. Add the yeast mixture, using a rubber spatula to scrape out the measuring cup. Process just to incorporate the yeast. Add egg and canola oil and process to bring the dough together, about 8 seconds. Stop and check the consistency of the dough. It should not be sticky. (If it is too wet, add additional bread flour, about 1 tablespoon at a time. Beat to blend the additional flour after each addition. If dough is too dry, add additional warm water about 1 tablespoon at a time, beating to blend after each addition.) When dough is the proper consistency, process for 29 seconds to knead the dough.

Turn dough out onto work surface and knead 5 or 6 times by hand to form a dough ball that springs back when tugged with fingers. Oil a large mixing bowl with canola oil and place dough in bowl, turning to coat all surfaces with the oil. Cover bowl tightly with plastic wrap and set aside to rise in a warm, draft-free spot, until doubled in bulk, about 1 hour. Preheat oven to 350 degrees.

While dough is rising, combine all ingredients for the filling, tossing to blend well. Butter two 12-muffin miniature (2-inch-diameter) muffin tins; set aside. Punch dough down, then divide in half. Turn one portion out onto a very lightly floured work surface and roll into a 17-by-11-inch rectangle. (If the dough begins to spring back and it is difficult to roll it into the proper dimensions, cover it loosely with plastic wrap and let it rest for about 10 minutes to relax the elasticity.) Scatter half of the filling over the surface of the dough to within 1 inch of the long edges and all the way to the edge on the short ends. Beginning at the long side of the dough nearest you, roll the dough into a cylinder. Pinch the edge of the dough to form a seal. Turn it seam side down and gently roll to flatten the seam. Repeat with remaining portion of the dough.

Using a sharp knife, slice the roll into slices about 1½ inches thick. Place the slices, cut side up, in the prepared muffin tins. Cover rolls loosely with plastic wrap and set aside to rise for 30 to 45 minutes, or until doubled in bulk.

Brush tops with the melted butter and bake in preheated oven until golden brown, about 25 minutes. Remove from oven and allow to cool for 5 minutes, then drizzle the Peach Glaze over the rolls, coating well. Remove rolls to a wire rack to cool just until the glaze sets. Serve slightly warm or at room temperature.

1 tablespoon instant-rise active dry yeast

⅔ cup sugar

1 cup warm water (105–115 degrees) plus additional as needed

2 tablespoons honey

3½ to 4 cups bread flour plus additional as needed

¾ teaspoon salt

1 egg, beaten

3 tablespoons canola oil

4 tablespoons (½ stick) melted butter

Filling

½ cup sugar

½ teaspoon ground cinnamon

½ cup chopped pecans

½ cup raisins

Peach Glaze

1 fresh peach, pureed until very smooth

2 cups powdered sugar

2 tablespoons melted unsalted butter

½ teaspoon almond extract

Broiled Red Snapper and Artichoke Hearts Benedict

★

1 (14-ounce) can artichoke hearts, 8–10 count, well drained and halved

2 tablespoons unsalted butter

1 small shallot, minced

Kosher salt to taste

4 (4-ounce) portions of red snapper fillet, skinned (see "Buying Fresh Fish [and Making Sure They're Fresh]" on page 146)

¼ pound (1 stick) butter, melted, with 1 tablespoon freshly squeezed lemon juice

Pinch of kosher salt, freshly ground black pepper, granulated garlic, and cayenne pepper

4 English muffin halves, toasted, and buttered

4 eggs, poached (see "Poaching Eggs" on page 239)

Prepared hollandaise sauce (see "Making Foolproof Hollandaise Sauce in the Food Processor" on page 201)

Paprika and minced parsley as garnish

I always considered this to be one of Don's most innovative creations. He started with the concept of a classic eggs Benedict—an English muffin topped with Canadian bacon, a poached egg, and hollandaise sauce. But the similarity stops there. Try this fabulous version at your next brunch (or even for dinner). You'll get rave reviews. It makes a sensational presentation if you serve a small portion of quickly seared fresh spinach on the plate.

Serves 4

Pat the halved artichoke hearts very dry using absorbent paper towels; set aside. Melt the butter in a heavy-bottomed 10-inch skillet over medium heat. When the foam subsides, add the shallot and cook, stirring, just until it is wilted, about 1 minute. Add the artichoke hearts and cook until lightly browned, turning once very carefully to avoid breaking them up. Season with salt. Drain off pan juices, set aside, and keep warm.

Remove any small bones in the fish with tweezers or needle-nose pliers, taking care not to tear the flesh. Place the fish on a heavy-duty baking sheet; set aside. Preheat broiler and place oven rack 6 inches below heat source. Pour the melted butter and lemon juice over the fish. Season each piece with a pinch of salt, pepper, granulated garlic, and cayenne pepper. Place pan under preheated broiler and cook until fish flesh is opaque throughout and fillets are lightly browned on top, about 2 to 3 minutes. Watch the fish very carefully so that they don't burn. Remove from oven.

To serve, place an English muffin in the center of each serving plate. Using a slotted spatula, top each muffin with a piece of fish, a poached egg, and a few of the artichoke hearts. Ladle a portion of the hollandaise sauce over the top. Garnish with paprika and parsley. Serve at once.

HERE'S HOW YOU DO IT

Poaching Eggs: Poaching an egg sounds like a simple task, but there's an art to it. And to be a great brunch cook, you must master the technique of poaching eggs.

Use the freshest eggs you can find and bring them to room temperature before poaching. Adding a small amount of vinegar to the poaching water will help coagulate the whites quickly and keep them from drifting off into wispy strands, making a neat, compact finished product. Never add salt to the water; it will toughen the eggs.

Fill a heavy, deep-sided 12-inch skillet two-thirds full of water. Add ¼ cup of plain white vinegar. Bring the water to a bare simmer. (The surface of the water should be barely rippling.) Break the eggs, one at a time, into a small bowl, then slide them into the water—up to 6 eggs at a time. Cook for 3 minutes for a nice soft yolk, or longer to set the yolks and give them a firmer texture. Remove the eggs from the pan carefully, using a slotted spoon and taking care not to break the yolks. Gently blot off excess water before using the eggs. Let the water return to a gentle simmer before poaching another batch.

Here's a time-saving trick when poaching eggs for a crowd. Poach all the eggs you will need but for only 2 minutes. Carefully remove them with a slotted spoon and float them in a large bowl filled with ice water. (The eggs can be held for an hour or two in the water bath if you keep replenishing the melting ice.) Finish the eggs at the last minute by returning them to the simmering water and poaching for 1 additional minute, or longer as desired.

Gulf Coast Red Snapper with Caper Cream Sauce

4 (5- to 6-ounce) portions of red snapper fillet, skinned (see "Buying Fresh Fish [and Making Sure They're Fresh]" on page 146)

¼ cup olive oil

4 tablespoons (½ stick) butter

3 cups all-purpose flour, seasoned with 1 tablespoon each: kosher salt, black pepper, granulated garlic, and paprika

Minced parsley and lemon wheels as garnish (see below "Making Lemon Wheels")

Caper Cream Sauce

4 tablespoons (½ stick) unsalted butter

1 tablespoon all-purpose flour

Pinch of cayenne pepper or to taste

⅓ cup well-drained capers

1 heaping teaspoon minced lemon zest

2 tablespoons freshly squeezed lemon juice

2 cups whipping cream

Kosher salt to taste

Red snapper was one of Don's favorite fish. Whenever we would go to our house in Rockport, he'd head to the waterfront fish markets to see if they had fresh snapper. If they did, it was a sure bet that he'd create something wonderful for our dinner. When a client wanted a fish dish for a party, Don would always try to get fresh red snapper to use. This is one of my favorites among his many snapper dishes—simple yet delicious.

Serves 4

Pat the fish fillets very dry using absorbent paper towels. Combine the olive oil and butter in a heavy-bottomed 12-inch skillet over medium heat. When the butter has melted and the foam subsides, dredge the fish pieces in the seasoned flour, coating well on both sides and shaking off all excess flour. Arrange the fish pieces, skinned side down, in the hot skillet so they don't touch. Cook just until the flesh turns opaque throughout, turning once, about 3 minutes per side. Do not overcook the fish (it should not be flaking apart). Transfer to a baking sheet and keep warm in a very low oven.

To make the Caper Cream Sauce, drain the skillet and return it to medium heat. Add the butter and swirl the skillet to melt it. Add the flour and cayenne, stirring to blend well. Cook, stirring, for 3 to 4 minutes. Add the capers and lemon zest. Stir to blend well, then add the lemon juice and cream. Stir again to blend. Cook at a brisk simmer until thickened, about 2 minutes. Season with salt. Remove from heat.

To serve, place a piece of fish on each serving plate and nap with a portion of the Caper Cream Sauce. Garnish with minced parsley and a lemon wheel. Serve at once.

HERE'S HOW YOU DO IT

Making Lemon Wheels: Lemon wheels are a great-looking garnish. They add a nice touch of color to the plate and they're decorative. Don especially liked to use them with fish and shellfish dishes. If you're serving a whole fillet of fish, twist the wheel right on top of the fish.

To make the lemon wheels, use a serrated bread knife to slice a lemon into thin slices, about ⅛-inch thick. Be sure that your slices are of uniform thickness. Using a sharp paring knife, make a cut from the outside peel to the center of the slice. To serve, twist the lemon slice in opposite directions at the cut so that the two sides form an S shape. Place the wheels on plates as desired.

Quail-Stuffed Chiles Rellenos with Mango and Papaya Pico de Gallo

This recipe is so typical of Don's unique versions of classic dishes. Grilled quail meat is mixed with cheese and stuffed into a fresh Anaheim chile—rather than the customary poblano chile—before it is battered and fried. The resulting taste is sublime, and the Anaheim chile is milder than the poblano, so it's perfect for guests who don't like a lot of spice.

Serves 8 to 10

Begin by making the pico de gallo. Combine all ingredients except salt in a bowl and toss to blend well. Season with salt. Cover and refrigerate until ready to use.

Using a small, sharp knife, make a 3-inch slit in the side of each blistered chile. Taking care not to tear the skin, scoop out the seeds and veins using your forefinger. Set chiles aside.

Remove the meat from the grilled quail, discarding skin and bones. Shred the meat using your fingers. (You should have about 12 ounces of meat.) Place meat in a bowl and add the cheese, green onions, garlic, cilantro, and salt. Toss to blend well and season with pepper. Stuff a portion of the quail mixture into each chile. Don't stuff them too tightly. Pinch the open edges of the chiles closed.

Heat 1 inch of canola oil in a heavy-bottomed 12-inch skillet over medium heat until the oil reaches a temperature of 350 degrees. Set a wire cooling rack over a baking sheet; set aside.

Dredge the stuffed chiles in the cornmeal mixture, shaking off excess. Next dip them in the egg wash, coating well on all sides; dip again in the cornmeal mixture, coating well and shaking off excess.

Lower the breaded chiles into the hot oil. Do not crowd the pan. Cook, turning once, until the chiles are golden brown, about 2 minutes per side. Remove with a slotted spatula and place on the cooling rack to drain. Serve hot with the Mango and Papaya Pico de Gallo.

14 Anaheim chiles, blistered and peeled (see "Blistering Chiles" on page 243)

12 semi-boneless quail, grilled

2 cups (8 ounces) shredded Monterey Jack cheese

4 green onions and tops, finely chopped

2 large garlic cloves, minced

2 tablespoons minced cilantro

1½ teaspoons kosher salt

Canola oil

Freshly ground black pepper to taste

2 cups yellow cornmeal mixed with 1 cup all-purpose flour and seasoned with 2 teaspoons kosher salt

4 eggs whisked into 3 cups milk

Mango and Papaya Pico de Gallo

2 ripe mangos, peeled, seeded, and cut into small dice (see "Peeling and Cutting Mangos" on page 121)

1 ripe papaya, peeled, seeded, and cut into small dice

1 small red onion, finely diced

1 large jalapeño, seeds and veins removed, minced

2 tablespoons minced cilantro

½ teaspoon ground cumin

Juice of 1 lime

1 heaping tablespoon minced cilantro

Kosher salt to taste

Barbecued Cabrito with Papaya and Lime Pico de Gallo

★

10 pounds goat legs and shoulder quarters

Brine (see recipe at right)

Olive oil

Cabrito Rub (see recipe below)

Mr. Strange's Barbecue Sauce, heated (see page 26)

Papaya and Lime Pico de Gallo (see recipe below)

Corn tortillas, warmed, or Pan de Campo (see page 169)

Cabrito Rub

1 cup kosher salt

1½ tablespoons granulated garlic

¼ cup coarse ground black pepper

1½ tablespoons ground cumin

¼ cup chili powder

2 tablespoons sweet paprika

2 tablespoons smoked paprika

Papaya and Lime Pico de Gallo

5 large papayas, peeled, seeded, and cut into tiny dice

2 large red bell peppers, blistered, peeled, seeds and veins removed, cut into tiny dice

1 large onion, cut into tiny dice

4 or 5 serrano chiles, seeds and veins removed, minced

2 Roma tomatoes, cut into tiny dice

2 large garlic cloves, minced

2 tablespoons minced cilantro

Juice of 1 large lime or to taste

Kosher salt to taste

Goats are raised all over the Texas Hill Country but remain underutilized as a meat source in this country. Don served it as often as he could talk clients into the idea! It's a delicious meat with very little fat and no gamey taste. And since goats roam free on Texas ranches, grazing on native grasses, they're not raised on feeds laced with antibiotics and chemicals.

Serves 8 to 10

Brine

2 gallons water, divided

2 cups kosher salt

8 bay leaves

2 tablespoons whole coriander seeds, toasted

2 tablespoon whole black peppercorns

1 cup loosely packed fresh thyme sprigs

2 cups brown sugar

2 oranges, quartered

2 large white onions, peeled and quartered

8 garlic cloves, peeled and crushed

Make the brine. Bring 2 quarts of the water to a simmer in a large deep pot. Add the salt, bay leaves, coriander seeds, peppercorns, thyme, and brown sugar. Whisk and simmer for 2 minutes, or until the salt has dissolved. Add the oranges, onion, and garlic. Simmer, covered, for 10 minutes. Remove from heat and stir in the remaining water. Chill.

Add the goat meat to the chilled brine mixture. Brine, refrigerated, for 24 hours.

Make the Cabrito Rub. Combine all ingredients in a bowl and toss with a fork or whisk to blend well; set aside.

To make the Papaya and Lime Pico de Gallo, combine all ingredients, except salt, in a stainless bowl and toss to blend well. Season with salt. Refrigerate, tightly covered, until ready to serve.

Build a hardwood charcoal fire in a large barbecue pit, preferably one with a separate fire box, so that the goat legs cook over indirect heat and get a good breath of smoke. Allow the fire to burn down until the coals are glowing red and covered by a layer of white ash, about 20 to 30 minutes. (The internal pit temperature should be about 275 degrees.) Rub the goat legs liberally with olive oil. Using your hands, rub the Cabrito Rub into the flesh, coating generously. Save any leftover rub in a storage container with tightly fitting lid for later use. Place the goat legs on the grill rack in the pit. Cook, covered, turning often, until an instant-read meat thermometer inserted in thickest part of the inside top of the leg registers 155 degrees, about 1½ hours. Baste the goat often with additional olive oil.

When the goat is cooked, remove from grill and pull the meat from the bones. Discard bones. Using your fingers, shred the meat, picking off any tendons or cartilage. Toss the meat with a small amount of barbecue sauce to moisten it. Pile the meat on a platter and serve hot. Place a basket of warm corn tortillas or Pan de Campo and a bowl of Papaya and Lime Pico de Gallo alongside so that guests can assemble their own soft tacos.

HERE'S HOW YOU DO IT

Blistering Chiles: You can use any of several methods to blister or roast all members of the chile, or *Capsicum,* genus, which includes bell peppers of all colors. Each method requires the use of a flame or another source of very high heat. Be very cautious when blistering chiles to avoid a nasty burn.

Probably the most common method is to place the chiles directly over the flame of a gas burner or light the gas grill and turn the temperature to high. Or you can turn on the broiler of an electric oven and set the rack about 3 to 4 inches below the heat source You can also use a small, hand-held butane burner (readily available at hardware stores) or a specially designed culinary torch, available at cookware shops. Whichever method you choose, cook the chiles, turning often with chef's tongs, until they are totally blackened and blistered on all sides. The skin should be peeling off.

Place the blistered chiles in a metal bowl and seal the top with plastic wrap. Set aside for about 20 minutes, or until the chiles are cool enough to handle comfortably. Then peel off the blistered skin. Remove and discard the veins and seeds and use the chiles as directed in the recipe.

Sweet Potato Brûlée

★

5 pounds sweet potatoes, peeled and cut into small chunks

¼ pound (1 stick) butter at room temperature

1 cup firmly packed light brown sugar

1 teaspoon ground cinnamon

1 teaspoon freshly grated nutmeg

¼ teaspoon ground cloves

¼ teaspoon ground white pepper

1 cup evaporated milk

3 eggs, beaten

Topping

1½ cups firmly packed light brown sugar

½ cup unsalted butter, softened and cut into ½-inch cubes

½ cup all-purpose flour

1 cup chopped pecans

While not a true "brûlée" that is flamed to caramelize the top, the topping on this delicious dish becomes caramelized during baking, giving it the crusty top of a brûlée. This is a great side dish for your Thanksgiving dinner, and it also complements ham or roast pork. Everyone loves it.

Serves 10 to 12

Place the sweet potato chunks in a heavy-bottomed 6-quart soup pot or Dutch oven and add cold water to cover by 2 inches. Bring to a full boil, reduce heat, and simmer until potatoes are very soft, about 25 minutes. Drain into a colander and transfer to a large mixing bowl. Add the butter and mash the potatoes and butter until smooth and well blended. Add remaining ingredients and stir to blend well, taking care that the spices are well distributed. Turn out into a 10-by-14-inch baking dish. Set aside. Preheat oven to 400 degrees.

To make the topping, combine brown sugar, butter, and flour in work bowl of food processor fitted with steel blade. Process until smooth and fluffy. Add the pecans and pulse just to blend, leaving the pecans fairly intact.

Spread the topping evenly over the potato mixture. Bake in preheated oven until set and caramelized on the top, about 45 minutes. Serve hot.

Hot Mustard Sauce

★

¾ cup ground dry mustard

¾ cup all-purpose flour

⅓ cup sugar

1¾ cups apple cider vinegar

½ teaspoon kosher salt or to taste

Hot Mustard Sauce is known far and wide as a really great sauce for roasted pork or ham. It's also good on sandwiches. It's so popular that guests have always wanted the recipe, so we included the sauce in the line of condiments and sauces available online through our Don Strange Market Place. The sauce keeps well in the refrigerator for a couple of weeks.

Makes about 3½ cups

Combine dry mustard and flour in a medium bowl. Whisk to blend and break up any lumps of mustard. In a separate bowl, whisk together the sugar, vinegar, and salt until the sugar has dissolved. Whisk the vinegar mixture into the mustard mixture until thick and well blended. Serve at room temperature.

A Helping Hand and a Few Accolades

The road to the level of success that Don Strange of Texas has achieved has not been an easy one. Not even a steady one. Bumpy, at best, but I think a more apt description of the road would be to compare it to a roller-coaster ride. The business has been subject to the perils of doing business in Texas—oil booms and oil busts, national economic woes, politics, escalating gas prices—all of which were unforeseen and, therefore, couldn't have been figured into the price of future business. It's certainly not been a paved road to wealth and fame. As to wealth, well, Don tallied up what the company made, paid the bills, took care of his staff, and then took his share from what was left, and we made do. That's all we ever counted on. And fame? Well, if fame tried to get in Don Strange's face, he would quickly turn away from it.

The bottom line is that Don never sought either wealth or fame. He was the most selfless man I ever met. He just wanted to make a decent living and establish a reputation as an honest, dependable person. *Success*, to Don, meant that each new event was at least as good as, and preferably better than, the last one. His road to that success had no end goal. He just wanted to be sure that every party was the best one the host had ever attended. His personal rewards along the road were the freedom to express his genius for innovation and creativity, using those talents to provide satisfaction and pleasure to others. To that end, no personal sacrifice was too great for him. Don would do anything to see that a job was done well.

Both Don and I were raised by parents who taught us that however much or little money you have, you have a responsibility to give something back. Neither of us ever understood how, or why, some people who, upon attaining a measure of success, become arrogant and lose sight of where that success came from. Don never took success for granted. To him, it was just a sideline of what he did—and the only thing to ensure continued success was the next great party.

In keeping with that philosophy, Don has given back to the San Antonio community in many, many ways over the years. His contributions to our local community had far-ranging benefits to the entire state. In 2003 Don launched his Helping Hands program as a community partnership with Roy Maas Youth Alternatives, Inc. Since its inception in 1976, Youth Alternatives, a private nonprofit organization, has provided shelter and counseling to more than 58,000 children and young adults in crisis, ranging in age from five to twenty-one, many of whom have been victims of physical, sexual, and emotional abuse. The organization operates the Bridge Emergency Shelter in San Antonio and MeadowLand, a campus providing long-term residential youth housing near Boerne.

Helping Hands is a multifaceted project that benefits the Youth Alternatives through a three-part program—nutrition, physical fitness, and mentorship.

In 2006 Don Strange of Texas launched a spin-off program that Don called Breakfast of Champions, bringing in corporate executives and other community leaders for monthly breakfast meetings with the children of Youth Alternatives. During the meetings, CEOs and others impart to the youngsters the importance of good nutrition and its impact on a sound body and mind. Meeting locations change each month to give the children exposure to different business and community settings. Don helped Roy Maas Youth Alternatives in a variety of other endeavors, too, such as providing the venue—the Don Strange Ranch—and all of the food and drinks for the RMYA Casino Night FriendRaiser. The company provides complimentary meals every month at RMYA's monthly Heart to Heart luncheons for potential supporters and also donates a portion of its e-commerce proceeds from the Don Strange Market Place to RMYA.

In 2007, in recognition of its work with RMYA, Don Strange of Texas was awarded the Mutual of America Community Partnership Award, which is given to private companies and nonprofit groups working to build strong collaborations that benefit social services. That year's award marked the first time a Texas collaboration was recognized since the national insurance company began honoring such partnerships in 1996. The award has recognized over 100 partnerships from cities and towns across America, each time helping recipients expand their programs and continue to attract additional sponsors.

Don was very dedicated to the RMYA programs and instilled that dedication within the entire company. The Helping Hands program will continue, both in honor of the work that Don did to establish it and as a testament to the company's passion for continuing the good work that he began.

In 2001–2002 Don partnered with the City of San Antonio to bring the Pan American Games to San Antonio, all on his own "dime." He was always willing to donate catered parties to many nonprofit organizations for their fund-raising live auctions. Among those: the Winston School; the Boerne School Foundation; and the Coastal Conservation Associations in San Antonio, Boerne, the Hill Country (New Braunfels), Corpus Christi, and the Rio Grande Valley. The Houston Livestock Show and Rodeo netted $55,000 over a consecutive two-year period through a live auction, which featured a fabulous dinner party that

Don catered. Don also gave parties annually to the American Cancer Society Cattle Baron's Balls live auctions in Austin, San Marcos, the Rio Grande Valley, Lubbock, and Corpus Christi. The company regularly opens the ropes course and team-building venue at the Don Strange Ranch for the Austin School for the Blind, the Center for the Intrepid—Wounded Warriors, and several children's homes around Texas. Each year the company donates a party to the Downtown San Antonio Rotary Club, where the funds raised benefit Diploma Plus, a program that pays youth to remain in school.

A San Antonio native, Don loved the city, and throughout his lifetime he worked to promote it. He encouraged similar businesses to help cement San Antonio's reputation as one of the premier destinations for tourists, conventions, and meetings by fostering the spirit of cooperation to forge new partnerships, even among competitors, and to showcase the diverse options afforded by the city. He encouraged businesses to always offer their best, in keeping with the goal of getting groups to come to San Antonio, and to treat them well so they would return again and again. By doing so, Don emphasized, it would mean expanded business for everybody. Meeting facilities, hotels, restaurants, and, yes, caterers too would benefit by earning their fair share of the business. He always said that businesses should bring visitors to San Antonio, and San Antonio to visitors!

Although Don always shunned the spotlight, I was so proud each time the company was presented with an award because he had earned each one of them through his hard work and dedication to providing the highest quality of service to his clients and to sharing with community members in need. Numerous articles featuring Don and the company have appeared in newspapers and magazines across the state. In 2007 Don Strange of Texas was named a Trendsetter by the *San Antonio Express-News*. These awards are given each year by the newspaper's Taste section to an individual restaurateur, chef, or caterer who exhibits the greatest visions in culinary trends.

Because of Don's untiring work with children and young adults, the company received the Corporate Service Award from the Texas Network of Youth Services in 2007. However, he really didn't feel that he needed to receive an award for doing something that he regarded as simply the right thing to do.

Don Strange of Texas received the Best Venue award at the first annual HOSPY Awards, presented by the San Antonio Hotel & Lodging Association in 2000. The following year, HOSPY accolades went to the Don Strange Ranch for Best Catering Cuisine as well as Best Venue. In 2008 Don Strange of Texas won the HOSPY Hero award.

In 2007 the company won a very prestigious award. Don Strange of Texas was awarded the Texas Treasure Business Award "for its historical contribution toward the economic growth and prosperity of the state," according to the Texas Treasure Business Award guidelines. The award honors businesses that have been in existence in Texas for more than fifty years, have remained committed to Texas for generations, and have helped create jobs and stimulate economic growth. To be considered for the award, a business must have a record of active involvement of employee or corporate community service. The award was created as Senate Bill 920, authored by Senator Leticia Van de Putte in the 79th Texas Legislative Session and signed into law by Governor Rick Perry.

This prestigious award was presented to Don at the San Antonio Convention and Visitors Bureau at one of his Breakfast of Champions breakfasts with kids from the Roy Maas Youth Alternatives and with the Convention and Visitors Bureau team. We were all immensely proud, both *for* him and *of* him. But, of course, he wanted no part of the limelight for doing what he felt just needed to be done.

After Don's death in November of 2009, I accepted two awards on his behalf. These were very bittersweet moments to me.

On November 20, only nine days after Don passed away, I accepted the Make a Difference Award, which Don won in the Outstanding Small Business category. These awards were established by Ruth's Chris Steak House owner Lana Duke, along with the San Antonio Hispanic Chamber of Commerce, to encourage other businesses to step up and make a difference in their community. The luncheon was hosted by Ms. Duke at the downtown Ruth's Chris Steak House.

On December 10, I accepted the 2009 Governor's Volunteer Award on Don's behalf in Dallas. Don was chosen by Governor Perry as the recipient in the Community Collaborator category. These awards honor some of Texas's most dedicated volunteers—individuals, organizations, corporations, and public entities—for community service exemplifying the power of volunteerism and civic engagement. It was an honor for me to accept this award for Don, but I so wished he had been the one accepting it and being honored in front of his peers as the example of the power of service and volunteerism that he was.

We raised our three sons to have the same deep sense of responsibility to give back to the community that we had. They are dedicated to continuing the company's involvement in the programs that Don began and that meant so much to their dad. I look forward to attending many more award programs in my life, watching Brian, Matt, and Jason follow in Don's footsteps. And each time, I'll be reminded of my pride for Don Strange, the man I loved and shared with so many.

My life with Don was a wonderful journey, and finishing this book without him has been a journey, too. Like all journeys, this one has had its smooth roads, bumpy roads, unexpected turns, and roadblocks. But as with any journey, it has been rewarding to reach the destination. Although Don was enthusiastic about the project, as it went on I sometimes had doubts. Was I doing the right thing? Was I doing the book like he would have done it? At some point I realized that, of course, I was not doing it like Don would have done it. But that's okay. Don was not the one doing it—I was, and I was working hard to make it the best I could.

On the last day of my active work on the project, after the manuscript was finally finished, I was at the Waring General Store to witness the last of the photographs being taken. Tracey Maurer, the photographer, Mary Ellen Rose, the food stylist, Lisa Dominguez Green, the photography assistant, and I all had a "last supper" together, and then they left for San Antonio. They were on the road between Waring and the Don Strange Ranch when storm clouds began threatening rain. As they drove on, suddenly the clouds cleared and they could see a rainbow. Looking closer, they all had an intuition about where the rainbow ended. Racing down the road, they pulled in at the ranch, and just as expected, the rainbow appeared to end right on the hill where we had scattered Don's ashes.

I guess everyone can make of it what they will, but for me, I felt Don had blessed our work and given it his stamp of approval. What a beautiful affirmation it was!

INDEX

CREDITS

Food Photography
Tracey Mauer
with Lisa Dominguez Green and Robert Amador

Food Styling
Mary Ellen Rose

Editor
Alison Tartt

Book Design
Barbara Jezek

Proofreader
Regina Fuentes

Type Styles
Goudy, Futura, and Bernhard Modern

Production
Asia Pacific representing Phoenix Offset

Photography
*Photographs not otherwise credited are part
of the Don Strange of Texas Collection.*
Food Network, 154 (right), 155. Elizabeth Horne Photography, 8,
245. Tracey Maurer Photography, 150, 152 (left), 157, 160–162,
168, 169–173, 174 (lower) 178, 179, 183–185, 188, 192, 193,
195, 196, 199 (right), 200, 201, 247, front endpapers (3rd row, 3rd
from right). National Chicken Council (David Veck Studios), 125, 146,
back endpapers (1st column, middle, 6th column, top). Cynthia Parish
Photography, 61. PartyPictures.com, 14. David Ross, 94, 95. Strange
Family, 20 (top), 21, 22, 27, 32, 33, 35. texasfreeways.com, 20
(lower). White House Staff Photograph, 116, 117. Wikipedia, 57.

DURANGO PUBLIC LIBRARY
DURANGO, COLORADO 81301